WRITING ACADEMIC ENGLISH

A Writing and Sentence Structure Workbook for International Students

ALICE OSHIMA
ANN HOGUE

 ADDISON-WESLEY PUBLISHING COMPANY

Reading, Massachusetts • Menlo Park, California • Don Mills, Ontario
Wokingham, England • Amsterdam • Sydney • Singapore • Tokyo
Madrid • Bogota • Santiago • San Juan

WRITING ACADEMIC ENGLISH:
A WRITING AND SENTENCE STRUCTURE WORKBOOK
FOR INTERNATIONAL STUDENTS

ISBN: 0-201-05479-5
HIJ-WC-89876

TO THE STUDENT

Good writing in English requires both good grammar and good organization. In this book, you will study both. You will learn selected* grammatical structures in order to perfect your grammar and improve your style. You will also learn to organize your thoughts in writing. At the end of the semester, you will know how to organize your ideas quickly and write about them clearly, and you will be able to write in the sophisticated*, mature style required in academic courses.

The *first part* of this book presents the basic principles* of English rhetoric*. Rhetoric has two aspects*: organization and style. English rhetoric is very different from the rhetoric of your native language. Good style in Chinese or Japanese is very different from good style in English; good organization in Arabic, Persian and Spanish is very different from good organization in English. Therefore, in order to write well in English, you must learn not only the rules of English grammar, but also the principles of English rhetoric. Learning the principles of rhetoric is just like learning the rules of grammar: first you must study them, then you must practice them.

The practice sections in this book will help you apply what you have learned about these basic principles of English rhetoric. There are also Writing Under Pressure exercises designed to help you organize your thoughts and write about them quickly. You will find this skill especially useful when taking essay examinations in your other courses.

The *second part* of this book presents some of the more difficult aspects of English grammar: verb tenses, active and passive voice, independent and dependent clauses, participial phrases, etc. Your goal in studying grammar should be to learn to use these structures in order to develop a more sophisticated writing style.

If you read carefully and do all of the exercises and practices thoughtfully, we guarantee* that your writing will improve. We also guarantee that you will find the task* of writing much, much easier.

---

* Certain words in this book are marked with an asterisk (*). Simple definitions for these words appear at the bottom of the page. These words include uncommon or technical words and words that were unfamiliar to students we have taught in the past. You may be unsure of other words as well. Try to "unlock" the meanings of these words by observing how they are used. If you still don't understand a word, look it up in your dictionary or ask your instructor for help.

---

selected: chosen   **sophisticated:** complex   **principles:** rules   **task:** job, work
rhetoric: the art of writing   **aspects:** parts   **guarantee:** promise

CONTENTS

Part I

WRITING A PARAGRAPH

Chapter 1

WHAT IS A PARAGRAPH?
An Overview

A **paragraph** is a basic unit of organization in writing in which a group of related sentences develops one main idea. A paragraph can be as short as one sentence or as long as ten sentences. The number of sentences is unimportant; however, the paragraph should be long enough to develop the main idea clearly.

The following model contains all of the elements of a good paragraph. Read it carefully two or three times and try to analyze its structure.

Model 1: Paragraph structure

Gold

1   Gold, a precious metal, is prized for two important characteristics. First of all, gold has a lustrous beauty that is resistant to corrosion*. Therefore, it is suitable for jewelry, coins, and ornamental purposes. Gold never needs to be polished and will remain beautiful forever. For example, a Macedonian* coin remains as untarnished* today as

5   the day it was minted twenty-three centuries ago. Another important characteristic of gold is its usefulness to industry and science. For many years, it has been used in hundreds of industrial applications. The most recent use of gold is in astronauts' suits. Astronauts wear gold-plated heat shields for protection outside the spaceship. In conclusion, gold is treasured not only for its beauty, but also for its utility.

THE THREE PARTS OF A PARAGRAPH

A paragraph has three major structural parts: a topic sentence, supporting sentences, and a concluding sentence.

The **topic sentence** states the main idea of the paragraph. It not only names the topic of the paragraph, but it also limits the topic to one or two areas that can be discussed completely in the space of a single paragraph. The specific area is called the controlling idea. Notice how the topic sentence of the model states both the topic and the controlling idea:

Topic Sentence

(Topic)   (*Controlling Idea*)

Gold, a precious metal, is prized for two important characteristics.

---

corrosion: chemical damage   **Macedonian:** from an ancient Mediterranean culture
untarnished: unchanged in color

Supporting sentences develop the topic sentence. That is, they explain the topic sentence by giving reasons, examples, facts, statistics, and quotations. Some of the supporting sentences that explain the topic sentence about gold are:

Supporting Sentences

First of all, gold has a lustrous beauty that is resistant to corrosion.
For example, a Macedonian coin remains as untarnished today as the day it was minted twenty-three centuries ago.
Another important characteristic of gold is its utility in industry and science.
The most recent application of gold is in astronauts' suits.

The **concluding sentence** signals the end of the paragraph and leaves the reader with important points to remember:

Concluding Sentence

In conclusion, gold is treasured not only for its beauty, but also for its utility.

TWO ADDITIONAL ELEMENTS

In addition to the three structural parts of a paragraph, a good paragraph also has the elements of unity and coherence.

Unity

Unity means that you discuss only *one* main idea in a paragraph. The main idea is stated in the topic sentence, and then each and every supporting sentence develops that idea. If, for example, you announce in your topic sentence that you are going to discuss two important characteristics of gold, discuss only those. Do not discuss anything else such as the price of gold, the history of gold, or gold mining.

Coherence

Coherence means that your paragraph is easy to read and understand because (1) your supporting sentences are in some kind of logical order, and (2) your ideas are connected by the use of appropriate transition signals. For example, in the paragraph about gold, there are two main supporting ideas: gold is beautiful, and gold is useful. Each of these supporting ideas is discussed, one after the other, and an example is given for each one. This is one kind of logical order. Furthermore, the relationship between the ideas is clearly shown by using appropriate transition words and phrases such as "first of all," "the second important characteristic," "for example," and "in conclusion."

In summary, a well-written paragraph contains five elements: a topic sentence, supporting sentences, a concluding sentence, unity, and coherence. In the first section of this book, you will study and practice each of these elements.

THE ASSIGNMENT FORMAT

Below are instructions and a model of one possible format for the assignments you will prepare for this class. Your instructor may ask you to use this format, or s/he may have other requirements.

1. Use only 8½″ × 11″ lined, 3-hole notebook paper.
2. Write a title in the center of the top line.
3. Write the practice number, page number and practice name in the upper left-hand corner.

4. Write your name, the course number and date in the upper right-hand corner.

5. Leave one-inch margins on both sides of the page.

6. Indent the first line of every paragraph.*

7. Write on every other line.

8. Number your pages.

9. Write in ink.

Model 2: Assignment format

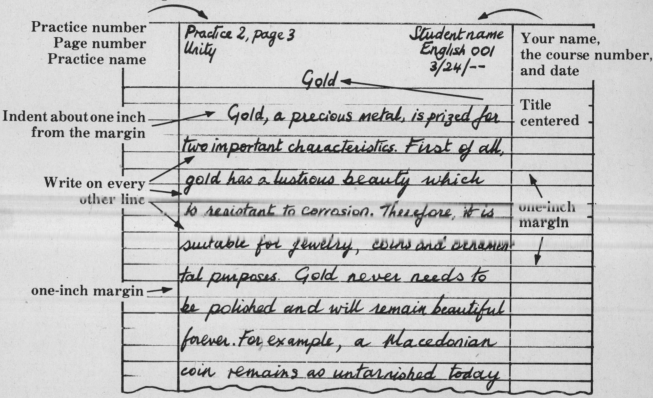

Notice that the first line in the paragraph is indented—moved to the right. While the practice of indenting is changing, particularly in business letter writing, it is still the accepted practice in academic writing.

HOW TO WRITE A TITLE

Single paragraphs do not usually have titles. Giving your practice paragraphs titles, however, may help you to organize and limit your thoughts. For longer essays or reports, though, the use of titles (as you will see in this book) will become more necessary.

A title tells the reader what the topic of the paragraph is. It is usually a word or phrase, not a sentence. It should be brief, but not so brief that it doesn't tell the reader what to expect.

*INDENT the first line of every paragraph. When typing, indent the first line 5 spaces. When writing by hand, indent the first line about one inch from the margin.

1. The first, last, and all important words in a title are capitalized. Prepositions and articles are not important words. Prepositions of more than five letters, however, may be capitalized. Articles that begin the title, of course, are capitalized.

2. The title is not underlined.

3. The title is not enclosed in quotation marks, nor is it ended with a period.

Example

My Greatest Culture Shock
How to Choose a Good Used Car
Inflation Affects Everybody
Backpacking in the Mountains
Writing Academic English
Riding the Subway in New York

The Topic Sentence

Every good paragraph has a topic sentence, which clearly states the topic and the controlling idea of the paragraph. It is a complete sentence. It is usually (but not always) the first sentence in the paragraph.

A topic sentence is the most important sentence in a paragraph. It briefly indicates what the paragraph is going to discuss. For this reason, the topic sentence is a helpful guide to both the writer and the reader. The writer can see what information to include (and what information to exclude). The reader can see what the paragraph is going to be about and is therefore better prepared to understand it.

There are three important points to remember about the topic sentence:

A topic sentence is a *complete sentence*; that is, it contains a subject, a verb, and (usually) a complement.

The following are *not* complete sentences.

Driving on freeways.
The importance of gold.
How to register for college classes.

A topic sentence contains both *a topic and a controlling idea*. It names the topic and then limits the topic to a specific area to be discussed in the space of a single paragraph.

The following examples show how a topic sentence states both the topic and the controlling idea in a complete sentence.

Driving on freeways requires skill and alertness.
Gold, a precious metal, is prized for two important characteristics.
Registering for college classes can be a frustrating experience for new students.

A topic sentence gives only the main idea; therefore, it is the most general statement in the paragraph. It does not give any specific details.

This is an example of a general statement that could serve as a topic sentence:

Good   *The Arabic origin of many English words is not always obvious.*

This sentence, on the other hand, is too specific to serve as a topic sentence:

Too   *The slang expression "so long" (meaning goodbye) is probably a*
Specific   *corruption of the Arabic "salaam."*

POSITION OF TOPIC SENTENCES

The topic sentence may be the first or last sentence in a paragraph. The topic sentence may also be the first *and* last sentence of the paragraph—"sandwich-style." A "sandwich-style" paragraph is especially helpful to your reader if the paragraph is very long. The second topic sentence in the "sandwich-style" paragraph also serves as a concluding sentence.

Study the following three paragraphs. Notice the different positions for the topic sentence in each. The topic sentences are underlined.

Model 2: Position of topic sentences

Hurricanes

Topic Sentence   Hurricanes, which are also called cyclones, exert tremendous power. These violent storms are often a hundred miles in diameter, and their winds can reach velocities* of seventy-five miles per hour or more. Furthermore, the strong winds and heavy rainfall that accompany them can completely destroy a small town in a couple of hours. The energy that is released by a hurricane in one day exceeds the total energy consumed by humankind throughout the world in one year.

Famous School "Failures"

Albert Einstein, one of the world's geniuses, failed his university entrance examinations on his first attempt. William Faulkner, one of America's noted writers, never finished college because he could not pass his English courses. Sir Winston Churchill, who is considered one of the masters of the English language, had to have special tutoring in **Topic Sentence** English during elementary school. These few examples show that failure in school does not always predict failure in life.

Synonyms

Topic Sentence   Synonyms, words that have the same basic meaning, do not always have the same emotional meaning. For example, the words "stingy" and "frugal" both mean "careful with money." However, to call a person stingy is an insult, while the word frugal has a much more positive connotation*. Similarly, a person wants to be slender but not skinny, and **Topic Sentence (Conclusion)** aggressive, but not pushy. Therefore, you should be careful in choosing words because many so-called synonyms are not really synonymous at all.

velocities: speeds   connotation: implied meaning

Practice 1: Recognizing Topic Sentences

Remember, the topic sentence indicates the main idea of a paragraph and is the most general statement in the paragraph.

STEP 1   Decide which of the following sentences is the topic sentence of the paragraph.

STEP 2   Write TS on the line next to that sentence.

STEP 3   Decide what order the supporting sentences should be in and number them 1, 2, 3, and 4.

Paragraph 1

_____ a. Next, add antifreeze to your windshield washer fluid; otherwise, the fluid will freeze and possibly break the container.

_____ b. First, put on snow tires if you plan to drive on snowy, icy roads very often.

_____ c. Driving in winter, especially on snowy, icy roads, can be less troublesome if you take a few simple precautions*.

_____ d. Finally, it is also a good idea to carry tire chains, a can of spray to unfreeze door locks and a windshield scraper in your car when driving in winter weather.

_____ e. Second, check the amount of antifreeze in your radiator and add more if necessary.

Paragraph 2

_____ a. Furthermore, researchers are continuing to work on the development of an efficient, electrically powered automobile.

_____ b. Researchers in the automobile industry are experimenting with different types of engines and fuels as alternatives to the conventional gasoline engines.

_____ c. One new type of engine, which burns diesel oil instead of gasoline, has been available for several years.

_____ d. Finally, several automobile manufacturers are experimenting with methanol, which is a mixture of gasoline and methyl alcohol, as an automobile fuel.

_____ e. A second type is the gas turbine engine, which can use fuels made from gasoline, diesel oil, kerosene, other petroleum distillates*, or methanol.

---

precaution: advance action to prevent something   **distillate:** a substance obtained from another substance

Paragraph 3

_____ a. Later on, people began to write on pieces of leather, which were rolled into scrolls.

_____ b. In the earliest times, people carved or painted messages on rocks.

_____ c. In the Middle Ages, heavy paper called parchment was used for writing; books were laboriously copied by hand.

_____ d. With the invention of the printing press in the middle of the fifteenth century, the modern printing industry was born.

_____ e. Some form of written communication has been used throughout the centuries.

Paragraph 4

_____ a. If there had been a big storm on the day of a baby's birth, the baby might have been named Thunder Cloud.

_____ b. American Indian names are very descriptive, for Indians were usually named for a physical attribute, for an occurrence in nature, or for an animal.

_____ c. Grey Eagle, Red Dog, Big Bear, and Spotted Wolf are examples of Indians named after animals.

_____ d. Indians with distinctive physical characteristics might be given such names as Big Foot or Crooked Leg.

Paragraph 5

_____ a. For one thing, individual I.Q.* scores vary considerably.

_____ b. Many experts also question whether I.Q. scores are related to intelligence.

_____ c. Furthermore, most psychologists agree that intelligence tests are biased* in favor of middle-class children.

_____ d. The validity* of standardized intelligence tests is being seriously questioned by educators and psychologists.

_____ e. In fact, motivation* seems to be just as important as intelligence in determining a person's ability to learn.

I.Q.: Intelligence Quotient   **biased**: prejudiced   **validity**: truth
motivation: desire

THE TWO PARTS OF A TOPIC SENTENCE

A topic sentence has two essential parts: the topic and the controlling idea. The *topic* names the subject or main idea of the paragraph. The *controlling idea* makes a specific comment about the topic, which indicates what the rest of the paragraph will say about the topic. It limits or controls the topic to a specific aspect of the topic to be discussed in the space of a single paragraph.

       TOPIC   CONTROLLING IDEA
    (Convenience foods) are <u>easy to prepare.</u>

In this example, the topic is named: convenience foods. A specific comment is then made about the topic: they are easy to prepare. From this sentence, the reader immediately knows that the supporting sentences in the remainder of the paragraph will explain or prove how quick and easy it is to prepare convenience foods, and perhaps give some examples (frozen dinners, canned soups, etc.).

       TOPIC   CONTROLLING IDEA
   (American cooking) reflects <u>the native foods of America's immigrant population.</u>

In this example, the topic is American food. The controlling idea of this topic sentence is that Americans eat a lot of food that originally came from other countries. Therefore, the reader should expect the paragraph to give examples of popular "foreign" foods such as fried rice (Chinese), tacos (Mexican), sauerbraten (German), sukiyaki (Japanese), spaghetti (Italian), and so on.

       TOPIC   CONTROLLING IDEA
  (The average American teenager) consumes <u>enormous quantities of junk food.</u>

In this example, the topic is the average American teenager. The controlling idea about the topic states that the American teenager eats a lot of junk food. Thus, the rest of the paragraph should discuss the quantities and types of junk food that American teenagers eat (soft drinks, potato chips, candy bars, etc.).

Practice 2: Identifying the Parts of a Topic Sentence

Circle the topic and underline the controlling idea in each of the following sentences.

Example   (Driving on freeways) requires <u>skill and alertness.</u>

1. Driving in Tokyo requires nerves of steel*.
2. Driving in Tokyo requires an aggressive attitude.
3. Living in a dormitory helps foreign students improve their English faster.
4. Living in a dormitory helps foreign students learn about American culture more quickly.
5. Living in a dormitory may cause severe culture shock for some foreign students.

---

nerves of steel: very strong
      nerves (idiom)

6. San Francisco is famous for its temperate climate.

7. San Francisco is well known for its many tourist attractions.

8. San Francisco has a great variety of ethnic* neighborhoods.

9. Meeting and making friends with Americans is a major problem for many foreign students.

10. Communicating in English is a major problem for foreign students.

11. In my opinion, many television commercials are misleading.

12. In the opinion of the nation's economic experts, the primary cause of inflation is our dependence on imported oil.

13. A good topic sentence has two essential parts.

14. Owning a large automobile is quickly becoming an expensive luxury.

WRITING TOPIC SENTENCES: TWO REMINDERS

One: **A topic sentence should be neither too general nor too specific. If it is too general, the reader cannot tell exactly what the paragraph is going to discuss. If it is too specific, the writer may not have anything left to write about in the rest of the paragraph.**

Think of a topic sentence like the name of a particular course on a restaurant menu. When you order food in a restaurant, you want to know more about a particular course than just "meat" or "soup" or "salad." You want to know *generally* what kind of salad it is. Potato salad? Mixed green salad? Fruit salad? You do not necessarily want to know all of its ingredients.

Similarly, the reader of a paragraph wants to know *generally* what to expect in a paragraph; the reader does not want to learn all of the specific details in the first sentence.

Too general	American food is terrible.
Too specific	American food is tasteless and greasy because Americans use too many canned, frozen, and prepackaged foods and because everything is fried in oil or butter.
Good	American food is tasteless and greasy.

Two: **Do not include too many unrelated ideas in your topic sentence; if you do, your paragraph will not be unified.**

Too many ideas	San Francisco is famous for its temperate climate, its many tourist attractions, and its cosmopolitan* atmosphere.

The three parts of this controlling idea are too unrelated for a single paragraph. They would require three separate paragraphs.

Good	San Francisco is famous for its many tourist attractions.

---

ethnic: of different racial and cultural backgrounds   **cosmopolitan:** international

Practice 3: Writing Topic Sentences

A. Write a topic sentence for each of the following topics. Remember to include both a topic (main idea) and a controlling idea.

Example

Topic: The effect(s) of television on children.

Topic Sentence: Television is harmful to children because it teaches them violence as a way of life.

                                            or

                  Television retards a child's reading ability.

1. The effect(s) of smoking on a person's health.
2. The benefits of foreign travel.
3. The importance of a college education for your field of study (engineering, medical technology, art, business, etc.).
4. The cause(s) of a current problem in your country (or in the United States).
5. A cultural difference between your country and the United States.

B. Choose, either individually or with your classmates as a group, five additional topics that interest you. Write these topics in the spaces below. Then write topic sentences for each.

6. _____

7. _____

8. _____

9. _____

10. _____

The Concluding Sentence

Now that you know how to write a good topic sentence for a paragraph, you should also learn how to write a good concluding sentence. A concluding sentence is not absolutely necessary, but it is very often helpful to the reader because it signals the end of the paragraph and because it reminds him/her of your important points.

A concluding sentence serves three purposes:
1. It signals the end of the paragraph. (Use an end-of-paragraph signal such as "In conclusion," "In summary," "Finally," etc.)
2. It summarizes the main points of the paragraph.
3. It gives a final comment on your topic and leaves the reader with the most important ideas to think about.

The examples below demonstrate two different types of concluding sentences. The first one paraphrases the topic sentence; i.e.,* the concluding sentence repeats the main idea of the topic sentence in different words. The second example summarizes the two main points of the paragraph, which were not specifically stated in the topic sentence.

Model 3: Concluding sentences

Synonyms

Synonyms, words that have the same basic meaning, do not always have the same emotional meaning. For example, the words "stingy" and "frugal" both mean "careful with money." However, to call a person stingy is an insult, while the word frugal has a much more positive connotation. Similarly, a person wants to be slender but not skinny, and aggressive but not pushy. Therefore, you should be careful in choosing words because many so-called synonyms are not really synonymous at all.

Gold

Gold, a precious metal, is prized for two important characteristics. First of all, gold has a lustrous beauty that is resistant to corrosion. Therefore, it is suitable for jewelry, coins, and ornamental purposes. Gold never needs to be polished and will remain beautiful forever. For example, a Macedonian coin remains as untarnished today as the day it was minted twenty-three centuries ago. Another important characteristic of gold is its usefulness to industry and science. For many years, it has been used in hundreds of industrial applications. The most recent use of gold is in astronauts' suits. Astronauts wear gold-plated heat shields for protection outside the spaceship. In conclusion, gold is treasured not only for its beauty, but also for its utility.

Practice 4: Writing Concluding Sentences

STEP 1 Underline the topic sentence in each paragraph.
STEP 2 Determine the main idea of each paragraph.
STEP 3 Add a good concluding sentence to each. You may either paraphrase the topic sentence or summarize the main points.
STEP 4 Begin each concluding sentence with an end-of-paragraph signal.

Paragraph 1

1   You can reduce gas consumption in your car by careful driving and good maintenance. Don't speed. Gas consumption is about 10 percent higher at 60 miles per hour than at 50 miles per hour and even greater at higher speeds. Avoid fast stops and starts because they wear your tires out in addition to using a lot of gas. Check your tire pressure often
5   because underinflated tires reduce gas mileage considerably. Get your car tuned up regularly because an inefficiently operating engine results in inefficient fuel consumption. _____

_____

_____

_____

_____

i.e.: that is (from the Latin abbreviation *id est*)

Paragraph 2

1 Alternative energy sources are becoming increasingly attractive as the energy crisis
becomes more severe. Solar heating systems, which use the sun's radiation as a source of
energy, are a promising alternative energy source. Nuclear power plants are already
in operation in several parts of the country. Government and private industry are even
5 investigating the possibility of capturing the power of ocean waves and tides for conversion* into usable energy. Coal is once again becoming an acceptable fuel as the nation
searches for solutions to the energy shortage. Even garbage is seen as a potential source
of energy. In some communities, garbage is burned to heat buildings and light city
streets. _____

_____

_____

_____

Paragraph 3

1 House construction in various parts of the world depends mainly on the availability
of building materials. For example, the Eskimos, living in a treeless region of snow
and ice, sometimes build temporary homes out of thick blocks of ice. People who live
in deserts, on the other hand, use the most available material, mud or clay, which
5 provides good insulation* from the heat. In Northern Europe, Russia, and other areas
of the world where forests are plentiful, people usually construct their homes out of
wood. In the islands of the South Pacific, where there is a plentiful supply of bamboo
and palm, people use these tough, fibrous* plants to build their homes. _____

_____

_____

_____

Paragraph 4

1 There are numerous everyday words in English that have come from other languages.
Americans relaxing at home, for example, may put on *kimonos**, which is a Japanese
word. Americans who live in a temperate climate may take an afternoon *siesta** on an
outdoor *patio**, without even realizing that these are Spanish words. In their garden,
5 they may enjoy the fragrance of *jasmine* flowers, a word that came into English from
Persian. They may even relax on a *chaise longue** while sipping a drink made with *vodka*,
words of French and Russian origin, respectively. _____

_____

_____

_____

---

conversion: change   **siesta:** afternoon nap
insulation: protection   **patio:** courtyard
fibrous: containing fiber   **chaise longue:** lounge chair
kimono: lounging robe

Paragraph 5

1   There are two major differences between the European and American university systems. In European universities, students are not required to attend classes. In fact, professors in Germany generally do not know the names of the students enrolled in their courses. In the United States, however, students are required to attend all

5   classes and may be penalized* if they don't. Furthermore, in the European system, there is usually just one comprehensive examination at the end of the students' entire four or five years of study. In the American system, on the other hand, there are usually numerous quizzes, tests, and homework assignments, and there is almost always a final examination in each course at the end of the semester. _____

_____

_____

_____

Review: What Is a Paragraph?

> These are the important points you should have learned from this chapter:
>
> 1. A good topic sentence:
>   a. is a complete sentence with a subject, a verb, and generally a complement.
>   b. states both the topic and the controlling idea of the paragraph.
>   c. is neither too general nor too specific. It states the main idea clearly, but it does not give the specific details.
>   d. is usually (but not always) the first sentence in the paragraph.
>
> 2. A good concluding sentence:
>   a. signals the end of the paragraph.
>   b. summarizes the important points briefly.

WRITING PRACTICE

Choose a topic from the list below and write a paragraph six to ten sentences in length.

STEP 1 Begin your paragraph with a good topic sentence and underline it.

STEP 2 Write several supporting sentences that explain or support the topic sentence.

STEP 3 Write a good concluding sentence and underline it.

STEP 4 Check your paragraph against the Paragraph Checklist on page 16 before you hand it in.

Topic Suggestions

Arranged marriages.

Uncontrolled population growth.

Computers, calculators, or machines in general.

Left-handed people.

The advantages of having a college education.

Owning a car.

---

penalized: punished

Paragraph Checklist

Form: _____ Does your paragraph have a title?
                             _____ Did you write on the correct side of the paper?
                             _____ Did you indent?
                             _____ Did you write on every other line?
                             (Refer to pages 4-5 for complete instructions)

Topic Sentence: _____ Does your topic sentence contain a control-
                                   ling idea?

Concluding Sentence: _____ Does your paragraph have a concluding sen-
                                   tence?

WRITING UNDER PRESSURE

Choose one of your best topic sentences from Practice 3 on page 12 and write a paragraph six to ten sentences long on the subject of that sentence. Check your paragraph against the Paragraph Checklist before you hand it in.

Your instructor will give you a time limit. Suggested limits:

Writing Time   — 13 minutes
Checking Time — 2 minutes

Total — 15 minutes

Chapter 2
UNITY AND SIMPLE OUTLINING

Another important element of a good paragraph is **unity**.

Every good paragraph has unity, which means that in each paragraph, only *one* main idea is discussed. If you start to discuss a new idea, start a new paragraph. Furthermore, every supporting sentence in the paragraph must be directly related to the main idea. Do not include any information that does not directly support the topic sentence.

Uni- is a Latin prefix meaning "one." When we talk about paragraph unity, we mean that you should discuss only *one* main idea in each paragraph. For example, if your paragraph is about the advantages of a college education, discuss only that. Do not discuss the disadvantages in getting a college education. To make it even easier, discuss only *one* advantage in each paragraph, such as the ability to get a better job. However, sometimes it is possible to discuss two or even three aspects of the same idea in one paragraph *if they are closely related to each other*. For example, it is possible to discuss both "better job" and "better salary" in the same paragraph because they are closely related, but it is not a good idea to discuss both "better job" and "better general knowledge about the world" in the same paragraph because they are not so closely related.

The second part of unity is that every supporting sentence must *directly* explain or prove the main idea, which is stated in the topic sentence. Sometimes students write supporting sentences that are "off the topic." For example, if you are writing a paragraph about the high cost of college tuition, you could mention inflation as a factor. But if you write several sentences about inflation, you are getting "off the topic," and your paragraph will not have unity.

Study the two paragraphs below. Both paragraphs discuss the same topic. In your opinion, which paragraph has unity and which one doesn't? Explain how individual sentences break the unity either by introducing a new idea or by being "off the topic."

Model 4: Unity

Surviving Cancer

Progress is gradually being made in the fight against cancer. In the early 1900s, few cancer patients had any hope of long-term survival. In the 1930s, less than one in five cancer victims lived more than five years. In the 1950s, the ratio was one in four. Currently, the ratio is down to one in three. The gain from one in four to one in three represents about 58,000 lives saved each year.

Surviving Cancer

Progress is gradually being made in the fight against cancer. In the early 1900s, few cancer patients had any hope of long-term survival. But because of advances in medical technology, progress has been made so that currently one in three cancer patients survives. It has been proven that smoking is a direct cause of lung cancer. However, the battle has not yet been won. Although cures for some forms of cancer have been discovered, other forms of cancer are still increasing. Heart disease is also increasing.

Practice 5: Unity I

The following short essay has not been divided into paragraphs, but it should contain six: an introductory paragraph, four "body" paragraphs, and a concluding paragraph.

STEP 1 Read the entire essay once or twice.
STEP 2 Decide where each new paragraph should begin. (Where does the author begin to discuss a different topic?)
STEP 3 Underline the first sentence of each paragraph.

Culture, Logic, and Rhetoric

1   Logic*, which is the basis of rhetoric, comes from culture; it is not universal. Rhetoric, therefore, is not universal either, but varies from culture to culture. The rhetorical system of one language is neither better nor worse than the rhetorical system of another language, but it is different. English logic and English rhetoric, which are
5   based on Anglo-European cultural patterns, are linear*—that is, a good English paragraph begins with a general statement of its content and then carefully develops that statement with a series of specific illustrations. A good English paragraph may also use just the reverse sequence: it may state a whole series of examples and then summarize those examples in a single statement at the end of the paragraph. In
10   either case, however, the flow of ideas occurs in a straight line from the opening sentence to the last sentence. Furthermore, a well-structured English paragraph is never digressive*. There is nothing that does not belong to the paragraph, and nothing that does not support the topic sentence. A type of construction found in Arabic and Persian writing is very different. Whereas English writers use a linear
15   sequence, Arabic and Persian writers tend to construct a paragraph in a parallel sequence using many coordinators*, such as *and* and *but*. In English, maturity of style is often judged by the degree of subordination* rather than by the degree of coordination. Therefore, the Arabic and Persian styles of writing, with their emphasis on coordination, seem awkward and immature to an English reader. Some Asian writers, on the
20   other hand, use an indirect approach. In this kind of writing, the topic is viewed from a variety of angles. The topic is never analyzed directly; it is referred to only indirectly. Again, such a development in an English paragraph is awkward and unnecessarily vague* to an English reader. Spanish rhetoric differs from English
25   rhetoric in still another way. While the rules of English rhetoric require that every sentence in a paragraph relates directly to the central idea, a Spanish-speaking writer loves to fill a paragraph with interesting digressions. Although a Spanish paragraph may begin and end on the same topic, the writer often digresses into areas that are not directly related to the topic. Spanish rhetoric, therefore, does not follow

---

logic: way of thinking or reasoning
linear: in a straight line
digressive: wandering away from
    the main topic
vague: unclear

coordinators: words that join equal elements
subordination: the joining of two unequal
    elements

30   the English rule of paragraph unity. In summary, a student who has mastered the
     grammar of English may still write poor papers unless the rhetoric of English is also
     mastered. Also, the student may have difficulty reading an essay written by the rules
     of English rhetoric unless (s)he understands the "logical" differences from those of
     his/her own native tongue.[1]

Practice 6: Unity II

A. Each of the following paragraphs breaks the rule of unity because it contains
one or more sentences that do not directly support the topic sentence.

STEP 1 Locate and underline the topic sentence of each paragraph.
STEP 2 Find the sentence(s) that do not support the topic sentence and cross
them out.

Paragraph 1

1   Tourism is the state of Hawaii's leading industry. Every year, some 3.2 million tourists
visit the islands. During the popular winter months, a planeload or shipload of tourists
arrives every fifteen minutes. New hotels, new resorts, and new restaurants are being
built every year to accommodate the increasing numbers of visitors. Sugar cane and
5   pineapples are also important industries in Hawaii.

Paragraph 2

1   The rapid increase in crime in Chicago is causing a great deal of concern to the city's
citizens. People are afraid to go out into the streets at night because they are afraid of
being robbed or even killed. More and more families are moving out of the city into the
suburbs* because of the high crime rate. The chief of police was fired last month
5   because of his inability to reduce crime. People are buying strong locks for their doors
and installing heavy iron bars across their windows to prevent burglaries. Some citizens
are even purchasing guns to protect themselves and their property. Indeed, it seems
that the increase in crime is turning the average home in Chicago into a prison for its
inhabitants.

Paragraph 3

1   The convenience and economy of small cars account for their popularity. They are easy
to park quickly and take smaller parking spaces. Small cars are also a means of conserving energy because they use less gas than big cars. Small cars are inconvenient and
uncomfortable on long trips, however, because of their limited passenger and trunk
5   space. They are also more economical to operate and maintain, and they cost less.
Because of all these advantages, the next car I buy is going to be an Econo-Midget.

---

[1] Adapted from Robert B. Kaplan, "Cultural Thought Patterns in Intercultural Education,"
Language Learning 16 (1966), pp. 1–20. Used with permission of the publishers.

---

suburbs: small communities surrounding a large city

B. Each of the following paragraphs has not only two or more topic sentences but also irrelevant sentences.

STEP 1 Decide where each paragraph should be divided into two or more paragraphs. Underline the topic sentence of each.
STEP 2 Find the irrelevant sentence(s) and cross them out.

Paragraph 4

1   The recent water shortage in California forced changes in Californians' lifestyles. When water was rationed*, Californians learned to conserve water. They didn't water their lawns and gardens or wash their automobiles. Also, they took fewer showers and baths. The water shortage lasted two years. Californians also learned to recycle*
5   water. For example, they used the rinse water from their washing machines to water their houseplants and gardens. California's agricultural industry was also severely affected by the water shortage. Because their water was also rationed, farmers planted fewer acres* and had to plan their crops more carefully. Many farmers planted crops that required less water and reduced the number of crops that needed
10   a lot of water. This eventually caused an increase in the price of food in supermarkets all over the country.

Paragraph 5

1   The United States and Canada will someday join the 95 percent of the world that uses the metric rather than the English system of measurement. No longer will North American schoolchildren have to memorize that there are 12 inches in a foot, 3 feet in a yard, 5½ yards in a rod, 40 rods in a furlong, and 8 furlongs in a mile. Inches
5   will become centimeters, pounds will become kilograms, quarts will become liters, and degrees Fahrenheit will become degrees centigrade (also called Celsius). The English system of measurement has been used in English-speaking countries since about the year 1200. The conversion to the metric system will not be easy, however, and will require enormous amounts of money and time. Proponents* of the change
10   argue that it is necessary in order for North American products to compete in world markets with metric products. For example, every piece of machinery in every factory and every office will have to be replaced. Furthermore, every machine and tool that makes, repairs, or supplies another piece of equipment will have to be changed. Not only every nut, bolt, and screw, but also every wrench, drill, and screwdriver will
15   have to be replaced, as any auto mechanic who has tried to fix an imported car with a set of American tools realizes. Therefore, although the United States and Canada are committed to "going metric," it will not happen next week or even next year. Because of the magnitude* of the problems that metric conversion will involve, the change will have to be gradual and, above all, carefully planned.

---

rationed: limited in amount
recycle: use again
acre: unit of area (1 acre
        = 4.047 square meters)

proponents: people in favor of something
magnitude: great size

Simple Paragraph Outlining

An outline is like an architect's plan for a house. An architect plans a house before it is built to make sure that all the parts will fit. Like an architect, you should plan a paragraph before you write it to make sure that all of your ideas will fit.

Learning to outline will improve your writing for three reasons. First of all, it will help you organize your ideas. Specifically, an outline will ensure that you won't include any irrelevant ideas, that you won't leave out any important points, and that your supporting sentences will be in logical order. Second, learning to outline will help you write more quickly. It may take some practice at first, but once you become used to outlining your ideas before you start to write, you will be surprised at how fast you will actually be able to write. Preparing an outline is 75 percent of the work. The actual writing becomes easier because you don't have to worry about what you are going to say; you already have a well-organized plan to follow. Finally, your grammar will improve because you will be able to concentrate on it, not on your thoughts or organization. Improved organization, speed, and grammar make learning to outline well worth the effort.

There are several different outline forms that can be used. The form used in this book is particularly helpful for students who have never practiced outlining before. However, your instructor may recommend a different form.

SIMPLE OUTLINES

A simple outline for a short paragraph might look like this:

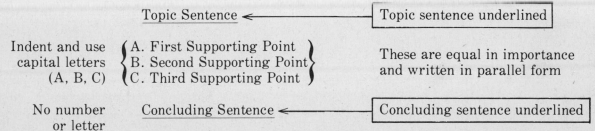

Of course, the number of main supporting points (A, B, C) will vary widely from paragraph to paragraph. This particular paragraph has three main supporting points; others may have only two or as many as ten or even twenty. Also, some paragraphs may not have a concluding sentence, and in others, the topic sentence may not be the first sentence.

Model 5: Simple Paragraph Outlining

Study the simple outline below for the second paragraph on page 21. Then re-read the paragraph to see how the writer used this plan to write a well-organized paragraph that is easy to understand.

Learning to outline will improve your writing for three reasons.
    A. It will help you organize your ideas.
    B. It will help you write more quickly.
    C. It will help you improve your grammar.
For these three reasons—improved organization, speed, and grammar—learning to outline is well worth the effort.

Writing Technique Questions

1. Are the three items in the support part of the outline above equivalent in value? (Are they all reasons or all examples?)
2. Are they all parallel in form? What is their form—nouns, verbs, adjectives, dependent clauses, or complete sentences?
3. Suggest shorter ways to write the support part of the outline.

THE "EQUIVALENT VALUE" RULE

In a formal outline, ideas that have the same kind of letter or number must have equal value. This means that every capital letter must be equal in value, and every idea given a small letter or Arabic numeral or Roman numeral must be equal. If, for example, your paragraph contains both reasons and examples, you should give the reasons one kind of letter or number, and examples another kind.

Incorrect

Topic Sentence
    A. Reason
    B. Example
    C. Example
    D. Reason
    E. Example
    F. Example
Concluding Sentence

Correct

Topic Sentence
    A. Reason
      1. Example
      2. Example
    B. Reason
      1. Example
      2. Example
Concluding Sentence

THE "PARALLEL FORM" RULE

Equal parts of a formal outline should be written in parallel form. This means that all ideas given the same kind of letter or number should be written in complete sentences, clauses, phrases, or single words such as adjectives, etc.

Incorrect

Rocks make excellent pets.
    A. They don't eat.
    B. Cleanliness.
    C. Obedient.
For these three reasons, rocks make great pets.

Correct

Rocks make excellent pets.
    A. They don't eat.
    B. They are clean.
    C. They are obedient.
For these three reasons, rocks make great pets.

In the incorrect outline above, the main supporting points are all different grammatical structures. A is a complete sentence, B is a noun, and C is an adjective. In the corrected outline, all three are complete sentences. Of course, you don't have to write complete sentences in the support part of an outline. You could write the same outline in these four ways:

1. A. Don't eat
   B. Are clean
   C. Are obedient

2. A. Because they don't eat
   B. Because they are clean
   C. Because they are obedient

3. A. Economical
   B. Clean
   C. Obedient

4. A. Economy
   B. Cleanliness
   C. Obedience

Remember to write your outline in parallel form by using the same grammatical patterns.

These are the important things to remember about simple outlining:

1. Give main supporting points capital letters.
2. Make sure that your main supporting points are equal. For example, do not give reasons and examples the same kind of letter or number.
3. Make sure that your main supporting points are written in parallel form.

Practice 7: Making Outlines Parallel

Rewrite each of these outlines to make the support part parallel in form.

1. San Francisco is famous for its tourist attractions.
   A. Golden Gate Park is very famous.
   B. Chinatown.
   C. Fisherman's Wharf attracts hundreds of tourists.
   D. Riding the cable cars.

For these four attractions alone, San Francisco is well worth a visit.

2. Gold, a precious metal, is prized for two important characteristics.
   A. It is beautiful.
   B. Useful to science and industry.

In conclusion, gold is treasured not only for its beauty but also for its utility.

3. Some of the world's most successful men had trouble in school.
   A. Albert Einstein failed his university entrance exams on his first attempt.
   B. William Faulkner's F's in English.
   C. Special tutoring necessary for Winston Churchill.

These few examples show that failure in school does not always predict failure in life.

Practice 8: Simple Paragraph Outlining I

Turn back to Practice 6A on page 19 and prepare a simple outline for each paragraph. Make sure that the support parts of your outlines are parallel.

Practice 9: Simple Paragraph Outlining II

Choose any three of the topic sentences below and write a simple outline for a paragraph for each of them. Follow the outline form in the model. Your supporting ideas can be reasons, examples, or simple facts.

1. Students who both work and attend school lead busy lives.
2. Technology is making people lazy.
3. Technology is making our lives easier.
4. A good doctor (teacher, scientist, businessperson, athlete) has two (three, four, five) important qualities.
5. Pollution is a growing threat to life on earth.

Review: Unity and Simple Outlining

These are the important points you should have learned from this chapter:

1. Every good paragraph has unity. Discuss only one idea in each paragraph. All supporting sentences must directly support the topic sentence.
2. A simple outline in the proper form includes a topic sentence, the main supporting points, and a concluding sentence.

WRITING PRACTICE

Choose one of the suggested topics listed below and write a paragraph ten to fifteen sentences in length. Be sure your paragraph is unified.

STEP 1 Write a simple outline that has all the parts (topic sentence, supporting ideas, and a concluding sentence). Make sure it is parallel in form.
STEP 2 Write your paragraph from your outline. Add enough sentences in the support part to make your main points clear.
STEP 3 Underline your topic sentence and your concluding sentence.
STEP 4 Check your paragraph against the Paragraph Checklist on page 25 before you hand in both your outline and your paragraph.

Topic Suggestions

Choose a famous person whom you admire. Explain why you admire that person, naming several qualities that make the individual admirable. If possible, cite instances when this person displayed these qualities.

The goals you will have achieved when you are forty years old. Discuss at least three different areas (family, job, house, finances).

The living arrangement (a college dormitory, a room with an American family, an apartment with some friends, a room in your parents' home) that, in your opinion, is the best for a person in your particular situation.

Paragraph Checklist

Form: _____ Does your paragraph have a title?
                           _____ Did you write on the correct side of the paper?
                           _____ Did you indent?
                           _____ Did you write on every other line?
                           (Refer to the Assignment Format on pages 4–5 for
                           complete instructions.)

Topic Sentence: _____ Does your topic sentence contain a controlling
                                 idea?

Supporting Sentences:
  Unity: _____ Do all of your sentences directly support your
                                 topic sentence?

Concluding Sentence: _____ Does your paragraph have a concluding sen-
                                 tence?

WRITING UNDER PRESSURE

Choose one of the topics from Practice 9 on page 24, and write a paragraph about it. Make a quick outline before you begin.

Check your paragraph against the Paragraph Checklist before you hand in both your outline and your paragraph.

Your instructor will give you a time limit. Suggested limits:

    Outlining Time — 3 minutes
    Writing Time   — 10 minutes
    Checking Time — 2 minutes

        Total — 15 minutes

Chapter 3

COHERENCE FROM TRANSITION SIGNALS

Another element of a good paragraph is **coherence**. *Co-* is a Latin prefix that means "together" or "with." The verb *cohere* means "hold together." In order to have coherence in writing, the movement from one sentence to the next (and in longer essays, from one paragraph to the next) must be logical and smooth. There must be no sudden jumps. Each sentence should flow smoothly into the next one.

There are two main ways to achieve coherence. The first way is to use *transition signals* to show how one idea is related to the next. The second way to achieve coherence is to arrange your sentences in *logical order*.

Transition Signals

Transition signals are words such as *first, second, next, finally, therefore*, and *however*, or phrases such as *in conclusion, on the other hand*, and *as a result*.

Think of transition signals as traffic signs that tell your reader when to go forward, turn, slow down, and stop. In other words, tell the reader when you are giving a similar idea (*similarly, moreover, furthermore, in addition*), an opposite idea (*on the other hand, however, in contrast*), an example (*for example*), a result (*as a result*), or a conclusion (*in conclusion*).

Using transition words to guide your reader makes it easier to follow your ideas. Transition words give your paragraph coherence.

Practice 10: Transition Signals

Compare paragraphs 1 and 2 on page 28. Both paragraphs give the same information, yet one paragraph is easier to understand than the other because it contains transition signals to lead the reader from one idea to the next.

Which paragraph contains transition signals and is more coherent? Circle all of the transition signals that you can identify.

Paragraph 1

1   A difference among the world's seas and oceans is that the salinity* varies in different
climate zones. The Baltic Sea in Northern Europe is only one-fourth as saline* as the
Red Sea in the Middle East. There are reasons for this. In warm climates, water
evaporates* rapidly. The concentration* of salt is greater. The surrounding land is dry
5 and does not contribute much fresh water to dilute* the salty sea water. In cold climate
zones, water evaporates slowly. The runoff created by melting snow adds a considerable
amount of fresh water to dilute the saline sea water.

Paragraph 2

1   Another difference among the world's seas and oceans is that the salinity varies in
different climate zones. For example, the Baltic Sea in Northern Europe is only one-
fourth as saline as the Red Sea in the Middle East. There are two reasons for this. First
of all, in warm climate zones, water evaporates rapidly; therefore, the concentration of
5 salt is greater. Second, the surrounding land is dry and, consequently, does not contribute much fresh water to dilute the salty sea water. In cold climate zones, on the other
hand, water evaporates slowly. Furthermore, the runoff created by melting snow adds a
considerable amount of fresh water to dilute the saline sea water.

Paragraph 2 is more coherent because it contains these transition signals:

Another tells you that this paragraph is part of a longer essay.

For example tells you that an example of the preceding idea is coming.

Two tells you to look for two different reasons.

First of all tells you that this is the first reason.

Second and *furthermore* indicate that additional ideas are coming.

Therefore and *consequently* indicate that the second statement is a result of the
first statement.

On the other hand tells you that an opposite idea is coming.

Each transition signal has a special meaning. Each one shows how the following
sentence relates to the preceding one. Of course, you should not use a transition
signal in front of *every* sentence in a paragraph. Using too many transition signals
can be just as confusing as using too few. However, good writing requires that you
use enough transition signals to make the relationships among your ideas clear.

Below is a chart showing some of the most common transition signals. You
should learn to use all of them, for they can be used with all kinds of writing. Later
on, you will learn about special transition signals that are used with certain types
of writing, such as chronological order, comparison, and contrast.

---

salinity: salt content
saline: salty
evaporates: dries up

concentration: amount
dilute: reduce the concentration of

TRANSITION SIGNALS FOR GENERAL USE

Meaning/ Function	Sentence Connectors	Clause Connectors		Others
		Coordinators	Subordinators	
To introduce an **additional** idea	furthermore moreover in addition	and		another (+ noun) an additional (+ noun)
To introduce an **opposite** idea	on the other hand however in contrast	but yet	although though even though whereas while	in spite of (+ noun) despite (+ noun)
To introduce a **choice** or **alternative**	otherwise	or	if unless	
To introduce an **example**	for example for instance e.g.*			an example of (+ noun) such as (+ noun)
To introduce a **restatement** or **explanation**	i.e.			
To introduce a **conclusion** or **summary**	in conclusion in summary to conclude to summarize			

e.g.: for example (from the Latin *exempli gratia*)

TYPES OF TRANSITION SIGNALS

Transition signals can be divided into four basic groups according to function: *sentence connectors*, *coordinators* (coordinating conjunctions), *subordinators* (subordinating conjunctions), *prepositions* and *determiners*.

Sentence Connectors

Examples: *however, therefore, furthermore, for example, on the other hand, in addition, still, otherwise*

Sentence connectors join one independent clause* with another to form a compound sentence, which is punctuated with a semicolon (;) and a comma (,).

INDEPENDENT CLAUSE ; SENTENCE CONNECTOR , INDEPENDENT CLAUSE .

I dislike mushrooms; therefore, I never eat them.
Mushrooms are good for you; however, I never eat them.

Notice that the sentence connector following the semicolon is *not* capitalized.

Sentence connectors may also come at the beginning, in the middle, or at the end of a simple sentence. In these cases, punctuate them with commas as follows:

1. At the beginning:
   Therefore, I never eat them.
   On the other hand, mushrooms are good for you.
2. In the middle:
   I, therefore, never eat them.
   Mushrooms, on the other hand, are good for you.

independent clause: subject + verb + complement

If the sentence connector is one word, the commas may be omitted:
I therefore never eat them.

3. At the end:
I never eat them, therefore.
Mushrooms are good for you, on the other hand.

Coordinators   **Examples:** *and, but, yet, or, nor, for, so.*

These seven coordinators join two independent clauses to form a compound sentence. Punctuate the sentence with a comma after the first clause.

INDEPENDENT CLAUSE   ,   COORDINATOR   INDEPENDENT CLAUSE   .

Mushrooms are good for you, but I dislike them.
I dislike mushrooms, so I never eat them.

Subordinators   **Examples:** *because, after, since, as, although, if, when*

Subordinators introduce a dependent clause* that is joined to an independent clause to form a complex sentence. There are two positions for the dependent clause:

1. If the dependent clause comes before the independent clause, use a comma after it.

DEPENDENT CLAUSE   ,   INDEPENDENT CLAUSE   .

Although mushrooms are good for you, I dislike them.
Because I dislike mushrooms, I never eat them.

2. If the dependent clause comes after the independent clause, do not use a comma.

INDEPENDENT CLAUSE   DEPENDENT CLAUSE   .

I dislike mushrooms although they are good for you.
I never eat mushrooms because I dislike them.

Prepositions and   **Examples:** *because of, due to, in spite of*   (prepositions)
Determiners   *another, additional, final*   (determiners)

This group of transition signals has no special rules for punctuation.

I dislike mushrooms because of a bad experience I once had.
Another reason I dislike mushrooms is their rubbery consistency.

Practice 11: Recognizing Transition Signals

STEP 1 Circle all of the transition signals in the following paragraphs. There are at least ten in each.
STEP 2 Punctuate the transition signals if necessary.

---

dependent clause: subordinator + subject + verb + complement

Paragraph 1

1   Genetic* research has produced both exciting and frightening possibilities. Scientists
are now able to create new forms of life in the laboratory due to the development of
gene splicing*. On one hand the ability to create life in the laboratory could greatly
benefit mankind. For example because insulin* is very expensive to obtain from
5   natural sources scientists have developed a method to manufacture it inexpensively
in the laboratory. Another beneficial application of gene splicing is in agriculture.
Scientists foresee the day when new plants will be developed using nitrogen from
the air instead of from fertilizer* therefore food production could be increased. In
addition entirely new plants could be developed to feed the world's hungry people.
10   Not everyone is excited about gene splicing however. Some people feel that it could
have terrible consequences. A laboratory accident for example might cause an epidemic*
of an unknown disease that could wipe out humanity. As a result of this controversy the
government has made rules to control genetic experiments. Still many people feel that
these rules are not strict enough even though the scientific community may feel that
15   they are too strict.

Paragraph 2

1   The "women's lib"* movement toward greater equality for women has produced some
permanent changes in the vocabulary of English. The first change is that new words
have been added. The words "feminist" "sexist" and "male chauvinist" for example
became common during the past ten years or so. Another new word is the title *Ms*
5   which is often used in place of both *Miss* and *Mrs*. A second change is that sexist titles
of many job occupations have been neutralized. A chairman is now a "chairperson" a
businessman is a "businessperson" and a salesman is a "salesperson." Moreover a mail-
man is now a "mail carrier" and an airline stewardess is now a "flight attendant."
10   Finally attempts to give equal treatment to masculine and feminine pronouns in English
have led to the search for a new pronoun form to replace *he* (as *he/she* or *s/he*) when
referring to neutral nouns such as *the student*. In my opinion some of the new words
such as *Ms* are quite useful; you can use *Ms* to address a woman when you don't
know if she is married. On the other hand the lack of a clear neutral pronoun can
lead to awkward sentence construction.

Practice 12: Choosing Transition Signals

STEP 1 Choose the transition signal that best shows the relationship between the
sentences in each group from the choices given in parentheses. Write the
signal in the space.

STEP 2 Add punctuation and change capital letters to small letters if necessary.

Note: All of the transition signals in this practice are sentence connectors. This is
to give you more practice in using and punctuating this type of transition signal
correctly.

Example   A recent article in *Era* magazine suggested ways to reduce inflation. The article
suggested that the president reduce the federal budget; *furthermore, it*
suggested that the government reduce federal, state and local taxes. (however, in
contrast, furthermore)

1. The same article said that the causes of inflation were easy to find _____
the cure for inflation was not so easy to prescribe. (however, for example,
therefore)

---

genetic: from *gene*, the unit of heredity
gene splicing: gene joining
insulin: a substance needed by people who
    have diabetes
fertilizer: food for plants

epidemic: rapidly spreading disease
controversy: disagreement
women's lib: abbreviation for the women's
    liberation movement

2. *Era* also suggested that rising wages were one of the primary causes of inflation _____ the government should take action to control wages. (however, therefore, for example)

3. In physics, the weight of an object is the gravitational force* with which the Earth attracts it _____ if a man weighs 150 pounds, this means that the Earth pulls him down with a force of 150 pounds. (moreover, therefore, for example)

4. The farther away from Earth a person is, the less the gravitational force of the Earth _____ a man weighs less when he is 50,000 miles from Earth than when he is only 5,000 miles away. (in conclusion, therefore, however)

5. A "tsunami" is a tidal wave produced by an earthquake on the ocean floor. The waves are very long and low in open water, but when they get close to land, they encounter friction* because of the shallow water _____ the waves increase in height and can cause considerable damage when they finally reach land. (on the other hand, as a result, in conclusion)

Review: Coherence from Transition Signals

These are the important points you should have learned from this chapter:

1. Every good paragraph contains appropriate transition signals that show the relationship of one idea to the next.
2. Transition signals can be sentence connectors, coordinators, subordinators, prepositions or determiners.
3. Each type of transition signal is punctuated differently.

WRITING PRACTICE

Choose one of the topics below and write one paragraph about it. Use transition signals in appropriate places.

STEP 1 Write a brief outline with a topic sentence, supporting points, and a concluding sentence.

STEP 2 Decide where transition signals would be appropriate to connect your supporting points and conclusion, and write them in the margin at the left of your outline.

STEP 3 Write your paragraph. Circle your transition words.

STEP 4 Check your paragraph against the Paragraph Checklist on the next page.

Topic Suggestions

Space exploration.

A current fad or fashion.

Movies.

The drug-abuse problem.

Test-tube babies.

---

gravitational force: the force that pulls   **friction:** resistance
things toward the Earth

NO

Paragraph Checklist

Form: _____ Does your paragraph have a title?
_____ Did you write on the correct side of the paper?
_____ Did you indent?
_____ Did you write on every other line?
(Refer to the Assignment Format on pages 4–5 for complete instructions.)

Topic Sentence: _____ Does your topic sentence contain a controlling idea?

Supporting Sentences:
Unity: _____ Do all of your sentences support your topic sentence?

Coherence— _____ Do you use transition signals at appropriate
Transitions points to make your sentences flow smoothly?

Concluding Sentence: _____ Does your paragraph have a concluding sentence?

WRITING UNDER PRESSURE

Choose one of the topic sentences below and write a paragraph that develops it. Use transition signals to connect the supporting sentences smoothly. You may use the transition signals suggested for each topic, or you may use others not listed. Make a quick outline before you begin.

1. Foreign travel is very educational.
   The first reason
   Another reason
   In addition
   Consequently

2. Last week, I witnessed a terrible accident.
   First
   After that
   Next
   Finally

3. Being an identical twin can be a lot of fun.
   For example
   Furthermore
   As a result
   In conclusion

4. Some people enjoy solitude.
   As an example
   Moreover
   On the other hand
   Therefore

Check your paragraph against the Paragraph Checklist before you hand in both your outline and your paragraph. Your instructor will give you a time limit. Suggested limits:

Outlining Time — 3 minutes
Writing Time — 10 minutes
Checking Time — 2 minutes

Total — 15 minutes

Chapter 4

COHERENCE FROM LOGICAL ORDER

In addition to using transition signals, a second way to achieve coherence is to arrange your sentences in some kind of logical order. Since there are different kinds of logical relationships, there are different ways to organize the ideas and sentences in a paragraph. Your choice of one kind of logical order over another will, of course, depend on your topic and on your purpose. You may even combine two or more different logical orders in the same paragraph. The important point to remember is to arrange your ideas in some kind of order that is logical to a reader accustomed to the English way of writing. The two most common kinds of logical order in English rhetoric are **chronological order** and **order of importance**.

Chronological Order

Chronological order is one of the easiest methods of organization to master. *Chronos* is a Greek word meaning time. Chronological order, therefore, is a way of organizing the ideas in a paragraph in the order of their occurrence in time.

Chronological order is used for something as simple as a recipe and for something as complex as a history book. In academic writing, chronological order has many uses. One of the primary ways you might use it is to write a historical review of the subject of a term paper. For example, you might review the history of labor unions before you discuss the current situation.

However, chronological order is not just used for historical events; it is also used in business, science and engineering to explain processes and procedures. For example, chronological order would be used to explain how to solve a math problem, how to perform a chemistry experiment, or how to set up an accounting system. Such paragraphs are called "how to" or "process" paragraphs.

Here are some typical test questions and/or term paper topics for which you could use chronological order as a method of organization:

Economics	*Trace the growth of labor unions in the United States since 1900.*
Business	*Describe the procedure for taking a year-end inventory in a small retail business.*

Chemical Engineering   *Describe the process of desalinization*.*

Biochemistry   *Discuss the function of the enzyme* pepsin in the digestion of food.*

There are two keys to writing a good chronological paragraph:
   1. **Discuss the events (in a history) or the steps (in a process) in the order in which they occur.**
   2. **Use chronological transition signals to indicate the sequence of events or steps.**

Analyze the following model paragraphs for their organization by time. Circle any words or expressions that indicate time order (*first, next, after that, in 1971,* etc.). The first paragraph reviews very briefly the history of computers. The second paragraph is an example of a process paragraph. It tells how to perform part of a simple chemistry experiment.

Model 6: Chronological Order

The Evolution* of Computers

1   In the relatively short span of twenty-five years, there has been an incredible evolution in the size and capabilities of computers. Today, computers smaller than the tip of your fingernail have the same capabilities as the room-sized machines of twenty-five years ago. The first computers were developed around 1945. They were so
5 large that they required special air-conditioned rooms. About twenty years later, in the 1960s, desk-sized computers were developed. This represented a gigantic advance. Before the end of that same decade, however, a third generation of computers, which used simple integrated circuits and which were even smaller and faster, had appeared. In 1971, the first microprocessor, less than one square centimeter in size, was developed.
10 Today, electronic engineers predict that even smaller and more sophisticated computers will be on the market before the end of this decade.

A Neutralization Experiment

1   To perform a neutralization experiment, proceed in the following manner. First, measure out about 2 cc. of laboratory NaOH solution. Second, pour the solution into a small casserole*. Next, add portions of HCl solution, stirring after each addition until the solution is acid when tested with litmus paper*. Then, place the casserole containing
5 the solution on a wire gauze over a Bunsen burner and heat it until the solution begins to boil. When it does, reduce the size of the flame immediately and allow the solution to boil gently. As it approaches dryness, sputtering* may occur. At this point, cover the casserole loosely with a watch-glass. Then, hold the casserole above the flame and move it back and forth until no further water vapor* is expelled*. Finally, allow the dish and
10 residue* to cool.

---

desalinization: removal of salt from sea water
enzymes: protein substances vital to cell
    metabolism
evolution: development
casserole: baking dish
litmus paper: a treated paper used to test
    acidity and alkalinity

sputtering: spitting out of small particles
water vapor: steam
expelled: given off
residue: remaining solid matter

Writing Technique Questions

1. What are the two uses of chronological order that the two model paragraphs exemplify?

2. What are the main time divisions in the paragraph about computers? How would you outline it?

3. What transition signals and time expressions are used in the first paragraph to show chronological order? Circle them.

4. What transition signals and time expressions are used in the second paragraph to show the steps in the process? Circle them.

5. What verb forms are used in the second paragraph? Why?

CHRONOLOGICAL ORDER: TRANSITION SIGNALS

Transition signals are especially important in a chronological paragraph. You have to be very clear about the sequence of events: did one event happen before, at the same time as, or after another event?

Some of the most common chronological transition signals are given in the chart below. Keep in mind, however, that *any* time expression can serve as a chronological transition signal. Such expressions as *in 1943*, or *since the war*, or *twenty-five years later* can all be used to signal the time order.

TRANSITION SIGNALS FOR CHRONOLOGICAL ORDER

Sentence Connectors	Clause Connectors		Others
	Coordinators	Subordinators	
first (second, third, fourth, etc.)		before	the first (+ noun)
		after	the second (+ noun)
next, last, finally		while	before the (+ noun)
first of all		until	in the year
after that		as soon as	since the (+ noun)
since then			

Practice 13: Chronological Transition Signals

Add appropriate chronological transition signals to the following essay and punctuate them. Consult the list in the preceding table or use others with which you are familiar.

How to Reduce the Danger of Smoking

1   The Department of Health, Education and Welfare (HEW) has outlined some steps to take some of the danger out of smoking for those people who are unable to quit smoking outright*. _____ choose a cigarette with less tar and nicotine to reduce your intake of these pollutants. _____ don't smoke your cigarette all the way down.

5   Smoke halfway, and you will inhale only about 40 percent of the total tar and nicotine. Remember, 60 percent of these substances* is contained in the last half of the cigarette. _____ take fewer draws on each cigarette—that is, reduce the number of puffs on each cigarette. This will cut down on your smoking. _____ reduce your inhaling. Don't open your lungs by inhaling deeply. Take short, shallow puffs. _____ smoke

10   fewer cigarettes each day. This may be the most difficult step of all. However, just follow these directions:

---

outright: all at once   **substances:** materials

1. Pick a time of day to start, and don't smoke before that time.

2. Don't think of it as cutting down; think of it as postponing.

15

3. Carry your cigarettes in a different pocket, or put them in a different place so that you can't reach for them automatically.

_____ think about the terrible diseases you are opening yourself up to each time you smoke a cigarette. _____ if you follow each of these steps without cheating, you should be able to at least control the number of cigarettes you smoke daily. Who knows, this might be the beginning of the end—of your smoking, that is.[1]

CHRONOLOGICAL ORDER: TOPIC SENTENCES

Notice that the topic sentence of a chronological paragraph in some way indicates the time order. In paragraphs such as the one on computers, phrases such as _the development of_, _the growth of_, or _the evolution of_ give the reader a hint that this is a chronological paragraph.

In a "how to" or process paragraph, such as the one on page 36 about the chemistry experiment, the process to be described is named in the topic sentence. Again, this is a hint to the reader to expect a chronological paragraph.

Practice 14: Chronological Topic Sentences

STEP 1 Put a check in the space to the left of every topic sentence suggesting that a chronological paragraph will follow.

STEP 2 Circle the word or words in the sentences you have checked that indicate chronological order.

Example ✓ (In the past twenty-five years,) (developments) in the field of electronics have revolutionized the computer industry.

_____ 1. The worst day in my life was the day I left my family and my friends to come to the United States.

_____ 2. In my opinion, television programs can be divided into three types: excellent, mediocre, and poor.

_____ 3. The life cycle of the Pacific salmon* is one of nature's most fascinating phenomena*.

_____ 4. Gold is prized for two important characteristics.

_____ 5. In the event of an earthquake, you should follow certain procedures in order to minimize the danger.

_____ 6. The tensions* that led to the race riots of 1964 had been building for years.

_____ 7. The election of a U.S. President is a very long and complex process.

_____ 8. Smoking damages not only your lungs, but also your heart.

_____ 9. There are three reasons I believe that women should be drafted* along with men.

_____ 10. The rise of terrorist groups in the past few years is an indication of the spread of anarchistic* tendencies in the world.

---

[1]DHEW Publication No. (CDC) 78-8705, U.S. Government Printing Office, 1978, 0-252-573.

salmon: a kind of fish
phenomena: things or events
tension: stresses

drafted: called into military service
anarchistic: total absence of government

OUTLINING A CHRONOLOGICAL PARAGRAPH

Writing an outline for a chronological order paragraph is very easy. Follow these steps:

STEP 1 Write a topic sentence that indicates chronological order by naming the event or the process you will explain.

STEP 2 List the events or steps in the order in which they occur or occurred.

STEP 3 Add transition signals to mark the most important points in the time sequence.

STEP 4 Write a concluding sentence if one is necessary.

Model 7: Outline for a Chronological Paragraph

Study the following outline for the model paragraph about computers from page 36.

The Evolution of Computers

Transition Signals	
	In the relatively short span of twenty-five years, there has been an incredible evolution in the size and capabilities of computers.
(Around 1945)	A. First computers were so large that they required special air-conditioned rooms.
(In the 1960s)	B. Desk-sized computers were developed.
(Twenty years later)	
(Before the end of that same decade)	C. A third generation of computers using simple integrated circuits appeared.
(In 1971)	D. Microprocessors less than one square centimeter in size were developed.
(Today)	E. Even smaller and more sophisticated computers will be on the market soon.

Practice 15: Outlining a Chronological Paragraph

Outline the paragraph, "How to Reduce the Danger of Smoking" on page 37. Include only the topic sentence, the six main steps, and the concluding sentence in your outline: do not write every sentence. Underline the topic and concluding sentences.

Put the transition signals that you added in parentheses to the left of each supporting point, as in the example above.

WRITING A CHRONOLOGICAL PARAGRAPH

To write a chronological paragraph, whether it is a history or a process:
1. Make a simple outline that lists the events (in a history) or the steps (in a process) in the order of their occurrence.
2. Add transition signals at appropriate points in the left margin of your outline.
3. Write a topic sentence that names the event or the process.
4. Write the paragraph, following your outline. Add enough details to make the chain of events or steps in the process very clear.

WRITING PRACTICE

STEP 1 Choose a topic from the suggestions listed below.
STEP 2 Write an outline, listing the main steps or main events that you will explain in your paragraph.
STEP 3 Add chronological transition signals at appropriate points in the left margin of your outline.
STEP 4 Write your paragraph from your outline.

Topic Suggestions

A. Process Topics

How to study for a test, take a test, or find a book in the library.
How to cure the hiccoughs, a hangover, "the blues," "the blahs*."
How to jump-start a car, wash and wax a car, change a tire.
How to put on makeup, put in contact lenses.
How to make a perfect cup of coffee, cup of tea, dry martini.

B. Historical Topics

Use some or all of the following data to write a brief history of manned space flights.

MANNED SPACE FLIGHTS

Crew/Date of Mission	Mission Name	Comments
Yuri Gagarin April 12, 1961	Vostok 1	First manned orbital* flight.
John Glenn, Jr. February 20, 1962	Mercury-Atlas 6	First American in orbit.
Aleksei Leonov March 18, 1965	Voskhod 2	First "space walk" (10 minutes).
4 Russian cosmonauts January, 1969	Soyuz 4 and Soyuz 5	First transfer of crew members from one spacecraft to another.
3 U.S. astronauts July 20, 1969	Apollo-Saturn 11	First landing on the moon.
2 Russian cosmonauts and 3 U.S. astronauts July, 1975	Soyuz 19 Apollo 18	U.S.-U.S.S.R. joint flight. Crews linked up in space, conducted experiments, and shared meals.
John Young and Robert Crippen April 12-15, 1981	Space Shuttle Columbia	First flight of a reusable space vehicle.

"the blahs": don't care attitude   orbital: in a circle around the Earth

Order of Importance

Another very common way to organize the ideas in a paragraph is to discuss them in the order of their importance. There are two ways to do this: you can discuss the most important point first and work down to the least important point, or you can begin with the least important and end your paragraph with the most important. The way you choose will depend on your topic and on your purpose; both ways can be effective.

You can use order of importance for all kinds of topics. Suppose, for example, you were asked on a history test to give the causes of the U.S. Civil War. There were three basic causes: the economic superiority of the northern states, the slavery issue, and the political question of the right of individual states to secede* from the United States and form a separate country. Which cause would you discuss first, and which last? It would depend on your point of view: do you want to emphasize economics, politics, or the slavery issue?

To use another example, suppose you were asked to write about the two most important influences on your life besides your family, and you chose to write about a particular teacher who had a big influence on you or perhaps a dramatic incident in your life that somehow changed you. Here, again, you would discuss the two influences in the order of their importance—how strongly each affected you.

Just as with chronological order it is important to use transition signals to guide your reader from one point to the next.

There are two keys to writing an effective paragraph using order of importance as a method of organization:

1. Discuss your points in the order of their importance, discussing the most important point either first or last.
2. Use order of importance transition signals to guide your reader from one point to the next and to indicate your most important points.

Model 8: Order of Importance

The Causes of Inflation

1   Inflation is an economic condition in which prices for consumer goods increase, and the value of money or purchasing power decreases. There are three important causes of inflation. The first and most important cause may be excessive government spending. For example, in order to finance a war or carry out social programs, the government

5   may spend more money than it has received through taxes and other revenue, thus creating a deficit. In order to offset this deficit, the Treasury Department can simply expand the money supply by issuing more paper money to meet the debts of government. This increase in the money supply will cause the value of the dollar to automatically decrease. The second cause of inflation occurs when the money supply increases

10   faster than the supply of goods. If people have more money, they will run out to buy popular goods like televisions and computers, for example, and a shortage will result. Industry will then produce more, at higher prices, to satisfy demand. Furthermore, if people think that the prices of popular goods are going up, they will buy and even borrow money at high interest rates to pay for them. Finally, if labor unions demand

15   that workers' wages be increased to cover the high cost of living, industry will meet this demand and add other costs of production on to the consumer. In summary, all of these causes can create inflationary problems that can affect the welfare of a nation. However, of these three causes, excessive government spending may be the most important.

---

secede: separate

Writing Technique Questions

1. What are the three main causes of inflation? In what order are they discussed? Why do you think the author used this order? Would the paragraph be more effective if government spending were discussed last?

2. If you had written this paragraph, would you have discussed the points in a different order? If so, how would you have done it? Why?

ORDER OF IMPORTANCE: TRANSITION SIGNALS

Notice that many of the transition signals for order of importance are the same as the transition signals for chronological order.

TRANSITION SIGNALS FOR ORDER OF IMPORTANCE

Sentence Connectors	Others
first, second, third, etc. next, last, finally above all more important, most important	the first (+ noun) the second (+ noun) the most important (+ noun)

Practice 16: Transition Signals for Order of Importance

Reread the model paragraph for order of importance and draw a circle around all the transition signals. If you find any that are not in the table, add them.

ORDER OF IMPORTANCE: TOPIC SENTENCES

Notice the topic sentence for the model paragraph on the causes of inflation:

There are three important causes of inflation.

Because this topic sentence mentions that there are several sources, a reader who is accustomed to the English way of writing will usually assume that the sources will be discussed in the order of their importance.
Sometimes the topic sentence actually names the subtopics:

In the United States, the vacuum cleaner, World War II, and the birth control pill were the three main factors that contributed to the liberation of women in the twentieth century.

And sometimes, the topic sentence specifically shows the order of importance:

In the United States, the two most important holidays are first, Christmas, and second, Thanksgiving.

Practice 17: Topic Sentences for Order of Importance

STEP 1 Put a check in the space to the left of every topic sentence that suggests order of importance organization.

STEP 2 Circle the word or words in the checked sentences which indicate this.

Example   ✔ A political leader today must possess (four important qualities.)

_____ 1. My twenty-first birthday was a day I will never forget.

_____ 2. In terms of salary, power, and status, women are behind men in most occupations.

_____ 3. Some meteorologists* believe that another ice age is approaching.

_____ 4. Living in a dormitory offers three advantages to a newly arrived foreign student.

_____ 5. Photosynthesis is the process by which plants manufacture their own food.

ORDER OF IMPORTANCE: OUTLINING

An outline for an order of importance paragraph follows one of the two following forms:

Topic Sentence

(Transition)   A. The most important point (reason, factor, example, etc.) is . . .
(Transition)   B. Next point
(Transition)   C. Next point
(Transition)   D. Final point

Concluding Sentence

If you decide that it is more effective to discuss your most important point last, your outline will look like this:

Topic Sentence

(Transition)   A. First point
(Transition)   B. Next point
(Transition)   C. The most important point (reason, factor, example, etc.) is . . .

Concluding Sentence

Practice 18: Outlining for Order of Importance

A. Write a simple outline for the Model 8 paragraph, "The Causes of Inflation," on page 41. In the left margin, note the transition signals used, following the Model 7 outlining example on page 39.

B. Write a simple outline for any two of the following topics. Follow the same directions as for A. above.

1. The problems of a foreign student in the United States.

2. The qualities of a good teacher (student, wife, husband, friend).

---

meteorologist: a specialist in weather and climatic conditions

3. The most important holidays in your country.
4. Important inventions in the twentieth century.
5. Important discoveries in the field of medicine.
6. Important developments in your major field.
7. Important influences on your life (people or events or both).

(*Note:* For 4, 5, and 6, you may want to get information from the library.)

Review: Coherence from Logical Order

> These are the important points you should have learned from this chapter:
>
> Every paragraph must have coherence, which means that your paragraph is easy to read and understand. Coherence results from two major structural techniques:
>
> 1. using transition signals in appropriate places to help your reader follow your ideas. Remember that there are different types of transition signals. Pay particular attention to the use of the sentence connector type (therefore, however, moreover, etc.).
> 2. stating your ideas in logical order. There are many kinds of logical orders; chronological order and order of importance are two of the most useful ones.

WRITING PRACTICE

Choose one of the topics below and write one or more paragraphs about it. If you write more than one paragraph, make sure that each paragraph division is logical and that each paragraph has a topic sentence. Pay particular attention to making your paragraph(s) coherent.

STEP 1   Decide which method of organization (chronological order or order of importance) best suits your topic.
STEP 2   Write an outline.
STEP 3   Write your paragraph or paragraphs.
STEP 4   Underline all topic and concluding sentences, and circle all of your transition signals.
STEP 5   Check your paragraph(s) against the Paragraph Checklist on page 45 before you hand in your paper.

Topic Suggestions

The traditional celebration of New Year's Day (or another important day) in your country.

The important milestones* in a person's life in your culture. Give reasons why they are important.

Your autobiography, or the biography of a famous person from your country.

The reasons for choosing your particular major field. If you have not yet chosen a major, you may write about one of the choices you are considering.

Any of the topics in Practice 18-B on pages 43-44.

---

milestone: important date or event

Paragraph Checklist

Form:	_____ Does your paragraph have a title?
	_____ Did you write on the correct side of the paper?
	_____ Did you indent the first line?
	_____ Did you write on every other line?
	(Refer to the Assignment Format on pages 4–5 for complete instructions.)
Topic Sentence:	_____ Does your topic sentence contain a controlling idea?
Supporting Sentences:	
Unity:	_____ Do all of your sentences support your topic sentence?
Coherence— Transition Signals:	_____ Do you use transition signals at appropriate points to make your sentences flow smoothly?
Coherence— Logical Order:	_____ Are your ideas arranged in logical order?
Concluding Sentence:	_____ Does your paragraph have a concluding sentence?

WRITING UNDER PRESSURE

Choose a topic from either Group A or Group B below and write a paragraph on that subject. Write a simple outline before you begin, using either chronological order or order of importance.

Group A—Order of Importance
Why it is important to: _____
  a. ___ learn English.
  b. ___ get a college education.
  c. ___ own an automobile.
  d. ___ earn a lot of money.
  e. ___ conserve energy.
  f . ___ reduce pollution.
  g. ___ stop smoking.

Group B—Chronological Order
The happiest day in your life.
The unhappiest day in your life.
A typical day in your life.
A perfect day in your "ideal" life.

Check your paragraph against the Paragraph Checklist before you hand it in. Your instructor will give you a time limit. Suggested limits:

      Outlining Time — 3 minutes
      Writing Time   — 10 minutes
      Checking Time — 2 minutes

           Total — 15 minutes

Chapter 5

CONCRETE SUPPORT

One of the biggest problems in student writing is that student writers often fail to prove their point. They fail because they do not support their points with concrete details. Their papers are too often full of opinions and generalizations without the factual details needed to support them.

Opinion versus Facts

Opinions are subjective* statements based on a person's beliefs or attitudes:

Smoking marijuana is harmful.

Engineering majors do not need to take a lot of English courses.

Americans are only superficially* friendly.

It is perfectly acceptable to express opinions in academic writing. In fact, most professors want you to express your own ideas. However, you must *prove* your opinions with concrete support. Moreover, the more specific you are, the better.

A paragraph contains concrete support for the topic sentence. You must prove your topic sentence by using specific and factual supporting details.

In very formal academic writing, even some statements that are considered facts need further support. In other words, they need specific supporting details in order to be completely convincing.

Here are some examples of statements that need further support to be acceptable in formal academic writing, and of replacement statements that include concrete evidence to support the statements.

Unsupported "Fact"   *On the average, heavy smokers die earlier than non-smokers.*

---

subjective: based on personal opinion and emotion   **superficially:** on the surface

47

Concrete Supporting Detail	*The life expectancy of a two-pack-a-day smoker at age 25 is 8.3 years less than that of a nonsmoker.*
Unsupported "Fact"	*Smoking causes lung cancer.*
Concrete Supporting Detail	*The U.S. Surgeon General's 1964 report on smoking and lung cancer states: "Cigarette smoking is causally related to lung cancer in men. . . . The risk of developing lung cancer increases with duration of smoking and the number of cigarettes smoked per day, and is diminished by discontinuing."*

Concrete Supporting Details

There are several kinds of concrete supporting details that you can use to support or prove your topic sentence. Among the most common are examples and illustrative incidents, quotations, and statistics. In academic writing, quotations are perhaps the kind of support most often used, but many academic disciplines* require the occasional use of statistics as well. The other two—examples and illustrative incidents—are also useful for explaining or proving your point.

Read the following article about the growing refugee problem in the world. Notice how the four different types of concrete supporting details support the author's main points.

Model 9: Concrete supporting details

World Refugees

Illustrative Incident   Duc Trong knew that the voyage would be risky, but he also knew that he had no choice. If he and his family stayed in their country, there was little hope for their future. So one night he, his wife, and ten other members of his family boarded a small, rickety* boat, taking with them only what they could carry, and set sail along with thirty-six other Vietnamese. Their voyage was a nightmare. Before they reached safety, they were attacked by two different groups of pirates, and during a terrible storm, their supplies were washed overboard. Eleven of the older people died, and the survivors were delirious* from lack of food and water.

Statistics   The rising tide of refugees around the world is rapidly becoming a flood. According to figures published by the United Nations, there are more than 6.2 million refugees and an additional 2.6 million people who are classified as "displaced persons." That makes a total of nearly 9 million.

Examples   No corner of the Earth is without a refugee problem, although the African continent has so far produced the greatest number. Ethiopia, with its 1.6 million refugees, has produced three times as many refugees as Vietnam and Cambodia combined. The Middle East has its Palestinian and, more recently, Afghan refugees. In the Western Hemisphere, Haiti, Cuba, and the Central American countries of El Salvador and Guatemala are producing refugees by the thousands.

Quotation   The refugees present problems not only for themselves, but also for the countries that take them in. As Victor Palmieri, the U.S. coordinator for refugee affairs, has put it, "The worldwide refugee explosion is a massive tragedy in human terms and a growing crisis in financial terms for the countries bearing the burden."[3]

---

[3]"6.2 Million Seek a Haven," *Newsweek* 95 (April 28, 1980), p. 45.

---

academic discipline: major field of study   **delirious:** temporarily crazy
rickety: in poor condition

Writing Technique Questions

1. What does the incident about Duc Trong in the first paragraph illustrate? What, then, is the author's main point in this paragraph? Notice that, even though it isn't stated directly in a topic sentence, the main idea is clear from the incident. What topic sentence could you write for this paragraph?

2. What is the main idea in the second paragraph? What statistics are given?

3. What is the main idea in the third paragraph? How is this supported?

4. What is the main idea in the last paragraph? What kind of specific supporting detail is given to support it? What is the source of the quotation?

In the following sections, you will practice using each kind of concrete supporting detail.

EXAMPLES AND ILLUSTRATIVE INCIDENTS

Examples and illustrative incidents are perhaps the easiest kind of supporting details to use. You don't have to search in the library for information; you can often take examples from your own knowledge and personal experiences. Furthermore, examples and illustrative incidents are usually interesting and make your writing enjoyable to read. Finally, since it is easy to remember a striking example or a good story, your reader is more likely to remember your point.

However, there are two cautions you should keep in mind if you use examples and illustrative incidents for support. First, remember that in formal academic writing—research papers, theses, and the like—examples and illustrative incidents are considered the weakest kind of support, so use them sparingly*. Second, be sure that your examples really prove your point. For instance, if you are trying to prove that, on the average, men are better drivers than women, don't use famous racing car drivers as examples of superior drivers because they aren't average.

Study the two models to see how examples and illustrative incidents can be used to support a topic sentence.

Model 10: Examples

Language and Perception*

1   Although we all possess the same physical organs for perceiving the world—eyes for seeing, ears for hearing, noses for smelling, skins for feeling, and mouths for tasting—our perception of the world depends to a great extent on the language we speak. In other words, we cannot perceive things that we have not named. Each
5   language is like a pair of sunglasses through which we "see" the world. A classic example of the relationship between language and perception is the word *snow*. In the English language, there is only that one word to describe all of the possible kinds of snow. In Eskimo languages, however, there are as many as thirty-two different words for snow. For instance, the Eskimos have different words for falling snow,
10 snow on the ground, snow packed as hard as ice, slushy snow, wind-driven snow, and what we might call "cornmeal" snow. In contrast, cultures that rarely experience cold weather and snow may have only one word to express several concepts that are differentiated in English. For example, the ancient Aztec languages of Mexico used only one word to mean snow, cold, *and* ice.

Writing Technique Questions

1. What is the main idea of this paragraph? Where is it stated?

2. How many supporting examples are given?

3. What transition signals introduce the examples?

---

sparingly: infrequently   **perception:** knowledge derived from the five senses

Model 11: Illustrative incidents

Nonverbal Communication*

1   Nonverbal communication, or "body language," is communication by facial expressions, head or eye movements, hand signals, and body postures. It can be just as important to understanding as words are. Misunderstandings—often amusing but sometimes
serious—can arise between people from different cultures if they misinterpret non-
5   verbal signals. Take, for example, the differences in meaning of a gesture* very common
in the United States: a circle made with the thumb and index* finger. To an American,
it means that everything is OK. To a Japanese, it means that you are talking about
money. In France, it means that something is worthless, and in Greece, it is an
obscene* gesture. Therefore, an American could unknowingly offend a Greek by
10   using that particular hand signal.
        The following true incident illustrates how conflicting nonverbal signals can
cause serious misunderstandings. While lecturing to his poetry class at Ain Shams
University in Cairo, a British professor became so relaxed that he leaned back in his
chair and revealed the bottom of his foot to the astonished class. Making such a gesture
15   in Moslem society is the worst kind of insult. The next day the Cairo newspapers carried headlines about the student demonstration that resulted, and they denounced
British arrogance and demanded that the professor be sent home.[4]

Writing Technique Questions

1. What is the main point of these two paragraphs? In which two places is it
   stated directly?
2. What examples are given to support the main point?
3. What story is told to support the main point?
4. What words and phrases are used to introduce the examples and the illustrative incident?
5. Why do you think this article was divided into two paragraphs?

When you use examples and illustrative incidents to support a point:
  1. Make sure that your example or illustration really supports your point.
  2. Introduce them with appropriate transition signals.

WRITING PRACTICE

Choose either A or B below and write a paragraph using examples and/or illustrative incidents to explain your topic sentence. Use at least two different supporting details.

STEP 1 Write an outline.
STEP 2 Write the paragraph from your outline.
STEP 3 Circle appropriate transition signals that introduce your examples and
            illustrations.
STEP 4 Check your paragraph against the Paragraph Checklist on page 45 before
            you hand it in.

A. Describe a body-language signal from your own culture that is different from
    English body language. Explain the confusion that can be caused when other
    people misunderstand it.

---

[4]Adapted from John C. Condon and Fathi S. Yousef, *An Introduction to Intercultural Communication* (Indianapolis and New York: The Bobbs-Merrill Company, 1975), p. 122.

---

nonverbal communication: communication   **index finger:** the finger next to the thumb
                                            without words   **obscene:** indecent, disgusting
gesture: hand signal

B. Explain a proverb* from your language by using examples. Some proverbs in English are:

> A stitch in time saves nine.
>
> Early to bed, early to rise, makes a man healthy, wealthy and wise.
>
> People who live in glass houses shouldn't throw stones.
>
> An apple a day keeps the doctor away.
>
> A rolling stone gathers no moss.

FIGURES AND STATISTICS

One of the most effective ways to support your position on a topic is to cite* figures and statistics. The use of this form of factual detail to support your point is essential in, for example, a scientific or business essay or report. Therefore, pay particular attention to the way in which numbers and percentages are written.

Underline all of the structure vocabulary for figures and statistics in the following paragraphs.

Model 12: Figures and statistics

The Population Time Bomb

1   The world's population is growing at a geometric rate*. It doubled from 1750 to 1900, a period of 150 years. It doubled again from 1900 to 1965, a period of only 65 years. At the current rate of increase, it is expected to double again by the year 2000, a period of only 35 years, according to a recent report published by the World Health Organization
5 of the United Nations. The world's population in 1978 had reached 4.3 billion and is increasing at the rate of 70 million each year. By the end of this century, there will be 7 billion people on Earth.

Living Alone

1   America is becoming a society of "loners." Since 1970, the number of Americans living alone has been increasing, according to a Census Bureau* report. The number of men living alone has more than doubled in the last several years, and the number of women living by themselves is up 35 percent. Among people under the age of 25, the number of
5 men living alone has nearly tripled since 1970, from 274,000 to 752,000, and the number of women has risen from 282,000 to 588,000. "There were 15.5 million people living alone in 1977," the Census Bureau said. Although the number of men living by themselves has increased rapidly since 1970, most of those living alone are still women—64 percent of the total.

Writing Technique Questions

1. What are the topic sentences for these two paragraphs?
2. What is the source of both these reports?
3. Which statistics are the most significant?

---

proverb: wise saying that gives a practical rule for living
cite: quote
geometric rate: growth or decline by an amount determined by a constant process, 2, 4, 8, 16, 32, etc.

Census Bureau: government agency responsible for population statistics

The following table illustrates some of the words and phrases that signify statistical information.

WORDS AND PHRASES USED WITH FIGURES AND STATISTICS

Vocabulary	Example of Structure
rate	The rate of inflation has skyrocketed.
ratio (of X to Y)	The ratio of smokers to non-smokers was 3:2.
percent	Twelve percent (or 12 percent) of the population is 55 or older.
percentage	Only a small percentage of personal income should go toward housing.
geometric rate arithmetic rate*	The world population is increasing at a geometric rate.
to double, triple, quadruple, etc.	The number of auto accidents has doubled.
to increase/decrease four-fold, by one-half; by three-tenths of 1 percent; 3.6 times	The number of computer companies has increased sevenfold.
to rise/fall by 20,000; by 6 percent (6%)	By 1990, oceanic levels will rise by 2 percent.

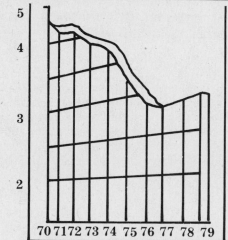

The Death Toll In Traffic Accidents

Death rate per 100 million miles driven

Source: National Highway Traffic Safety Administration, 1980.

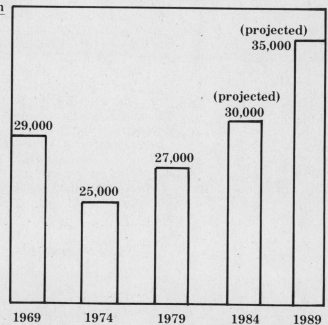

The Number of Automobile Traffic Deaths

Source: National Highway Traffic Safety Administration, 1980.

arithmetic rate: growth or decline by a constant amount; as 1, 2, 3, 4, 5, 6

Practice 19: Using Figures and Statistics

Complete the following essay by choosing the correct word from those given in parentheses and writing it in the blank. Refer to these two graphs for information.

The Hazards of Driving Small Cars

1   Small cars may be hazardous to your health, according to a recent study conducted by the National Highway Traffic Safety Administration. The number of Americans dying in automobile accidents is _____ (increasing, decreasing, gaining, reducing) again after _____ (rising, falling, inclining, declining)

5 sharply in 1974, when the national 55 mile per hour speed limit was imposed. Safety authorities warn that as drivers increasingly shift to fuel-saving smaller, lighter cars, the rise in the death toll will accelerate _____ (geometrically, arithmetically).

10   In 1979, the last year for which full statistics are available, small cars were involved in 55 _____ (rate, ratio, percentage, percent) of all fatal crashes even though they constituted only 38 _____ (rate, ratio, percentage, percent) of the cars on the road, according to the National Highway Traffic Safety Administration. Projecting from current trends, the agency and other

15 safety officials _____ (estimate, guess, predict) that automobile traffic deaths will increase _____ (to, from, of, by) 30 percent by 1989, or _____ (to, from, of, by) about 27,000 a year _____ (to, from, of, by) about 35,000 a year, almost exclusively because of the inherent vulnerability* of smaller cars.

20   Perhaps more significantly, the death rate per hundred million miles driven has begun to increase over the last three years, reversing a fifty-year downward trend. According to the safety council, the rate _____ (increased, decreased, raised, rose) from a record low of 3.33 deaths _____ (per, pro, of, from) hundred million miles in 1977 _____ (to,

25 from, of, by) 3.40 in 1978 and 3.53 in 1979.

    Based on its analysis of highway deaths, the highway safety council says occupants of a subcompact car are 3.4 _____ (times, double, triple) more likely to die than those in a compact if two such cars collide; 6.3

30 _____ (ratio, times, lose) more likely to die in a crash with a midsize car; and 8.2 _____ (times, quadruple, rate) more likely to die in a collision with a large car.

WRITING PRACTICE

Choose either Graph 1 or Graph 2 below and write a paragraph explaining its significance. Graph 1 compares the percentages of A, B, C, and D grades at Stone Mountain Jr. College in the fall semesters of 1968 and 1978. The second graph shows average annual costs for public and private colleges in the United States in 1981.

STEP 1 Decide what general trend the graph shows. Write this trend as your topic sentence.

STEP 2 Write five to eight supporting statements, using the statistical information shown in the graphs.

STEP 3 Mention the source of your data somewhere in your paragraph. Use a "reporting" phrase, such as *according to* _____ or _____ *reported that* _____.

STEP 4 Check your paragraph against the Paragraph Checklist on page 45 before handing it in.

---

inherent vulnerability: "natural" weakness (in this case due to small size)

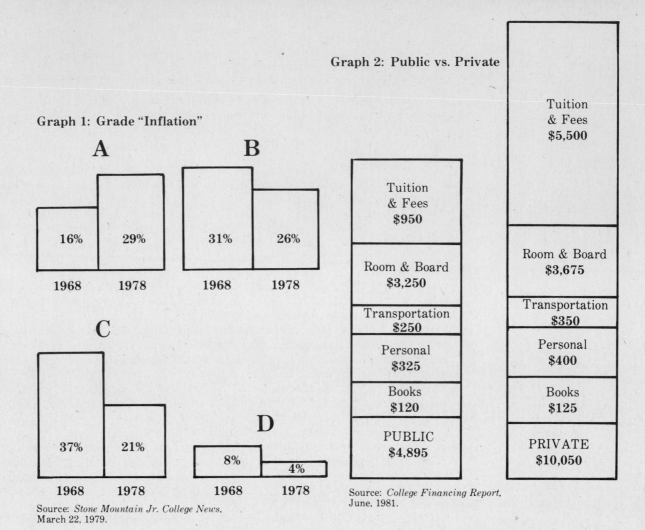

Graph 2: Public vs. Private

Graph 1: Grade "Inflation"

Source: *Stone Mountain Jr. College News,*
March 22, 1979.

Source: *College Financing Report,*
June, 1981.

Note: Advanced classes may want to develop their own topics for practice in using statistics meaningfully. This could involve obtaining statistics from library sources or from student-initiated surveys.

Quotations

Quotations are essential in academic writing. In all kinds of academic writing, from term papers to doctoral dissertations, you are expected to use quotations to support your ideas.

Your goals in studying this section are to learn how to insert quotations smoothly into a paragraph by using various "reporting" phrases and clauses and how to punctuate them correctly.

REPORTING PHRASES AND CLAUSES

Reporting phrases and clauses are expressions used to introduce a direct or indirect quotation, or any other information that has been borrowed.

There are many different reporting phrases and dependent clauses used in academic English. Some of the more common ones are:

___ said (that)	___ maintains (that)	*according to*
___ reported (that)	___ believes (that)	*as* ___ *stated*
___ stated (that)	___ insists (that)	*as* ___ *reported*
___ mentioned (that)	___ later said (that)	*as* ___ *said*
___ further stated (that)	___ continued to say (that)	

There is a difference in the grammar of the phrases and clauses listed above.

According to .... is a phrase. It is followed by an independent clause:

> *According to Professor Jones, abortion is murder.*

As ... *stated* is a dependent clause. It is followed by an independent clause, which can be a direct or indirect quotation:

> *As Jones stated at the Senate Hearings, "Abortion is murder."*

... *states* is an independent clause. It is followed by a dependent "that" clause or by a direct quotation:

> *Jones stated that abortion is murder.*
> *Jones stated, "Abortion is murder."*

DIRECT AND INDIRECT QUOTATIONS

There are two kinds of quotations: direct and indirect.

**Direct
Quotation**

Direct quotations are quotations in which another person's words are quoted exactly. Direct quotations are enclosed in quotation marks. Note the punctuation of the following direct quotations.

> *As Dr. David Doom, President of Planned Parenthood*, said, "Unless we control population growth, the world will be uninhabitable* by the year 2000."*

> *"Since the world's food production cannot keep up with the growing population," he further stated, "famine* in many parts of the world will be a certainty by the end of this century."*

**Indirect
Quotation**

Indirect quotations are quotations in which another person's words are not quoted exactly. They are written without quotation marks. Indirect quotations are usually put into a "that" clause, and you may need to change the verb tense. Refer to the grammar section on Direct and Indirect Speech on page 152.

> *Dr. David Doom, President of Planned Parenthood, stated that unless we <u>controlled</u> population growth, the world <u>would</u> be uninhabitable by the year 2000.*

> *He further stated that since the world's food production <u>could</u> not keep pace with the growing population, famine in many parts of the world <u>would</u> be a certainty by the end of this century.*

The explanations and practices in this section give an overview of the problems involved with direct and indirect quotations. For more detailed information, refer to the appropriate sections in the grammar and punctuation part of the book:

> Direct and Indirect Speech, page 152
> Sequence of Tenses, page 142
> Quotation Marks (punctuation), page 237

Planned Parenthood: an organization that supports birth control
uninhabitable: unable to support life
famine: widespread lack of food

Model 13: Quotations

Read the following model paragraphs and study how both direct and indirect quotations are used to support the topic sentences.

The Population Time Bomb
(continued)

1   The dangers of overpopulation cannot be underestimated. Dr. David Doom, President of Planned Parenthood, maintains that the world will be uninhabitable by the year 2000 unless the rate of growth is reduced. According to Dr. Doom, the world's food production cannot meet the needs of 7 billion people, so famine is an inevitable consequence of

5   uncontrolled population growth.[5] The World Health Organization agrees with Dr. Doom. It recently published a report noting that famine already exists in many parts of Africa and Asia.[6]

The Crime of the Future

1   The increased use of computers in business has been accompanied by a corresponding increase in computer crime. Computers are used in business in ever-increasing numbers to store, process and distribute information. At the same time, thefts by computer are on the rise.

5   The costs to the victims of computer crime are very high. In his book, *Crime by Computer*, computer expert Donn B. Parker estimated that financial losses to business from computer thefts would exceed $10 billion in 1978.[7] Although Parker's estimate is based on documented cases, no one really knows the extent of computer crime because thefts by computers are almost impossible to discover. "There is just no reliable way to

10   detect computer thefts," Parker said. "It is not just the money they control; they control data, and data is power."[8]

Writing Technique Questions

1. Does the first paragraph use direct or indirect quotations? How many quotations are used? What reporting phrases are used?

2. How many direct and/or indirect quotations are used in the paragraphs on computer crime? What main idea do they support?

3. What is the purpose of the superscribed* numbers? Are they used only for direct quotations?

When you use other people's ideas:

Be accurate. Whether you use a direct quotation or an indirect quotation, do not change the meaning of the original.

1. If you use a direct quotation, do not omit any words.

2. If you have a very good reason to omit part of a quotation, use an ellipsis (. . .) in place of the missing words:

   "The first reason . . . is the inability of underdeveloped nations to produce enough food," Dr. Doom stated.

---

[5]David R. Doom, "We are Sitting on a Time Bomb," *Newsday* 88 (March 2, 1980), p. 45.

[6]*World Population: Facts and Figures,* World Health Organization Publication No. 274 (New York: United Nations Press, 1978), p. 13.

[7]Michael Smith and Peter Gorner, "Crime's New Breed—Computer Super Crooks," *San Francisco Chronicle* (June 27, 1978), p. 6.

[8]*Ibid.*

---

superscribed: written above the line.

3. If you have a very good reason to *add* words to the original, put brackets ([. . .]) around the added words.

> *"The second reason [for the inevitability of famine] is that developed nations, which have only 30 percent of the population, consume 70 percent of the food," he said.*

4. If you use an indirect quotation, you may summarize or paraphrase* the author's words. However, be careful not to change the meaning.

> *Dr. Doom stated that the two causes of famine were the inability of underdeveloped nations to produce enough food and the dispropor-tionate* consumption of food by developed nations.*

Punctuate direct quotations correctly. The rules for punctuating direct quotations are given in the punctuation section.

Shift verb tenses in indirect quotations if necessary. The rules for shifting verb tenses are given in the grammar section under Sequence of Tenses.

Document the source of your quotation. In academic writing, it is *ALWAYS* necessary to state the exact source of your information.

1. In the body of your paper, you may document the source of your information informally by naming the author and the title of the publication.

2. In addition to informal documentation, formal academic papers (term papers, theses, etc.) require formal footnotes, which must be in a particular form. See the unit on footnoting in the next chapter for general information.

Practice 20: Punctuating and Writing Direct and Indirect Quotations

STEP 1 Add punctuation marks to the following direct quotations. Change the capitalization if necessary.

STEP 2 Rewrite them as indirect quotations. Shift the verb tenses if necessary.

The sentences in this practice are all about black holes, which are invisible masses in space larger than giant stars. The discovery of black holes is causing enormous excitement in the fields of astronomy and physics.[9]

1. Dr. John Miller, a well-known astrophysicist who has been studying black holes, said it is the greatest challenge we astrophysicists have ever faced.

_____

_____

_____

2. He further explained in black holes the long-held laws of nature simply do not apply.

_____

_____

_____

[9]All quotations from "Black Holes: The Bermuda Triangles of Space," *Popular Astronomy* 44 (March 15, 1978), pp. 78–81.

paraphrase: state in other words
disproportionate: not according to proportion or size

3. A black hole is a huge, great, enormous, big nothing explained Miller's associate, Kathleen Parker. It is an invisible vacuum cleaner in space she added.

_____

_____

_____

4. Black holes are created by the death of a very large star she stated.

_____

_____

5. Since they cannot be seen, even with the most powerful telescopes she continued
their existence can only be proven mathematically.

_____

_____

_____

WRITING PRACTICE

Write three short paragraphs that explain the idea stated in the topic sentences.
Use the quotation for support somewhere in each paragraph.

STEP 1 Copy the topic sentence exactly as it is given.
STEP 2 Add two or three supporting sentences of your own.
STEP 3 Incorporate the quotation somewhere in your supporting sentences:
        Quote directly or indirectly.
        Use different reporting phrases in each paragraph.
        Mention the source of the quotation informally in the paragraph.
STEP 4 Write a formal footnote for each quote at the bottom of your paper. (See
page 74 for information on how to write footnotes.)

Topic Sentence:	There is also a sociological reason for Japan's spectacular eco-nomic growth.
Quotation:	The Japanese prefer to work as members of groups rather than individually. This characteristic is often cited as one of the most important in explaining Japan's economic success.
Example Author:	Howard Van Zandt
Article:	"How to Negotiate in Japan"
Publication:	*Harvard Business Review*, Volume 48, No. 6 (November-December, 1970), page 47.
Editor:	None

    There is also a sociologial reason for Japan's
spectacular economic growth. In Japan, the emphasis is on
group cooperation rather than individual achievement. As
Howard Van Zandt stated in a recent article in the Harvard
Business Review. "The Japanese prefer to work as members of
groups rather than individually." He added that this
characteristic was often cited as one of the most important in explaining Japan's economic success.

Footnote: [1]Howard Van Zandt, "How to Negotiate in Japan," *Harvard Business Review* 48 (November-December, 1970), p. 47.

1. Topic Sentence: The quality of education in American high schools has declined.
   Quotation: Two out of every three American high school graduates don't feel that they have received an adequate education.
   Author: Robert W. Henderson
   Article: "The Crisis in American High Schools"
   Publication: *Issues in American Education* (New York: Broadway Publishing Co., 1975), p. 156
   Editor: Thomas E. Brown

2. Topic Sentence: The Earth's wildlife is in danger of disappearing.
   Quotation: Between 1771 and 1870, twelve mammal species became extinct*. Between 1871 and 1970, at least forty-three more species disappeared. Of the ten million species of animals and plants on Earth today, perhaps 25 percent could become extinct before the end of this century.
   Author: Robert F. Ferguson
   Article: "Endangered Species"
   Publication: *Environmental Studies* (New York: Educational Services Publishers, Inc., 1978), p. 33
   Editor: Loraine H. Walker

3. Topic Sentence: Business offices will undergo a radical transformation in the next ten or twenty years.
   Quotation: In the next ten years, the use of automated word-processing equipment and portable computers will drastically affect the way in which business is conducted. The changes . . . will be so radical and will occur so quickly that one can truly speak of an office "revolution." In the past five years alone, there have been more developments in office equipment than there were in the previous fifty.
   Author: Carole S. Clewley
   Article: "The Office of the Future"
   Publication: *Newsday* 154 (May 27, 1981), p. 68
   Editor: None

Detailed Paragraph Outlining

In Chapter Two, you learned how to organize a simple outline for a paragraph containing the three main parts: topic sentence, main supporting ideas, and concluding sentence. A simple outline, you will remember, looks like this:

Topic Sentence

A. First main supporting point

B. Second main supporting point

C. Third main supporting point

D. Fourth main supporting point

Concluding Sentence (if there is one)

As stated earlier in the book, the outline helps you to organize your main ideas and the supporting points of those ideas in the proper order. Furthermore, as your assignments require more complex paragraphs, writing a detailed outline before you begin the writing process becomes an important tool.

---

extinct: no longer in existence

In this section you will learn to write a more detailed outline. When you add details to your basic outline, you follow the same principles as before:

1. Indent.
2. Give equivalent details the same kind of number or letter.
3. Use parallel structures.

If you add details to the simple outline above, it will look like this:

Topic Sentence
A. First main supporting point → capital letters
   1. Specific detail
   2. Specific detail → Arabic numbers
   3. Specific detail
      a. Further specific detail → small letters
      b. Further specific detail
B. Second main supporting point
   1. Specific detail
   2. Specific detail
Concluding Sentence

Notice that each smaller detail is indented farther and farther to the right

Notice that each group of points and details consists of at least two items: A and B; 1 and 2; 1, 2, and 3; a and b. The rules of formal outlining require that there be at least two items in a group in order to give them letters and numbers. In other words, there must be a B if there is an A; there must be a 2 if there is a 1 and so on.

Practice 21: Detailed Paragraph Outlining I

A. Complete the outline for the following composition.

Public Transportation in San Francisco

1   San Francisco has one of the worst public transportation systems in the United States. The first problem is that the buses and streetcars are never on schedule. You often have to wait thirty minutes or more for your bus. Frequently, several buses going in the same direction arrive at the same time, and then another one may not come for thirty more
5   minutes. Second, maintenance is very poor. The buses and street cars often break down, causing long delays. City officials admit that there is an average of five such breakdowns every day. Furthermore, the buses and streetcars are in terrible condition. They are always dirty, the windows are frequently broken, and the seats are torn. The third problem is the poor attitude of many of the drivers. They refuse to give information
10 about transfer points, they drive like mad, and they show little consideration for the comfort and safety of their passengers. Recently, a friend of mine was actually injured when the driver of a streetcar closed the doors on his fingers. When you are riding a bus, you feel as if you are being tossed around like a bowl of jello because of the sudden stops and starts. A fourth, and by far the most serious problem is the increase in crime.
15 A report from the San Francisco Police Department shows that thefts and assaults have increased forty-three percent over the three previous months. A few days ago, an old man was killed when he tried to resist a thief. In conclusion, because of all these problems, it is becoming increasingly inconvenient and even dangerous to ride public transportation in San Francisco.

Outline   San Francisco has one of the worst public transportation systems in the United States.
   A. Schedule problems
      1. Long waiting time
      2. Simultaneous bus arrivals

B. Maintenance problems
   1. Breakdowns
      a. Buses and streetcars
      b. Average of five breakdowns per day
   2. Bad condition of buses and streetcars

      a. _____

      b. _____

      c. _____

C. _____

   1. _____

   2. _____

   3. _____

      a. _____

      b. _____

D. _____

   1. _____

   2. _____

In conclusion, _____

_____

_____

B. Complete the outline for the following composition.

The Confusing English Spelling System

1   One of the most difficult and confusing aspects of the English language is its spelling system. There is often a discrepancy* between the pronunciation of a word and its spelling. One cannot always tell how to spell a word by its pronunciation nor how to pronounce it by its spelling. For example, there are twelve different ways to spell the
5   sound *sh* in English: *sh*oe, na*ti*on, *sch*ist*, o*c*ean, *s*ure, mi*ss*ion, ma*ch*ine, spe*ci*al, man*si*on, nau*se*ous, con*sci*ous, and an*xi*ous. To give an opposite example, the vowel combination *ou* can be pronounced in at least five different ways, as in the words *through, although, thought, tough,* and *out.*

    In order to understand the discrepancies in the English spelling system, it is
10 good to know something about the history of the language. First, it is helpful to realize that English was originally the spoken language of people in England who could neither read nor write. While the uneducated people spoke English, the educated upper classes spoke in French and wrote in Latin. Later, when English
15 became a written language, there was no system for spelling English words. Moreover, the first writers of English were French-speaking scribes* who knew English only slightly; therefore, they carried many French spelling habits into English. In addition, these scribes, who were used to writing in Latin, often inserted letters into words even when they were not pronounced because the corresponding
20 word in Latin was spelled that way. The *b* in *debt* and *doubt,* for example, came from Latin *debitum* and *dubitare.* Finally, the confusion increased when the pronunciation of certain words changed while the spelling remained the same. This is the case with the words *light* and *night,* where the *gh* originally represented a distinct sound.

    In conclusion, although it may not improve your spelling, it may soothe your
25 feeling of frustration to know that English spelling is just as difficult for native speakers as it is for foreign learners.

---

discrepancy: difference   **schist:** a crystalline rock
scribes: writers, copiers

Outline   I. One of the most difficult and confusing aspects about the English language is its spelling system.

    A. _____

    B. _____

       1. _____

       2. _____

II. In order to understand the discrepancies in the English spelling system, it is helpful to know something about the history of the language.

    A. English was originally the spoken language of people in England who could neither read nor write.

      1. Uneducated people spoke English.

      2. Educated _____

                            _____

    B. _____

                  _____

    C. _____

                  _____

       1. _____

                     _____

       2. _____

                     _____

          a. Scribes added the b in debt from the Latin *debitum.*

          b. Scribes added the b in doubt from the Latin *dubitare.*

    D. _____

                  _____

                  _____

III. In conclusion, although it may not improve your spelling, it may soothe your feeling of frustration to know that English spelling is just as difficult for native speakers as it is for foreign learners.

Practice 22: Detailed Paragraph Outlining II

A. Organize the items in the list below into a logical outline. Remember to give the items with equal importance the same kind of letter or number.

Europe	France	Thailand
England	Saudi Arabia	Texas
Southeast Asia	Turkey	Malaysia
Canada	China	North America
The United States	The Middle East	Asia
Mexico	California	Cambodia
New York State	Los Angeles	San Francisco
The Far East	Iran	Vietnam
Japan	Quebec	Ontario

B. The sentences below are in scrambled order. Arrange them into a logical outline.

American high schools are facing problems on four fronts.

Vandalism* in the schools is increasing.

Teachers who have had to take teacher certification examinations show very low scores.

In 1975, according to an N.E.A.* report, acts of vandalism and theft cost the schools $200 million.

Colleges report that some new freshmen read and write at the sixth-grade level.

Students aren't learning anything.

Taxpayers are protesting the increasing costs by voting against tax increases to pay for schools.

During the last ten years, there have been numerous strikes by teachers demanding higher pay and less work.

On the national Scholastic Aptitude Test (SAT), a national test for high school seniors, the average scores in verbal ability have fallen by ten percent.

Teachers are also creating problems for the schools.

A large school in Chicago, Illinois, reported that one window is broken and two typewriters are stolen every week.

Math scores on the SAT have declined by six percent since 1962.

Traditional methods of financing the schools are breaking down.

The schools in Cleveland, Ohio, were closed for three months last winter because they simply ran out of money.

Review: Concrete Support

> These are the main points you should have learned from this chapter:
> 1. Use concrete supporting details to prove your points.
> 2. Do not use opinions for support.
> 3. Use examples, illustrative incidents, figures and statistics, simple statements of fact, and direct or indirect quotations.
> 4. Use appropriate reporting phrases or clauses to introduce your supporting details.
> 5. Document the source of *all* borrowed information.

WRITING PRACTICE

Write one long paragraph in which you argue either *for* or *against* a controversial* topic.

STEP 1 Write a detailed outline of your paragraph before you begin.
STEP 2 Begin your topic sentence with an opinion phrase, such as *In my opinion* . . . or *Many people feel that . . .*
STEP 3 Add as many reasons as you can think of. Try to use at least three.

---

vandalism: willful destruction of property
N.E.A.: National Education Association
controversial: something about which
people disagree

STEP 4 Support each reason with some kind of specific supporting detail. Vary the kind of support you use—that is, do not use examples only or statistics only.

STEP 5 Write a brief concluding sentence.

STEP 6 Before you hand in your outline and paragraph, check it against the Paragraph Checklist that follows.

Topic Suggestions

Birth control and/or family planning
Abortion
Capital punishment*
Living together without being married
Euthanasia*
Your college's English requirement
Legalization of marijuana

Strikes by public employees— police officers, firefighters, teachers
Strikes by health professionals— doctors, nurses
Nuclear power plants

Paragraph Checklist

Form:
____ Does your paragraph have a title?
____ Did you write on the correct side of the paper?
____ Did you indent the first line?
____ Did you write on every other line?

Topic Sentence:
____ Does your topic sentence contain a controlling idea?

Supporting Sentences:
Unity:
____ Do all of your sentences support your topic sentence?

Coherence— Transition Signals:
____ Do you use transition signals at appropriate places to make your sentences flow smoothly?

Coherence— Logical Order:
____ Are your ideas arranged in logical order?

Concrete Support:
____ Does your paragraph contain enough specific supporting details to prove your main points?

Concluding Sentence:
____ Does your paragraph have a concluding sentence?

WRITING UNDER PRESSURE

Make a general opinion statement about one of the groups of people listed below under Topic Suggestions and support your opinion with specific supporting details. Your goal is to convince your reader that your opinion is correct, so you must present very strong arguments.

Make a simple outline before you begin to write, and hand in your outline with your paragraph.

---

capital punishment: death penalty   **euthanasia:** mercy killing

Check your paragraph against the preceding Paragraph Checklist before you hand it in.

Topic Suggestions

Americans.

English teachers.

Politicians.

In-laws.

Businesspeople.

Rock musicians.

Engineers.

Professional athletes.

Your instructor will give you a time limit. Suggested limits:
Outlining Time — 3 minutes
Writing Time — 10 minutes
Checking Time — 2 minutes

Total — 15 minutes

Chapter 6

PARAPHRASING, SUMMARIZING, AND FOOTNOTING

Paraphrasing is a writing skill in which information from published sources is written in different words (rephrased) without changing its original meaning. It is often used in place of directly quoting what a writer has said. Paraphrasing is used to rewrite short selections, such as sentences, a series of sentences, or paragraphs. A paraphrase is usually as long as the original text in order to communicate its full meaning.

Writing a Paraphrase

Here are some techniques you can use to write a paraphrase:

1. Use synonyms wherever possible. Some of the words from the original passage may appear in your paraphrase, but try to use synonyms.
2. Change active sentences to passive sentences or vice-versa.
3. Change direct quotations to indirect quotations.

Follow these steps to write a paraphrase:

STEP 1 Read the selection carefully several times until you understand it fully.
STEP 2 Look up any words you do not understand; find synonyms for them.
STEP 3 Write a brief outline, including:
    a. the main idea (topic and controlling ideas)
    b. the main supporting points
    c. primary and secondary supporting details
STEP 4 Write the paraphrase. Use your own words, but do not omit any essential ideas. Above all, do not change the meaning of the original.

Note: When you include paraphrased information in a formal report or research paper, *always* footnote it. (For general information on footnoting, see page 74.)

The following are examples of paraphrases.

Model 14: Paraphrases

Original   When the Maracaña soccer stadium [in Rio de Janeiro, Brazil] was opened to the public in 1950, and Brazil lost the World Cup to the Uruguayan team, the Brazilians were so disheartened one had the impression that the country itself had died. And people did die of sadness. Mere threats of defeat in a championship match can cause heart attacks and the despair of the public is so great that many beat their heads against the cement posts. Such is the Brazilian's passion for soccer.[1]

---

[1]Vinicius de Moraes and Ferreira Gullar, *The Joy of Rio* (New York: The Vendome Press, 1980), p. 13.

Outline   A. Brazil lost the World Cup in 1950
　　　　　　 1. Entire country was sad
　　　　　　 2. Some people died
　　　　　　B. Possible defeat causes strong reaction
　　　　　　 1. Some experience heart attacks
　　　　　　 2. Some beat their heads
　　　　　　C. Brazilians are very emotional about soccer

Paraphrase　　　In 1950, Brazil lost the World Cup in soccer to Uruguay in Rio de Janeiro. The entire country was overcome by sadness; some people even died from it. Brazilians react very strongly to potential defeat in championship soccer games. Some people have heart attacks, and others beat their heads against cement posts. Brazilians are very emotional about soccer.

Original　　　Howard Van Zandt, who studied Japanese business practices extensively, said, "The Japanese prefer to work as members of groups rather than individually. This characteristic is often cited as one of the most important in explaining Japan's economic success."[2]

Outline   A. The Japanese people would rather work in groups.
　　　　　　B. This trait is responsible for Japan's economic success.

Paraphrase　　　Van Zandt maintains that the Japanese people would rather work together in groups, not individually. He believes that this trait is one of the most important factors which has contributed to the success of Japan's economy.

Practice 23: Paraphrasing I

Paraphrase each of the following selections. Follow the steps outlined on page 67.

Paragraph 1
However great the powers of the President of the United States, they are restricted by the "checks and balances" represented in the Congress, in the Supreme Court of the United States, and in the force of public opinion. However, of all the elective officers of our government, only the President and the Vice President are chosen by all the voters of the United States.[3]

_____

_____

_____

_____

_____

_____

_____

[2]Howard Van Zandt, "How to Negotiate in Japan," *Harvard Business Review* 48 (November–December, 1970), p. 47.
[3]"The President Proposes but Congress Disposes," *The Capitol*, 6th Edition, House Document No. 93–139, p. 38.

Paragraph 2

The Smithsonian Institution is an independent establishment dedicated to the increase and diffusion* of knowledge. It is a great complex of museums and art galleries, scholars, and experts in many fields. It is devoted to public education, basic research, and national service in the arts, sciences, and history, with major facilities in Washington, around the country, and overseas.[4]

_____

_____

_____

_____

_____

_____

Paragraph 3

"Vitamin C in large doses* not only protects against the common cold, but also offers considerable protection against other infectious diseases, both viral and bacterial. I believe that Vitamin C in adequate amounts could considerably decrease the incidence and severity of the flu."[5]

_____

_____

_____

_____

_____

Practice 24: Paraphrasing II

Write paraphrases of the following:

Two selections from a textbook.

Two quotations from any source.

Copy the original selections and write the paraphrases below them as in the preceding exercise. Follow the steps outlined on page 67.

For additional practice in paraphrasing, any of the material in this book may be assigned by your instructor.

Writing a Summary

A summary is similar to a paraphrase except that a summary is usually shorter. When you summarize, you compress large amounts of information into the fewest possible sentences. In order to do this, you include only the main points and main supporting points, leaving out the details.

---

[4]"The Smithsonian Today," *Official Guide to the Smithsonian* (CBS Publications, Inc., 1976), p. 11.
   [5]Interview with Dr. Linus Pauling and Dr. Arthur Robinson, "When Is It Finally Going to Dawn on Us?" *The Body Forum* (January, 1977), p. 9.

---

diffusion: spreading out
doses: amounts

To write a summary, follow the same steps as you did to write a paraphrase, but omit all unnecessary details. For example, a possible summary of the paragraph on Brazilian soccer enthusiasm (Model 14 on page 67), is as follows:

> *The Brazilian people become so emotionally involved with their national soccer team that in 1950, when their team lost the World Cup to Uruguay, the entire country was saddened, and some people even died. The mere possibility of defeat causes genuine physical suffering.*

Again, as when you paraphrase, you must not change the original meaning, and you must document the source of the original.

Model 15 shows an original paragraph, an outline, and a summary written from the outline.

Model 15: A summary

Original For generations, Americans have researched their pasts to discover who their ancestors were. In recent years, many more people have developed an avid interest in their genealogy* and the cultural heritage of their ancestors. This interest was sparked for two reasons. First, Americans celebrated the bicentennial* of the United States in 1976 and paid tribute to this country's history. Second, and more recently, the book *Roots*, which traces the family history of an American black man named Alex Haley back to Africa, was serialized* on national television. As a result of these two events, a new pastime for thousands of Americans was created.[6]

Outline A. American research into background

   1. Ancestors
   2. Cultural heritage

   B. Reasons for research
   1. Bicentennial celebration
   2. *Roots*

Summary Recently, many Americans have become interested in researching their backgrounds in order to identify their ancestors and learn about their cultural heritage. This interest in genealogy began with the U.S. Bicentennial celebration and intensified with the televising of the family history of Alex Haley, a black American.

Practice 25: Writing Summaries I

Read each of the following paragraphs and write a summary of it. These paragraphs discuss the basic categories of consumer goods.[7]

STEP 1 Make a brief outline.
STEP 2 Write your summary from your outline.

---

[6]Stephen Longsworth, "In Search of Roots," *American Genealogical Journal* 68 (June, 1978), p. 132.
[7]E. Poe, *Enterprise of American Business* (New York: MacMillan Publishing Co., 1978).

---

genealogy: study of one's ancestors   **serialized:** shown in parts on successive days
bicentennial: two-hundred-year anniversary

Paragraph 1

Convenience goods may be classified as staples, impulse goods, and emergency goods. Staples are bought and used frequently without much consideration being given to their purchase. Many food products and nonprescription drug items are staple goods. Brand identification may have some weight in the buying decision, but usually easy availability will be more important than the brand. Items such as bread, milk, and aspirin are considered staples, and easy availability to consumers is important in their distribution.

_____

_____

_____

_____

_____

_____

_____

Paragraph 2

Impulse goods are items that customers buy on sight without having gone out specifically for their purchase. Their unit price is usually low. The purchase of an impulse good satisfies a need that is strongly felt at the moment. Items that customers will buy on an impulse are frequently placed near store doors or at cash registers. Candy bars, chewing gum, cigarettes, and magazines are frequently displayed in this way.

_____

_____

_____

_____

_____

_____

_____

Paragraph 3

A good may be either a staple or an impulse item, depending on the purpose of the good's use and on whether the good was purchased because of an immediately felt need. Candy bars may be considered staple goods if they are purchased for lunch boxes as part of a weekly grocery shopping trip. But a candy bar might be viewed as an impulse item if it were purchased and eaten on the spot because a person just happened to see it.

_____

_____

_____

_____

_____

Paragraph 4

Emergency goods are bought only when an urgent need is felt. In this situation price is not too important, because the customer needs the goods at once. Tire chains purchased at a turnpike* service station during a snowstorm, or ambulance service for the victim of a heart attack are examples of emergency goods.

_____

_____

_____

_____

_____

Paragraph 5

Shopping goods are in a totally different category. Shopping goods are compared with competing products for price, quality, style, or service by the customer before purchase. This presents an opportunity for selling by sales personnel. Shopping goods typically have a relatively high unit price and are bought less frequently than convenience goods. Examples of shopping goods include apparel, jewelry, furniture, and appliances.

_____

_____

_____

_____

_____

Paragraph 6

Since the customer will probably want to compare shopping goods with those sold by the competition, retail stores selling such goods find it desirable to be located close together. In some cases the name of the retail store is more important to the customer than the name of the manufacturer. Therefore, the retailer has considerable opportunity to increase sales of shopping goods through promotion.

_____

_____

_____

_____

_____

Paragraph 7

Specialty goods is yet another classification of consumer items. Specialty goods are identified by customers with strong brand preference or with features that justify a special buying effort. The customer usually has knowledge of the product before the buying trip and is willing to go out of the way to find a certain brand. Examples of specialty goods include photographic equipment, expensive clothing, and stereo sets. An automobile may be considered a specialty good by the customer who has a strong preference for a particular manufacturer's models.

_____

turnpike: freeway

_____

_____

_____

_____

_____

_____

Practice 26: Writing Summaries II

Summarize a five-paragraph section from a textbook, journal, or magazine article on a subject of your choice.

STEP 1 Write an outline for each paragraph.
STEP 2 Write your summary for each paragraph from your outline.
STEP 3 Footnote your selection.
STEP 4 Hand in a copy of the original selection, your outlines, and your summaries.

Footnoting

When you write a research paper or do any kind of academic writing on a subject in which your goal is to inform or persuade your reader, you would first seek information from other sources by doing library research. Research official records and original works as well as books, journals and magazines to collect facts, opinions, statistics, etc. to strengthen your discussion.

But when you take someone else's works or ideas and integrate them into your paper, you must acknowledge the source of that borrowed material, generally by using footnotes. Footnotes also tell the reader where to look to verify this information or to learn more about the subject.

It is not necessary to footnote information that is considered common knowledge or factual, such as the boiling point of water, the dates and events of history, the results of a public election, etc. On the other hand, it *is* necessary to footnote the following:

1. Information that is not common knowledge, such as the reasons for recent Congressional redistricting*.

2. Opinions, theories, or statements of another writer, whether written in direct or indirect speech, paraphrases or summaries, such as the results of Dr. Linus Pauling's research on the common cold or Erich von Däniken's theories of prehistoric visitors from outer space.

3. Statistics, graphs, and figures, such as the gross national product (GNP) in the United States for the past five years or the current population of China.

There are several acceptable styles for writing footnotes, but each academic discipline has its own preferred style; therefore, you should ask your instructors which style they prefer.

The form of the footnotes depends on whether the material is from a book, a magazine, an encyclopedia article, etc. It will also vary if there is one author or

---

Congressional redistricting: determining areas for election purposes

several, or if the name of the author is unknown. There are many possible variations. Also, there are several abbreviations commonly used with footnotes. We suggest that you consult a term paper manual for complete information. For the exercises in this workbook, you need to learn only two basic footnote forms: one for books and one for magazine or journal articles.

BOOK FOOTNOTES

When you use information from a book, your footnote should contain this information:

Author's name, first name before last name
Title of the book, underlined
Publishing information, the city, a colon (:), then the publisher's name and the
   year of publication
Page, number or numbers on which the borrowed information appears.

There are rules for punctuating footnotes. Titles of books are *always* underlined. Generally, commas separate the various parts (author's name, title, etc.). Publishing information is usually placed inside parentheses. The first line is indented, and a period is placed at the end.

Here is an example of a book footnote:

**Book
Footnote**   ¹E. Adamson Hoebel, *Anthropology: The Study of Man* (New York: McGraw Hill Book Company, 1972), p. 145.

ARTICLE FOOTNOTES

When you use information from an article in a magazine or professional journal, or from a chapter of an anthology*, your footnote should contain this information:

Author's name, first name before last name
Title of the article or chapter, in quotation marks
Title of the magazine or book, underlined, in which the article appears
Publishing information—
   Magazines and journals: volume number and exact date
   Books: name of the editor, city, publisher, and year
Page number or numbers on which the borrowed information appears

Here is an example of a footnote for an article from a professional journal:

**Article
Footnote**   ¹Howard Van Zandt, "How to Negotiate in Japan" *Harvard Business Review* 48 (November-December, 1970), p. 47.

---

anthology: collection of essays, articles or poems by one or several authors

Part II

WRITING AN ESSAY

THE ESSAY

Writing an Essay

An essay is a piece of writing several paragraphs long instead of just one or two paragraphs. It is written about one topic, just as a paragraph is. However, the topic of an essay is too long and too complex to discuss in one paragraph. Therefore, you must divide the topic into several paragraphs, one for each major point. Then you must tie all of the separate paragraphs together by adding an introduction and a conclusion.

Writing an essay is no more difficult than writing a paragraph, except that an essay is longer. The principles of organization are the same for both; so if you can write a good paragraph, you can write a good essay.

An essay has three main parts:

1. An *introductory paragraph*
2. A *body* (at least one, but usually two or more paragraphs)
3. A *concluding paragraph*

Introductory Paragraph

The **introductory paragraph** consists of two parts: a few *general statements* about your subject to attract your reader's attention, and a *thesis statement*, to state the specific subdivisions of your topic and/or the "plan" of your paper. A thesis statement for an essay is just like a topic sentence for a paragraph: it names the specific topic and the controlling ideas or major subdivisions of the topic.

Body

The **body** consists of one or more paragraphs. Each paragraph develops a subdivision of your topic, so the number of paragraphs in the body will vary with the number of subdivisions. The paragraphs of the body are like the main supporting points of a paragraph. Furthermore, just as you can organize the ideas in a paragraph by chronological order or by order of importance, you can organize the paragraphs in an essay in the same ways.

Conclusion

The **conclusion** in an essay, like the concluding sentence in a paragraph, is a summary or review of the main points discussed in the body.

The only additional element in an essay is the linking expressions between the paragraphs of the body. These are just like transitions within a paragraph. You use transitions *within* a paragraph to connect the ideas between two sentences. Similarly, you use transitions *between* paragraphs to connect the ideas between them.

You can see that writing an essay is essentially the same as writing a paragraph; an essay is just longer. The chart below shows you how the parts of a paragraph correspond to the parts of an essay.

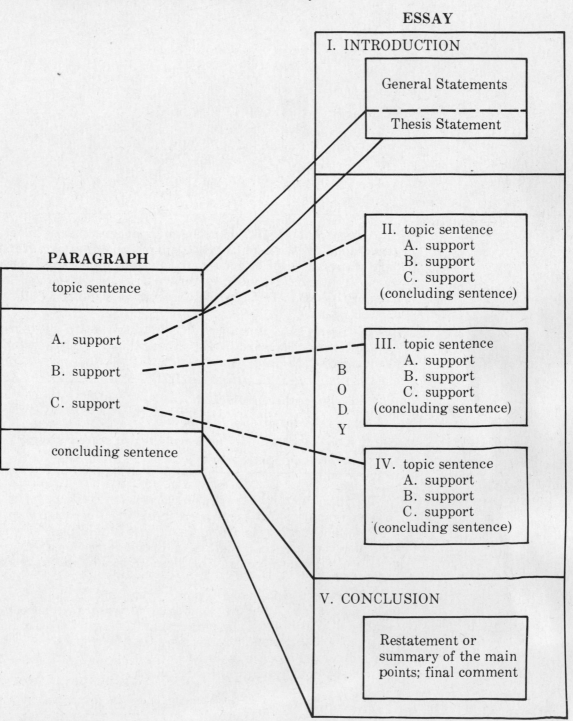

Note: The body is the longest part of the essay and can contain as many paragraphs as necessary to support the controlling ideas of your thesis statement.

THE INTRODUCTORY PARAGRAPH

All writers (even professionals) complain that the most difficult part of writing is getting started. How many times have you wasted valuable minutes during an essay examination trying to think of your first sentence? Getting started, or writing an introduction, can be easy if you remember that an introduction has four purposes:

1. It introduces the topic of the essay.
2. It gives a general background of the topic.
3. It often indicates the overall "plan" of the essay.
4. It should arouse the reader's interest in the topic.

The Introduction has two parts:

I. General Statements
II. A thesis statement

Notice the two parts of the following introductory paragraph.

Model 1: The introductory paragraph

Introduction   A person born in the twentieth century has seen a lot of changes take place in almost all areas of human life. Some people are excited by the challenges that these changes offer; others want to return to the simpler, less automated life style of the past. Living in the twentieth century has certain advantages such as a higher standard of living, but it also has some disadvantages such as a polluted environment, the depersonalization of human relationships, and the weakening of spiritual values.

The first sentence in an introductory paragraph should be a very general comment about the subject. Its purpose is to attract the reader's attention and to give background information on the topic. Each subsequent sentence should become more specific than the previous one and finally lead into the thesis statement.

General statements:

1. introduce the topic of the essay.
2. give background information on the topic.

The thesis statement is the most important sentence in the introduction. It states the specific topic and lists the major subtopics that will be discussed in the body of the essay. Furthermore, it often indicates the method of organization such as chronological order, or order of importance.

The thesis statement:

1. states the main topic.
2. lists the subdivisions of the topic.
3. may indicate the method of organization of the entire paper.
4. is usually the last sentence in the introductory paragraph.

To sum up, an introductory paragraph is like a funnel: very wide at the top, increasingly narrow in the middle, and very small at the neck or bottom.

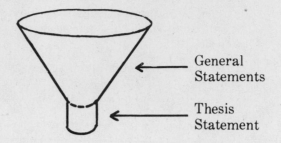

General
Statements

Thesis
Statement

Practice 1: Recognizing the Parts of an Introduction

STEP 1 Read the following introductory paragraphs, each of which is in incorrect order.

STEP 2 Rewrite each paragraph, beginning with the most general statement first. Then add each sentence in the correct order until the introduction becomes more specific. Write the thesis statement last.

Paragraph 1

(1) The heavy traffic problem can be solved by building rapid transit systems from the suburbs to the cities, by improving public transportation systems within the cities, and by forming car pools. (2) Traffic congestion is caused by the thousands of cars that come into the cities from the suburban areas as well as from the thousands of cars within the city limits. (3) One of the most serious problems that most big cities are faced with is traffic congestion. (4) This mammoth problem must be resolved before it gets worse.

_____
_____
_____
_____
_____
_____
_____
_____
_____
_____
_____

Paragraph 2

(1) However, in others, the nuclear family is the norm, with only the parents and young children sharing the same house. (2) People in different cultures all over the world have different systems for family life. (3) In most cultures, people live in extended families in which several generations share the same house. (4) If this new system becomes widespread, it could have enormous

effects on American society. (5) On the positive side, living together might reduce the divorce rate in the United States; on the negative side, it might lead to the eventual disintegration of the family altogether. (6) In the United States, young people are experimenting with still another system of family life: living together without marriage.

_____

_____

_____

_____

_____

_____

_____

_____

_____

_____

Paragraph 3

(1) Although scientists have experimented with different methods of prediction, from observing animal behavior to measuring radio signals from quasars*, they have not proven successful. (2) Earthquakes are the most destructive natural disasters known to man, in terms of the millions of deaths and billions of dollars in property loss that they cause. (3) Despite these heavy losses, scientists are still unable to predict earthquakes. (4) This paper will review the history of the science of earthquake prediction, then discuss each of the methods in more detail, and finally present data indicating the success–failure ratios of each method.

_____

_____

_____

_____

_____

_____

_____

_____

_____

_____

_____

quasars: star-like objects in space

Practice 2: Thesis Statements I

A. Study these thesis statements from two different essays on the topic of the status of women in Xanadu, an imaginary country. Which method of organization (chronological order or comparison and contrast) does each one indicate?

1. Beginning in World War II and continuing through the period of economic boom, the status of women in Xanadu has changed remarkably.

   Method of organization: _____

2. Although the status of women in Xanadu has improved remarkably in recent years, it is still very low when compared to the status of women in the countries of the Western world.

   Method of organization: _____

B. In the following two thesis statements, both the method of organization and the major subdivisions of the topic are indicated. Each subdivision will be the topic of a paragraph in the body. How many paragraphs will the body of each essay probably contain? Underline the topics of each paragraph.

3. The status of women in Xanadu has changed remarkably in recent years due to increased educational opportunities and changes in the country's laws.

   Probable number of paragraphs: _____

4. The status of women in Xanadu has improved remarkably in recent years in the areas of economic independence, political rights, educational opportunities, and social status.

   Probable number of paragraphs: _____

C. Analyze the following thesis statements.

   STEP 1 Locate the main topic and the subtopics in each of the following thesis statements.
   STEP 2 Underline the subtopics.
   STEP 3 Draw a circle around the words or punctuation marks that are used to introduce the subtopics.

   Example

   Capital punishment should be abolished (not only) because it deprives another person of life, (but also) because it does not stop crime.

   1. Women generally live longer than men for two main reasons: they tend to take better care of their health, and they lead less stressful lives.
   2. Drug and alcohol abuse among teenagers can be traced to the following causes: lack of parental supervision, lax enforcement of drug laws, and the social and psychological problems of teenagers themselves.
   3. In choosing a major, a student has to consider various factors, such as personal interest, job opportunities, and the availability of training institutions.
   4. An architect should be both an artist and an engineer.
   5. The purpose of this report is to analyze the influence of Chinese culture on Japanese language and literature.

Practice 3: Thesis Statements II

STEP 1 Complete the following thesis statements by adding topics to them.
STEP 2 Circle your topics.
If you use correlative conjunctions (both . . . and, not only . . . but also, etc.), be sure your structures are parallel.

1. The life expectancy of the average person is increasing because of _____ _____

2. Technology is changing our lives in three important areas: _____ _____

3. Foreign students have a difficult time taking notes in class due to _____ _____

4. A teacher must have the following qualities: _____ _____

5. The purpose of this paper is to _____ _____ _____

6. Television commercials are insulting to the average viewer because _____

7. Owning an automobile is a necessity both _____ _____

8. The basic causes of inflation are _____ _____

9. Poverty creates negative consequences for society, such as _____ _____

10. Living together without marriage is becoming increasingly popular for three reasons: _____ _____

WRITING PRACTICE

Write a good thesis statement for essays on each of the following topics:

Foreign travel.   Choosing a career.
Culture shock.   Space exploration.
Technology.

THE CONCLUDING PARAGRAPH

The final paragraph is the conclusion, a very important part of the essay. In this paragraph you tell the reader that you have completed the essay. This is achieved by either writing a summary of the main points discussed in the body of the essay or by rewriting the thesis statement in different words. Then you add your final comments on the subject—food for thought. Since this is your last opportunity to make your point, you should write a strong, effective message that will be remembered.

The concluding paragraph consists of:

1. a summary of the main points

or

2. a restatement of your thesis in different words

and

3. your final comment on the subject.

Note: Introduce the concluding paragraph with a transition signal.

Study the introduction and conclusion for the following model essay on the advantages and disadvantages of living in the twentieth century. Is the concluding paragraph a summary of the main points of the essay or is it a paraphrase of the thesis statement? Is there a final message for the reader?

Model 2: The concluding paragraph

Introduction   A person born in the twentieth century has seen many changes take place in almost all areas of human life. Some people are excited by the challenges that these changes offer; others long to return to the simpler, less automated life-style of the past. Living in the twentieth century has certain advantages, such as a higher standard of living, but it also has some disadvantages, such as a polluted environment, the depersonalization of human relationships, and the weakening of spiritual values.

Conclusion   In conclusion, although the twentieth century has indeed given us a lot of advantages by making us richer, healthier and freer to enjoy our lives, it has, in my opinion, not made us wiser. The twentieth century has also made our Earth dirtier, our people less humane, and our spiritual lives poorer. We should continue to enjoy the benefits of technological advancements because they free us to pursue our interests and goals. However, we must make a concerted effort to preserve our natural environment for future generations. Moreover, we should take the time now to make our lives more meaningful in an increasingly impersonal, mechanized world.

Practice 4: Writing Concluding Paragraphs

A. Write concluding paragraphs for the following introductions.

STEP 1 Summarize the main points or paraphrase the thesis statement.
STEP 2 Add your own comments as a final message to the reader.

Paragraph 1

The busy schedules that most Americans face from day to day have created a rising health problem in the United States. Stress affects almost everyone, from the highly pressured executive to the busy homemaker or student. It can cause a variety of physical disorders, ranging from headaches to stomach ulcers and even alcoholism. Stress is not a problem that can be cured like a common cold; however, it can be controlled. A person can learn to control stress by setting realistic goals, enjoying a hobby and/or physical exercise, and by maintaining a good, warm relationship with family and friends.

_____

_____

_____

_____

_____

_____

_____

_____

_____

Paragraph 2

Television is the most popular form of entertainment in the American household. People of all ages use this medium to entertain themselves for an average of four hours a day. Thus, television has had a tremendous influence on its viewers, especially children. Scientists now say that children can be adversely affected by constantly watching television. This is due to the fact that they participate less in physical activities, spend less time reading and studying, and see a world of violence that can affect their own feelings of security.

_____

_____

_____

_____

_____

_____

_____

_____

B. Write concluding paragraphs for the introductory paragraphs 1, 2, and 3 that you reorganized in Practice 1, pages 80 and 81.

Essay Outlining

Because an essay is longer and more complex than a paragraph, it is even more important to organize your thoughts and to plan your essay before you begin to write. The best way to do this is to make an outline.

The principles and techniques that you have already learned for paragraph outlining can be applied to essays. The only additional element is the numbering of each paragraph with Roman numerals. For example, in a five-paragraph essay, the introduction is paragraph I; the three paragraphs of the body are II, III, and IV; and the conclusion is paragraph V.

Here is a list of Roman numerals:

1 - I	5 - V	9 - IX	13 - XIII
2 - II	6 - VI	10 - X	14 - XIV
3 - III	7 - VII	11 - XI	15 - XV
4 - IV	8 - VIII	12 - XII	

Study the following model outline for an essay on the advantages and disadvantages of living in the twentieth century. Only the paragraphs of the body of the essay have been outlined; only the thesis statement in the introductory paragraph has been given.

Model 3: Essay outlining

The Advantages and Disadvantages
of Living in the Twentieth Century

Thesis Statement I. Living in the twentieth century offers certain advantages, such as a higher standard of living, but it also has some disadvantages, such as a polluted environment, the depersonalization of human relationships, and the weakening of spiritual values.

II. The biggest advantage of living in the twentieth century is the high standard of living we enjoy.

A. More money for less hard work.

1. More office workers than manual laborers
2. Higher salaries
3. Increased government services

a. Social security
b. Unemployment benefits
c. Disability insurance

B. Longer life expectancy

1. Better medical care

a. More hospitals, doctors, nurses
b. Advances in medical technology

2. Improved nutrition
3. More leisure time

C. Modern conveniences

1. Communication

a. Telephones
b. Radio and television

2. Labor-saving machines in the home

a. Dishwashers
b. Washing machines
c. Vacuum cleaners

3. Faster transportation

III. One of the main disadvantages of living in the twentieth century is that we are living in an increasingly polluted environment.

A. Air pollution

1. Smog
2. Nuclear fallout

B. Water pollution
   1. Chemical wastes from factories

      a. Dead fish
      b. Contaminated drinking water supplies

   2. Raw sewage from cities
   3. Oil spills from ships

IV. A second disadvantage of living in the twentieth century is the depersonaliza-
    tion of human relationships.

    A. People and machines

       1. Automated vending machines, banks, etc.
       2. Tape recorded telephone answering
       3. Computerized dating services

    B. People and numbers

       1. Social security numbers
       2. Credit card numbers

V. The final disadvantage of living in the twentieth century is the weakening of
   spiritual values.

   A. Materialistic culture

   B. Faith in science instead of in religion

VI. In conclusion, although the twentieth century has indeed given us a lot of
    advantages by making us richer, healthier and freer to enjoy our lives, it has,
    in my opinion, not made us wiser. The twentieth century has also made our
    earth dirtier, our people less humane, and our spiritual lives poorer. We
    should continue to enjoy the benefits of technological advancements because
    they free us to pursue our interests and goals. However, we must make a
    concerted effort to preserve our natural environment for future generations.
    Moreover, we should take the time now to make our lives more meaningful
    in an increasingly impersonal, computerized world.

Writing Technique Questions

1. How many paragraphs does this essay contain?

2. How many paragraphs are in the *body* of the essay?

3. Look at the contents of paragraph II. How many main points are given? Do you
   think there are too many ideas for one paragraph? Would you recommend
   dividing it into several paragraphs? How many? What would be your new
   topic sentences?

Transition Signals Between Paragraphs

Transition signals are important not only *within* paragraphs but also *between*
paragraphs. If you write two or more paragraphs, you need to show the relationship
between your first and second paragraph, between your second and third paragraph, and so on.

Think of transitions between paragraphs like the links of a chain. The links of
a chain connect the chain; they hold it together. Similarly, a transition signal
between two paragraphs links* your ideas together.

---

link: join, connect

Two paragraphs are linked by adding a transition signal to the topic sentence of the second paragraph. This transition signal may be a single word, a phrase, or a dependent clause that repeats or summarizes the main idea in the first paragraph.

Study the following model, and notice how the paragraphs are linked by a single word, a phrase, or a clause.

Model 4: Paragraph Transitions

Flextime

One of the most important changes that management has made in industry in recent years is the scheduling of flexible work hours for their employees. Workers are given the option of choosing when they will work. This allows them more leisure time for family and fun. Flextime has obvious advantages for both workers and management although it may not be practical in all types of businesses.

Transition Word   The (first) advantage is increased production per work-hour. (+ supporting sentences)

Transition Word   A (second) advantage is that factory workers are happier. (+ supporting sentences)

Transition Phrase   (In addition to increased output and worker satisfaction,) factory managers report that absenteeism has declined. (+ supporting sentences)

Transition Clause   (Although flextime has produced these three positive results in some industries,) it is not as advantageous in all types of businesses. (+ supporting sentences)

Practice 5: Transitions Between Paragraphs

Connect the ideas in the following paragraphs by adding a transition word, phrase, or clause to the topic sentences of the second, third, fourth, and fifth paragraphs. Try to vary the linking expressions that you use. You may rewrite the topic sentences if necessary.

Icebergs: A Potential Source of Water

The supply of fresh water has not been a major problem for most countries in the world because a rainy season is part of their yearly climatic conditions. However, in countries where the rainy season is very sparse, scientists must constantly seek ways to increase fresh supplies of this precious element. Government planners in South America and the Middle East have been trying to devise new ways of increasing their nations' supplies of fresh water. The first method being considered is the use of desalinization plants, which would remove salt from sea water. Another method being considered is towing icebergs. According to this method, large icebergs from Antarctica would be wrapped in cloth or plastic, tied to powerful tugboats by strong ropes, and towed to the dry country. While this plan may have some potential, there are certain practical problems that must be solved.

_____

_____ is the expense. According to estimates, it would cost between $50 and $100 million to tow a single 100-million-ton iceberg from Antarctica to, for example, the coast of Saudi Arabia.

_____ is the possibility that the iceberg would melt en route*. No one knows if an iceberg could be effectively insulated during such a long journey. At the very least, there is the possibility that it would break up into smaller pieces, which would create still other problems.

_____

_____ there is the danger that a huge block of ice off an arid* coast could have unexpected environmental effects. The ice could drastically change the weather along the coast, and it would almost certainly affect the fish population.

_____

_____ the cost of providing fresh water from icebergs would be less than the cost of providing water by desalinization, according to most estimates. It would cost between 50¢ and 60¢ per cubic meter to get water from an iceberg, as opposed to the 80¢ per cubic meter it costs to get the same amount by desalinization.

Review: The Essay

An essay has at least three main parts: an introduction, a body, and a conclusion.

1. The introductory paragraph attracts the reader's attention and informs the reader what your main topic of discussion will be. An introductory paragraph has two parts:

   a. Several general sentences that give background information on your subject and gradually lead your reader into your specific topic.

   b. A thesis statement that states the subdivisions (topics of each paragraph). It may also indicate your method of development.

2. The body of an essay discusses your subdivided topics, one by one. It contains as many paragraphs as necessary to explain the controlling ideas in the thesis statement.

3. The concluding paragraph reminds your reader of what you have said. Remember to use a "conclusion" transition signal. Your concluding paragraph has a summary of the main ideas, or a restatement of the thesis, and your final comment on the topic.

Outlining an Essay

1. Always make an outline of an essay before you begin to write. Follow the same outlining form that you learned in the section on paragraph outlining.

2. Number each paragraph with Roman numerals: I, II, III, IV, V, etc. The introduction is paragraph I, the first paragraph of the body is paragraph II, and so on.

Transitions Between Paragraphs

Remember to show the relationship *between* paragraphs by using appropriate linking words, phrases, or clauses.

---

en route: during the journey   **arid:** dry

Chapter 8

PATTERNS OF ESSAY ORGANIZATION

Organizing an essay is essentially the same as organizing a paragraph; the only difference is that instead of working with single sentences, you are working with paragraphs. You can use the same patterns (or combination of patterns) for essays as you use for paragraphs. You simply decide what information belongs in each paragraph, and then in what order you should arrange the paragraphs.

You already know something about the different patterns of organization in English. You are familiar with chronological order and order-of-importance as ways of sequencing ideas. So far, however, you have practiced these different orders only within a paragraph.

In the following section, we will analyze in some detail four of the most useful patterns of essay organization: chronological order, logical division, cause and effect, and comparison and contrast.

Chronological Order

As you know, chronological order is order by time. It is used in almost all academic fields to describe historical events as well as to write biographies and autobiographies. In addition, chronological order has an important use in scientific and technical writing. It is used in these fields to explain physical, chemical, biological, and mechanical processes, such as how a machine works, how a chemical reaction takes place, how a certain biological process occurs, and so on. It is also used to give directions or instructions—how to perform a chemistry experiment, how to operate a piece of equipment, etc.

In a chronological process essay, the main steps in the process are the topics of the paragraphs.

In this section, you will practice using chronological order to explain the steps in a technical process. The following practice essay explains the process for treating sewage*. In the writing practice for this section, you will be asked to explain a similar process.

sewage: waste matter

If necessary, review the section on chronological order in paragraphs on page 39. Pay particular attention to the chronological order transition signals, such as:

First,   *The second step,*
Next,   *Before continuing,*
Finally,   *After that step has been accomplished,*

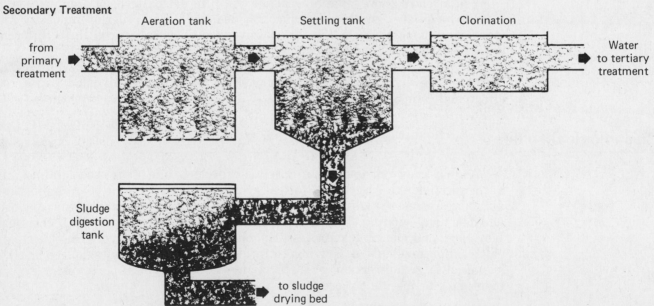

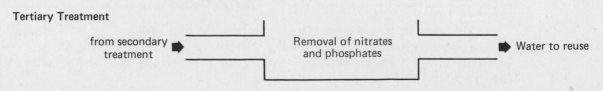

Three stages of sewage treatment.

Practice 6: A Chronological Process Essay

The following essay explains the process of treating sewage, to make impure water pure again. A flow chart on the facing page demonstrates the process; the essay explains it.

STEP 1 Underline the thesis statement twice.
STEP 2 Underline the topic sentences of those paragraphs that explain a major step in the process (as mentioned in the thesis statement).
STEP 3 Draw a circle around the between-paragraph transition signals.

A Sewage Treatment Process

1   Sewage treatment requires the removal of major contaminants* from waste water in order to purify it for reuse. This process takes place in sewage treatment plants and requires the use of special equipment and chemicals. The sewage treatment process is divided into three stages: primary treatment, secondary treatment and tertiary* treat-
5   ment.
    During the primary stage of treatment, large, heavy, suspended solids are removed from the sewage inflow. The polluted water passes through a screen into a grit chamber. Large organic solids drop to the bottom of the grit chamber. Then the polluted water continues to flow into a settling tank, where sludge* from the water drops into the
10   sludge digestion tank. From there, it flows out to a drying bed. The water continues to flow through the system, to begin the next phase of the treatment process.
    In the secondary stage, organic matter is further broken up and removed. As the water flows from the settling tank into the aeration tank, it combines with air. This process increases the oxygen content of the water and also increases the number of
15   microorganisms that feed on dissolved wastes. Then the water flows into a second settling tank, where more sludge drops out. From there, the water flows into a chlorination chamber. In this phase of the process, chlorine kills most of the harmful bacteria*.
    After leaving the chlorination chamber, the water begins the tertiary or final stage of treatment. In this stage, remaining chemical impurities, mainly phosphates and
20   nitrates, are removed by chemical and physical means. Now the water is ready for reuse.
    To summarize, waste water can be made reusable in sewage treatment facilities by undergoing a three-stage treatment process. These stages include primary treatment, which removes about 35 percent of the organic pollutants; secondary treatment, which
25   removes up to 90 percent of the remaining organic pollutants by chlorination; and finally, the tertiary treatment, in which the last impurities—nitrates and phosphates—are dissolved.

Writing Technique Questions

1. Remembering that the previous essay is an example of technical writing, explain the structure of the introductory paragraph. Does it give general, introductory information about the topic, or does it give a rather specific definition of the topic?

2. How many *main* steps are named in the thesis statement? How many paragraphs does the body of the essay have?

3. What is the structure of the concluding paragraph? Is this the same as or different from the kind of conclusion you have learned to write?

---

contaminants: impure elements
tertiary: third
sludge: oily mud
bacteria: germs

Practice 7: Outlining Essays

Make an outline of the previous essay. Make your outline as detailed as possible, listing all the steps in the process. Include the thesis statement and concluding sentence in your outline.

Practice 8: Transition Signals Between Paragraphs

In the spaces below, write out the transition signals that connect the paragraphs of the essay. Identify the grammatical form of each: word, phrase, or clause.

Between paragraphs I and II: _____

Between paragraphs II and III: _____

Between paragraphs III and IV: _____

Between paragraphs IV and V: _____

WRITING PRACTICE

Choose one of the topics from the list of suggestions below and write a chronological process essay similar to the model.

STEP 1 Make an outline before you begin.
STEP 2 Write an introduction in which you name the process and list the main steps.
STEP 3 Complete the body of the outline.
STEP 4 Write a conclusion summarizing the main steps.
STEP 5 Write the body of the essay, using appropriate transition expressions between paragraphs.

Check your essay against the Essay Checklist on page 117 before you hand it in.

Topic Suggestions

How solar collectors use the sun's energy to heat water.
(Use the flow chart on page 95.)

How to find and check out a book from your college library.

How to register for classes at your college or university.

Explain a technical or scientific process which you are familiar with.

Note: If you choose one of the last three topics, you should prepare a flow chart and attach it to your finished essay.

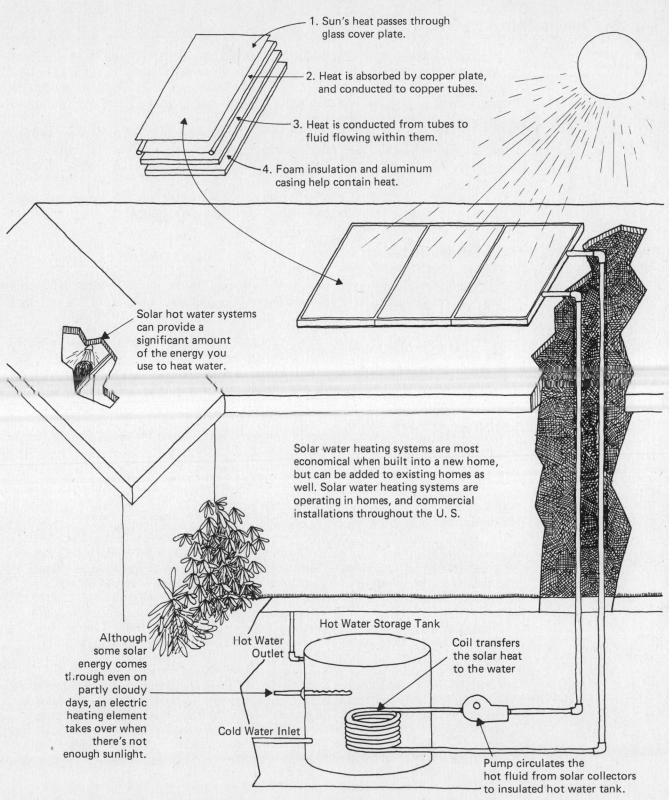

1. Sun's heat passes through glass cover plate.

2. Heat is absorbed by copper plate, and conducted to copper tubes.

3. Heat is conducted from tubes to fluid flowing within them.

4. Foam insulation and aluminum casing help contain heat.

Solar hot water systems can provide a significant amount of the energy you use to heat water.

Solar water heating systems are most economical when built into a new home, but can be added to existing homes as well. Solar water heating systems are operating in homes, and commercial installations throughout the U. S.

Although some solar energy comes through even on partly cloudy days, an electric heating element takes over when there's not enough sunlight.

Hot Water Storage Tank

Hot Water Outlet

Coil transfers the solar heat to the water

Cold Water Inlet

Pump circulates the hot fluid from solar collectors to insulated hot water tank.

How solar collectors use the sun's energy to heat water. Construction of a solar heat collector.

Logical Division

Logical division is a form of essay organization that is used to group related items according to some quality they have in common. Logical division can be useful in planning a paper because a broad subject can be subdivided into several categories or groups that will narrow the topics for discussion. Then, each subdivided topic can be discussed in order.

For instance, as an engineer, you might write a paper in which you classify the various options available to students in the field of engineering. You might divide engineering, the main class, into the following subclasses: civil engineering, electrical engineering, mechanical engineering, chemical engineering, and electronic engineering. By dividing the field into subclasses, you can discuss each one separately, which simplifies the task of explaining a broad subject.

Practice 9: A Logical Division Essay

The following essay discusses some of the influences of the American Indians on modern American culture. It uses logical division as a method of organizing the information.

STEP 1 Locate and underline the thesis statement twice. How many subtopics does it list?

STEP 2 Locate the main sentence in the concluding paragraph and underline it twice. Is it a paraphrase of the thesis statement or a summary of the main points?

STEP 3 Underline the topic sentence in each paragraph once, and circle all of the transition signals. (*Note:* The topic sentence is not necessarily the first sentence in every paragraph.)

STEP 4 Notice especially the transition expressions between paragraphs. Do all of the paragraphs contain one?

Native American Influences on Modern American Culture

1   When the first Europeans began to settle the North American continent, they encountered a completely new culture: the Indian tribes of North America. The Indians, who had a highly developed culture in many respects, must have been as curious about the strange European manners and customs as were the Europeans
5   about the Indians. As always happens when two cultures come into contact, there was a cultural exchange. The Indians adopted some of the Europeans' ways, and the Europeans adopted some of the Indians' ways. As a result, the Indians have made many valuable contributions to American culture, particularly in the areas of language, art, government, and cuisine.
10   First of all, the Indians left a permanent imprint on the English language. The early settlers borrowed words from several different Indian languages to name the new places and new objects that they had found in their new land. All across the country, one can find cities, towns, rivers, and states with Indian names. For example, the states of Delaware, Iowa, Illinois, and Alabama are named after Indian tribes, as are
15   Chicago, Miami, and Spokane. In addition to place names, English has adopted many everyday words from various Indian languages. The words *chipmunk, moose, raccoon, skunk, moccasin,* and *potato* are just a few examples.

Although the vocabulary of English is the area that shows the most native influence, it is not the only area of American culture that was changed by contact
20   with the Indians. Art is another area showing the mark of Indian contact. Wool rugs woven by women of the Navajo tribe in Arizona and New Mexico are highly valued works of art in the United States. Also, Indian jewelry made from silver and turquoise is very popular—and very expensive. Especially in the western and southwestern regions of the United States, Indian pottery, handcrafted leather

25 products, and beadwork can be found in many homes. Indeed, Indian art and handicrafts have become a treasured part of American culture.

In addition to language and art, it may surprise some people to learn that Americans are also indebted to one Indian tribe for our form of government. The Iroquois Indians, who were an extremely large tribe with many branches and sub-

30 branches (called "nations"), had developed a highly sophisticated system of government to keep the various branches of the tribe from fighting one another. Five of the nations had joined together in a confederation called "The League of the Iroquois." Under the League, each nation was autonomous in running its own internal affairs, but the nations acted as a unit when dealing with outsiders. The

35 League kept the Iroquois from fighting among themselves and was also valuable in diplomatic relations with other tribes. When the thirteen American colonies were considering what kind of government to establish after they won their independence from Britain, someone suggested that they use a system similar to the League of the Iroquois. Under this system, each colony or future state would be autonomous in

40 managing its own affairs but would join forces with the other states to deal with matters that concerned them all. This is exactly what happened. As a result, the present form of government of the United States can be traced directly back to an Indian model.

The final area in which Indian culture has affected American culture is agriculture.

45 Being skilled farmers, the Indians of North America taught the newcomers many things about farming techniques and crops. Every American schoolchild has heard the story of how the Indians taught the first settlers to place a dead fish in a planting hole to provide fertilizer for the growing plant. Furthermore, the Indians taught the settlers irrigation methods and crop rotation. In addition, many of the foods we eat today were introduced

50 to the Europeans by the Indians. For example, potatoes, corn, chocolate, and peanuts were unknown in Europe. Now they are staples in the American diet.

In conclusion, we can easily see from these few examples the extent of the Indian influence on our language, our art forms, our government, and our eating habits. Modern Americans are truly indebted to the North American Indians for their contribu-

55 tions to their culture. Hopefully, the cultural exchange will one day prove to be equally positive for them.[1]

Practice 10: Outlining

Make an outline of the previous essay. Make your outline as detailed as possible by dividing the topic into as many subtopics as possible. Include the thesis statement and concluding sentence in your outline.

Practice 11: Transitions Between Paragraphs II

Copy the words, phrases or clauses that serve as links between the six paragraphs of the model essay.

Between I and II: _____

Between II and III: _____

Between III and IV: _____

Between IV and V: _____

Between V and VI: _____

[1]Some of the material in this essay is based on "The Influence of the American Indian on American Culture," in *Writing English: A Composition Text in English as a Foreign Language* by Janet Ross and Gladys Doty (New York: Harper & Row, 1975). Adapted with permission of the publishers.

ORGANIZING BY LOGICAL DIVISION

Usually there is more than one way to organize information by logical division. The only rule is that your system of dividing and subdividing must be consistent.

When you organize information by logical division:

1. Establish a single principle of division:

   The main classes of division for the newspaper are News, Sports, Entertainment, Business, and Classified Ads.

2. Divide each main class into subclasses, which are determined by the general subject. Include all of the subclasses relevant to the discussion of your essay:

   The News Section is subdivided into three sections: International News, National News, and Local News.

   The Classified Section is divided into two main subdivisions, Want Ads and Real Estate. Each of these is further subdivided.

The technique of logical division is illustrated in the following diagram, in which the Sunday edition of a big city newspaper is the subject of an essay.

The Big City Newspaper

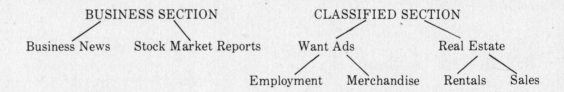

In outline form, the information about the newspaper might look like this:

I. News Section
   A. International
   B. National
   C. Local

II. Sports Section
   A. Professional
   B. Amateur

III. Entertainment Section
   A. Films
   B. Radio
   C. TV

IV. Business Section
   A. Business News
   B. Stock Market Reports

V. Classified Section
   A. Want Ads
      1. Employment
      2. Merchandise
   B. Real Estate
      1. Rentals
      2. Sales

Practice 12: Organizing by Logical Division

Select one of the topics suggested below and list as many items as you can think of. Then divide your list into as many classes and subclasses as you can, using at least two different systems of dividing. Finally, arrange all of the information into outlines as on the preceding pages.

For example, if you choose the first topic, cars, you might list as many different car models as you can think of: Volkswagen Rabbit, Mercedes 450SL, Ford Fiesta, Cadillac Seville, etc. Then establish your bases for subdividing the list. You might choose two or more of these: import/nonimport, size, cost, fuel economy, speed. Finally, put the information into outline form.

Topic Suggestions

Car models.
Types of transportation.
Types of communication.
Kinds of entertainment.
Kinds of teachers.
Kinds of students.
Fields within your major field.
Kinds of animals.

Sources of energy.
Food.
The students in your school.
The students in your class.
Objects in a desk drawer.
Objects in a kitchen drawer.
Kinds of books.

WRITING PRACTICE

Write an essay in which you explain the influence of one culture on another. You should write about two cultures with which you are familiar. For example, a student from Japan might choose to write about the influences of Japanese culture on the United States or the influences of U.S. culture on Japan. (Remember: Cultural exchanges work in both directions.)

Select three or four areas in which one culture has influenced the other, and use specific examples to support your topic sentences. Some areas of possible influence are language, food, clothing, home furnishings, music, family customs, religion, government, education, political organization, business methods, and art.

Prepare an outline before you write your essay. Hand in both the outline and the essay.

Be sure to use transition signals both *within* and *between* paragraphs.

Check your essay against the Essay Checklist on page 117 before you hand it in.

Cause and Effect

Another common method of organizing an essay is by cause and effect. In a cause and effect essay, you discuss the reasons for something, and then you discuss the results of it.

The following are examples of typical cause and effect essay examination questions. Each is followed by a logical sequence outline that might be used to answer the questions. Notice how an outline will help you to keep your answer in the correct order.

Sociology   I. Discuss alienation* in American society.

    A. Define "alienation."

    B. List its causes and explain each in detail.

        1. American mobility*

        2. Decline of the nuclear family system

alienation: feeling of separation from society
mobility: frequent moves from one area to another

         C. List its effects and explain each in detail.
           1. Effects on the individual
            a. Loneliness
            b. Mental illness
             (1) Depression
             (2) Suicide
           2. Effects on society as a whole
            a. Political apathy
            b. Club-joining phenomenon

Science   I. Discuss the relationship between temperature inversion*
       and the formation of smog.

       A. Define "temperature inversion."
       B. Explain its causes.
       C. Explain its effect. (It produces smog.)

Business   I. Discuss the reasons behind the passage of the Sherman
       Antitrust Act of 1890 and the Clayton Act of 1914.

       A. Explain the provisions of each law.
       B. State the reasons the two laws were passed.
       C. Explain the effects of the two laws on business prac-
       tice.

Practice 13: A Cause and Effect Essay

STEP 1 Read the following essay on women's liberation in the United States.
STEP 2 Underline the thesis sentence twice.
STEP 3 Underline the topic sentences once.
STEP 4 Which paragraph is the transition paragraph? Which part of this para-
     graph concludes the discussion of the causes? Which part of this paragraph
     introduces the discussion of the effects? (See page 103 for discussion of
     transition paragraphs.)
STEP 5 Circle all of the cause and effect structure words in the essay. (See page 102
     for a list of cause and effect structure words.)

Women's Liberation

1   Since the middle of this century, women around the world have been seeking
greater independence and recognition. No longer content with their traditional roles as
housewives and mothers, women have joined together to create the so-called "women's
liberation movement." While the forces behind this international movement vary from
5 culture to culture and from individual to individual, the basic causes in the United
States can be traced to three events: the development of effective birth-control
methods, the invention of labor-saving devices for the home, and the advent* of World
War II.
   The first cause of the liberation of women was the development of effective birth-
10 control methods, freeing women from the endless cycle of childbearing and rearing.
As a result of having a choice as to *when* and *if* to bear children, women acquired
the freedom and the time to pursue interests outside of the home. Because of the
development of birth control, women could delay having children or avoid having
them altogether; consequently, women had the opportunity to acquire an education
15 and/or pursue a career.

---

  temperature inversion: a layer of warm air trapped
       below a layer of cool air

  advent: beginning

The second event was the development of mechanized labor-saving devices for the home, resulting in more leisure time and freedom for women. For example, fifty years ago, a housewife spent an average of twelve to fourteen hours per day doing housework. Due to the invention of machines such as vacuum cleaners, washing

20 machines and dishwashers, a housewife can now take care of her daily housework in about five hours.

The third event that, at least in the United States, gave impetus* to the liberation of women was World War II. During the war, most men were serving in the military. Consequently, women had to fill the vacancies in the labor force. Women

25 by the thousands went to work in factories and even took over businesses for their absent husbands. This was a great change for the majority of American women, for they discovered that they could weld* airplanes and manage a business as well as change diapers and bake cookies.

These three events planted the seeds of a great change in society, and the effects

30 of this change are being felt at all levels: in the family, in business, and in government.

One of the biggest effects of the greater independence of women is being felt in the home. The traditional husband-wife relationship is undergoing a radical transformation*. Because so many women are working, men are learning to share the

35 household tasks of cooking, cleaning, and even caring for children. In some families, there has been a complete reversal of the traditional roles: the husband stays home while the wife earns the family's income. It should be pointed out, however, that this is the exception, not the rule. In most families in the United States, the husband still earns most of the money, and the wife still does most of the housework.

40 The effects of women's liberation are being felt not only in the home, but also on the job. More and more women are working, and they are demanding equal salaries and equally responsible positions. It is not uncommon for a woman to be the president of a corporation these days. Many businesses encourage women to advance to high management positions, and every year, the nation's schools produce more

45 women doctors, lawyers, and accountants.

Politics and government are still other areas that are feeling the effects of the women's movement. Although the United States doesn't appear ready to accept a woman president, as some countries of the world have, women are being elected to public office in increasing numbers. The United States currently has three women

50 governors, which is the highest office in a state. A few years ago, this would have been unthinkable. Furthermore, the increasing political power of women has resulted in the proposal of an amendment* to the U.S. Constitution, called the Equal Rights Amendment, which will give women complete equality with men by law if passed.

In conclusion, women in the United States are acquiring greater independence,

55 which is causing sweeping changes in society—at home, at work, and in politics. While men may not be happy with these changes, they should always remember that it was they, the men, who created the conditions leading to the liberation of women: men made war, male scientists developed birth control, and businessmen earned a lot of money selling vacuum cleaners and dishwashers.

Writing Technique Questions

1. Which paragraphs discuss the causes of the liberation of women in the United States? Which paragraphs discuss the effects?

2. What is the function of the paragraph that begins on line 29?

3. Does the thesis statement list both causes and effects, or just causes?

4. Does the conclusion review both causes and effects, or just effects?

---

impetus: stimulation   radical transformation: extreme change
weld: to join metal parts using heat   amendment: addition

There are two keys to writing good cause and effect essays:

1. Use an appropriate method of organization.
2. Use cause and effect structure words accurately.

CAUSE AND EFFECT ORGANIZATION

There are basically two main ways to organize a cause and effect essay: "block" organization and "chain" organization. In *block organization*, you first discuss all of the causes as a block (in one, two, three, or more paragraphs, depending on the number of causes). Then you discuss all of the effects together as a block. In *chain organization*, you discuss a first cause and its effect, a second cause and its effect, and a third cause and its effect, in a "chain."

BLOCK	CHAIN
Causes	Cause / Effect
	Cause / Effect
Effects	Cause / Effect

The type of cause and effect organization you choose will depend on your topic. Some topics are more easily organized one way, and some the other way. A chain pattern is usually easier if the causes and effects are very closely interrelated. If there is no *direct* cause and effect relationship, the block style may be easier. Some topics may require a combination of block and chain organization as in the model essay on the preceding page.

TRANSITION PARAGRAPHS

In the middle of the preceding essay there is a short paragraph that separates the "causes" part from the "effects" part. This is called a transition paragraph, which is sometimes useful in long block organization essays.

The function of transition paragraphs is to conclude the first part of the essay and introduce the second part. It is not always necessary to write a transition paragraph, but it is helpful when your topic is long and complex.

Note: Since this paragraph is only one sentence, it could also be placed at the beginning of the next paragraph or at the end of the previous one.

CAUSE AND EFFECT STRUCTURE WORDS

Just as there are transition signals that show time and order of importance relationships, there are words and phrases that show cause and effect relationships. They are called cause and effect structure words.

In writing a cause and effect essay, there are many possible structure words you can use. These words show whether you are discussing a reason or result.

You are probably already familiar with many.

Cause structure words
    Examples:

Effect structure words
    Examples:

The first cause _____	*The first effect* _____
The next reason _____	*As a result* _____
Because of _____	*Therefore* _____

To keep clear the difference between these two different groups of signals, remember that cause structure words signal a reason for something:

In 1975, the speed limit in the U.S. was lowered from 70 to 55 miles per hour.

Conversely, effect structure words signal the result of some action:

The number of traffic deaths in the U.S. decreased sharply in 1975.

The first sentence is the *reason* for the decrease in the number of traffic deaths. The second sentence is the *result* of the lowering of the speed limit.

Many of the most common cause and effect structure words are listed in the chart below. Learn to use several different ones so that you don't always use *because* or *as a result* in your sentences.

CAUSE AND EFFECT STRUCTURE WORDS

	Sentence Connectors	Coordinators	Subordinators	Others
To introduce a cause or reason		for	because since as	because of due to to result from the result of the effect of X on Y the consequence of
To introduce an effect or result	as a result as a consequence therefore thus consequently hence	so		the cause of the reason for to result in to cause to have an effect on to affect

Practice 14: Recognizing Cause Structure Words

STEP 1 Underline the part of the sentence that states a cause.
STEP 2 Circle the word or words that introduce the cause.
STEP 3 Be able to discuss the use of each structure word or phrase that you have circled. What kind of grammatical structure follows each one? Notice especially the difference between the use of *because* and *because of*.

1. The computer is a learning tool since it helps children to master math and language skills.
2. Due to the ability of computers to keep records of sales and inventory, many big department stores rely on them.

3. A medical computer system is an aid to physicians because of its ability to interpret data from a patient's history and provide a diagnosis*.

(How would you rewrite this sentence using *because* instead of *because of*?)

4. Lowering the speed limit to 55 MPH has caused a sharp decrease in the number of traffic deaths.

5. Public transportation is becoming popular because the cost of gasoline has been rising.

(How would you rewrite this sentence using *because of* instead of *because*?)

6. Since carpools cut expenses, many commuters are joining them.

7. Smog results from chemical air pollutants being trapped under a layer of warm air.

8. The patient's death was the result of the doctor's negligence.

9. Little is known about life on the ocean floor, for scientists have only recently developed the technology to explore it.

10. The effect of prolonged weightlessness is the loss of muscle tone*, which can be a problem for astronauts who spend long periods of time in space.

Practice 15: Recognizing Effect Structure Words

STEP 1 Underline the part of the sentence that states an effect.
STEP 2 Circle the word or words that introduce the effect.
STEP 3 Be able to discuss the use of each structure word or phrase. What kind of grammar follows each one? How have you punctuated the sentence?

1. The performance of electric cars is inferior to the performance of cars with conventional internal combustion engines; consequently, some improvements must be made in them if they are to become popular.

2. However, electric cars are reliable, economical and nonpolluting; therefore, the government is spending millions of dollars to improve their technology.

3. Electric cars use relatively inexpensive electricity for power; thus, they cost less to operate than cars that use gasoline.

4. His refusal to attend classes resulted in his dismissal from the school.

5. The cost of gasoline is rising; as a result, many people are using their cars less often.

6. The cause of the patient's death was the doctor's negligence.

7. When he finally arrived, he gave no reason for his tardiness*.

8. It has been documented that heavy cigarette smoking affects the heart as well as the lungs.

9. Cold water is denser than warm water and will therefore sink.

10. Fresh water is less dense than salt water, so it tends to float on the surface of a body of salt water.

Practice 16: Using Cause and Effect Structure Words

STEP 1 Using various cause and effect structure words from the chart, combine these sentences to emphasize a cause or an effect relationship as indicated.
STEP 2 Use different structure words in each sentence. Circle the words you use.

---

diagnosis: identification of a disease   **tardiness:** being late
muscle tone: healthy elastic quality

Example   The death rate among women from lung cancer is increasing. Women are smoking more.

Emphasize the cause: (Because) women are smoking more, the death rate of women from lung cancer is increasing.

Emphasize the effect: The increase in the death rate of women from lung cancer is the (result of) their smoking more.

1. Cancer is increasing in industrialized nations. Air pollution and the use of chemicals in food are increasing in these countries.

   Emphasize the cause: _____
   _____
   _____

   Emphasize the effect: _____
   _____
   _____

2. Mr. Williams received a promotion last week. Mr. Williams is a clever administrator, a capable personnel manager and a financial wizard.

   Emphasize the cause: _____
   _____
   _____

   Emphasize the effect: _____
   _____
   _____

3. The saltiest water is found at the bottom of the ocean. Salt water, being denser than fresh water, sinks.

   Emphasize the cause: _____
   _____
   _____

   Emphasize the effect: _____
   _____
   _____

4. Heat energy is carried by electrons. Metals have many free-moving electrons. Metals are good conductors of heat.

   Emphasize the cause: _____
   _____
   _____

Emphasize the effect: _____

_____

_____

5. Some businesses now have flexible working hours. Productivity has increased. Absenteeism has decreased.

Emphasize the cause: _____

_____

_____

Emphasize the effect: _____

_____

_____

WRITING PRACTICE

Choose one of the suggested topics from below and write an essay that discusses it in terms of cause and effect. Be sure to use a variety of cause and effect structure words, and begin each paragraph with a transition expression.

Use either block or chain organization. If you use block organization, be sure to insert a transition paragraph between the two parts of the body.

Before you write your essay, prepare an outline. Hand in both your outline and your essay. Check your essay against the Essay Checklist on page 117 before you hand it in.

Topic Suggestions

Culture shock.

Pollution.

Inflation.

Discrimination by age, sex, race, religion, etc.

The increase (or decrease) in the birth rate in a country.

The increase (or decrease) in life expectancy in a country.

The refugee problem.

Any social, economic or political problem in your country or in the United States that interests you.

Comparison and Contrast

A very common and useful method of essay organization is comparison and contrast. It is a form of writing that is used frequently in college work, and in business and the professions as well. Anything can be compared or contrasted such as periods in history, characters in stories, kinds of equipment, or the qualifications of two job applicants. The only important rule to observe is to compare or contrast things of like nature, or else the comparison or contrast will not be valid. In other words, you can compare and contrast apples and bananas, but you can't compare apples and typewriters.

When you make a comparison, you show how certain aspects of one item are similar to the same aspects of another item in the same general class. A comparison answers the question, "What features do X and Y have in common?" or "How are X and Y similar?"

When you contrast two things, you point out the differences between them, i.e. you point out how they are *not* alike. A contrast answers the question, "What are the differences between X and Y?" or "How are X and Y different?"

As with every other kind of writing, there are specific techniques you need to learn in order to write good comparison and contrast essays. The two major techniques are:

1. Appropriate use of comparison and contrast structure words.
2. Logical organization of the points of comparison and contrast.

Practice 17: A Comparison and Contrast Essay

STEP 1 Read the following model essay which analyzes two models of cars by the comparison/contrast method.

STEP 2 Locate and underline the thesis sentence twice and the topic sentences once. Does the thesis statement indicate comparison/contrast?

STEP 3 Circle all of the structure words for comparison/contrast. (Refer to the charts on pages 108 and 111.)

STEP 4 Analyze the organization: Which paragraph discusses similarities? Which paragraphs discuss the differences? Is there a transition between the two parts? What is the purpose of the conclusion? Does it make a judgement about the two cars?

The T-Bird versus the Rabbit

1   Buying a new car can be fun, but since there are so many fine models on the market to choose from, the final decision can be a very difficult one to make. After narrowing the choices down to two cars, a person can make a comparison and contrast analysis by noting first the similarities and then the differences between, for example, the
5   Ford Thunderbird (popularly termed the T-Bird) and the Volkswagen Rabbit.

The T-Bird and the Rabbit have several similarities. The T-Bird is an attractive car; the Rabbit is too. The T-Bird will seat five people comfortably, as can the Rabbit. In addition, the seats in the T-Bird as well as in the Rabbit are upholstered in tough vinyl. Furthermore, both the Rabbit and the T-Bird have a 12,000-mile
10   warranty.

Despite these similarities, the T-Bird and the Rabbit have some very important differences in the following areas: physical dimensions, equipment, and fuel consumption and economy.

The first major difference between the T-Bird and the Rabbit is in their physical
15   dimensions. The T-Bird measures 199 inches in length, whereas the Rabbit measures only 156 inches. The difference in size between the two cars is more than three feet. This means that the longer T-Bird has more leg room than the Rabbit. On the other hand, the T-Bird requires a larger parking space, while the smaller Rabbit is easier to maneuver in crowded city streets. However, just as the T-Bird is longer, it is also
20   much heavier; therefore, the T-Bird will give you a much smoother and quieter ride than the compact Rabbit.

Another obvious difference between the two cars lies in their equipment. The T-Bird has more luxury features than the Rabbit. For example, the T-Bird has power windows, power steering, power front disc brakes, and reclining bucket seats. Although the
25   Rabbit has none of these extra features, it has a sunroof; the T-Bird merely has a vinyl

roof. Thus, while the driver of the T-Bird can enjoy the power of a big car, the driver of the Rabbit can enjoy sunshine and fresh air through the sunroof.

The final difference between these two cars is in fuel consumption and economy. The Rabbit can be filled up with $10.00 worth of gas, but it will cost twice that amount to
30   fill up the T-Bird. The Rabbit also has a fuel injection system, which helps to give the car easier starts; it also uses the most economical grade of gas. In contrast, the T-Bird requires the most expensive gas. The most important feature, however, is that the Rabbit gets 38 miles per gallon on the highway and 24 miles in the city, whereas the T-Bird averages only 14 miles per gallon.

35   In conclusion, then, although there are some superficial similarities between the two cars, there are quite a number of important differences. The T-Bird is much larger and more luxurious, but the Rabbit is compact and easier to maneuver. Furthermore, even though both cars have unique features, the Rabbit uses fuel much more economically. Therefore, considering the high cost of gas these days, the Volkswagen Rabbit is
40   definitely the car to own.

Writing Technique Questions

1. On how many points are the two cars compared and contrasted? What are they? Where are they named?

2. In which paragraph(s) are the similarities discussed? In which paragraph(s) are the differences discussed?

3. What is the function of the third paragraph?

4. Is this similar to block style organization, which was discussed in the last section?

COMPARISON AND CONTRAST STRUCTURE WORDS

The first key to writing successful comparison and contrast essays is the appropriate use of comparison and contrast structure words. These are words that introduce points of comparison and points of contrast.

Comparison Structure Words   The following table lists some of the words and phrases used to write about similarities.

COMPARISON STRUCTURE WORDS

Sentence Connectors	Subordinators	Coordinators	Others
similarly likewise also too†	as just as	and	like just like alike similar (to) the same as both . . . and†† not only . . . but also†† compare to‡

†Unlike most sentence connectors, *too* cannot come at the beginning of a sentence.
††These are correlative conjunctions, a special group of conjunctions. See the section on Parallelism, page 135.
‡See the note on page 111 on the use of *compare to* and *compare with*.

Practice 18: Recognizing Comparison Structure Words

The following sentences discuss the similarities between the British and the American systems of government.

STEP 1 Underline the items being compared in each sentence.
STEP 2 Circle the comparison signal.
STEP 3 Identify the kind of grammatical structure that follows the comparison signal: Noun Phrase, Clause, etc.

Example   The United States has a democratic <u>form of government</u>, (just as) Great Britain does. *(clause)*

1. The United States operates under a two-party system; Great Britain does also.
2. Similar to the British Parliament, the United States Congress has two separate houses, the Senate and the House of Representatives.
3. The U.S. House of Representatives is like the British House of Commons, and the U.S. Senate is similar to the British House of Lords.
4. The members of the U.S. House of Representatives are elected by district, just as the members of the British House of Commons are.
5. The method of selecting cabinet members is the same in both countries.
6. In Great Britain, there is a cabinet appointed by the prime minister; similarly, the U.S. president also appoints a cabinet.
7. Both the British monarch and the U.S. president have the right to veto* any law.
8. The U.S. Congress can override* a veto by the president. In theory, the British Parliament could also override a veto by the monarch, but this has never happened because the British monarch has never vetoed a law.
9. The method of getting a law passed in Great Britain is almost the same as the method of getting a law passed in the United States.

Practice 19: Using Comparison Structure Words

STEP 1 Add comparison structure words to the following sentences and connect them. Rewrite each sentence, and use a variety of comparison words.
STEP 2 Double check your sentences for correct punctuation. (Refer to the section on Punctuation, page 229, for more information.)

1. A bicycle is an excellent form of transportation. A moped* is an excellent form of transportation.

   _____

   _____

2. A bicycle is constructed of a metal frame with two wheels, a handlebar for steering, a saddle seat, and two pedals. A moped has the same basic construction.

   _____

   _____

---

veto: not approve   **moped:** motorized bicycle
override: overrule

3. A bicycle is propelled by pedalling. A moped can be pedalled.

_____

_____

4. A bicycle requires almost no maintenance. A moped needs little upkeep.

_____

_____

5. New York City has a nickname; it is called "The Big Apple." San Francisco is called "The City by the Golden Gate."

_____

_____

6. New York has several famous bridges which connect Manhattan to the other boroughs*. San Francisco has two bridges that connect it to neighboring counties*.

_____

_____

_____

7. New York is well known for its Chinatown, Harlem, and Little Italy. San Francisco has many ethnic districts, such as North Beach (Italian), Chinatown, Japantown, and the Mission District (Spanish-speaking).

_____

_____

_____

_____

8. New York has a financial district called Wall Street. San Francisco's financial district is called Montgomery Street.

_____

_____

_____

boroughs: civic divisions of New York City
counties: civic divisions of a state

Now learn to use the words and phrases needed to write about differences.

Contrast Structure Words

CONTRAST STRUCTURE WORDS

Sentence Connectors	Subordinators	Coordinators	Others
on the other hand in contrast however by (in) comparison††	although though even though whereas while	but yet	different (from) dissimilar unlike to differ (from)
			to compare to† to compare with

†In strict usage, there is a difference between compare to and compare with. Compare to is used to express similarities only:

In this poem, the poet compares love to a rose.

Compare with is used to express both similarities and differences:

Compared with some languages, English has a simple grammar.

††*By (in) comparison* is listed here as a contrast signal because it introduces differences, not similarities:

A Volkswagen Rabbit gets 38 miles per gallon; by (in) comparison, a Datsun gets only 33.

Practice 20: Recognizing Contrast Structure Words

STEP 1 Underline the items being contrasted in each sentence.
STEP 2 Circle the contrast structure words.
STEP 3 Identify the kind of grammatical structure that follows each signal: Noun Phrase, Clause, etc.

Example The governments of Great Britain and the United States are quite dissimilar in several aspects. (Prepositional phrase)

1. Whereas the chief executive in Great Britain is called the prime minister, the chief executive in the United States is called the president.

2. In the United States, the president fulfills the functions of both political leader and head of state while these two functions are separate in Great Britain.

3. In other words, Great Britain has both a monarch and a prime minister, but the United States has only a president.

4. The president of the United States may be of a different political party than the majority of Congress; in contrast, the British prime minister is the head of the political party that has the most seats in Parliament.

5. Unlike the United States, which has a written constitution, Great Britain has no written constitution.

6. The scheduling of elections in the two countries is quite different.

7. In the United States, elections are held on a regular schedule, no matter how popular or unpopular the government is. In Great Britain, on the other hand, elections are held whenever the prime minister loses a vote of confidence*.

8. The members of the U.S. Senate are elected; however, the members of the British House of Lords are appointed or inherit their positions.

9. As you can see, the two systems of government, although they are both democracies, differ in several major aspects.

vote of confidence: vote indicating approval or disapproval

Practice 21: Using Contrast Structure Words

Add contrast structure words to each of the following pairs of sentences.

STEP 1 Choose a signal of the type suggested for each group.

STEP 2 Write it in the blank space and add any necessary punctuation marks. Also change the capitalization, if necessary.

A. Use a sentence connector

1. Junior colleges offer programs that can be completed in two years _____ _____ colleges and universities offer programs that take four years to complete.

2. Junior colleges award associate of arts degrees to their graduates _____ _____ colleges and universities award baccalaureate degrees, master's degrees, and Ph.D.'s.

3. Many junior colleges are free _____ almost all colleges and universities charge tuition.

B. Use a subordinator

4. Active solar heating systems require mechanical means to harness* the sun's energy _____ passive systems rely on natural forces to collect solar radiation.

5. Passive systems work well only in hot, dry climates _____ active systems can work efficiently in any area.

6. _____ passive systems are limited by seasonal conditions, active systems work throughout the year.

C. Use a coordinator

7. An electric car is designed to carry a maximum of four people _____ _____ a medium-sized gasoline-powered car can carry up to six passengers comfortably.

8. It takes six hours to recharge the batteries of an electric car _____ _____ it takes less than five minutes to fill up the gas tank of a conventional car.

D. Use any type of contrast signal, and rewrite the sentences.

9. The analog computer is used mainly for scientific work. The digital computer is useful in business.

_____

_____

_____

10. The analog computer is used to measure temperatures, flows and voltages. The digital computer can count, print, reproduce facts, sort data into numerical order, and so on.

_____

_____

_____

_____

harness: control

11. The output from the analog computer is represented as a continuous, unbroken flow. The output from the digital computer is in the form of discrete* letters and numbers.

_____

_____

_____

_____

E. Write four sentences of your own, using contrast structure words from the OTHERS group in the table. Write sentences contrasting the subjects given.

12. Lemons/limes

_____

_____

13. Communism/capitalism

_____

_____

_____

14. American food/another country's food

_____

_____

_____

15. City life/suburban life

_____

_____

_____

COMPARISON AND CONTRAST ORGANIZATION

There are several ways to organize a comparison and contrast essay. However, in this section you will learn only two basic forms: point-by-point organization and block organization. Each type of organization is illustrated in the following models.

Study each model very carefully. Notice how the thesis statement tells the reader what type of organization will be used in the body of the essay. In addition, notice the different ways in which the outlines are written, depending upon the controlling idea(s) in the thesis statement.

Model 5: Point-by-point organization

In point-by-point comparison and contrast organization, you make a sentence-by-sentence comparison of two (or more) items or subjects. For example, if you were comparing two jobs, you might make an outline like the following:

Thesis   One way to decide between two job offers is to make a point-by-point
Statement   comparison of their features.

---

discrete: individual

I. *The salaries of Job X and Job Y are approximately equal.*
   A. Job X's salary
   B. Job Y's salary

II. *Job X offers the same fringe benefits* as Job Y.*
   A. Job X's fringe benefits
   B. Job Y's fringe benefits

III. *In contrast to Job Y, Job X offers good opportunities for advancement.*
   A. Job X's opportunities for advancement
   B. Job Y's opportunities for advancement

IV. *Unlike the high-pressure and competitive atmosphere at Company X, the atmosphere at Company Y seems congenial and supportive.*
   A. Atmosphere at Company X
   B. Atmosphere at Company Y

Model 6: Block Organization—Type 1

In Type 1 block organization, you discuss the features of your items or subjects in blocks. That is, in the first paragraph you discuss all of the features of the first item. Then in the second paragraph, you explain all of the same features of the second item in the same order that they were discussed in the first paragraph.

Thesis Statement   One way to decide between two job offers is to consider the advantages of Job X and Job Y.

I. *Job X offers several advantages.*
   A. Salary
   B. Fringe benefits
   C. Opportunity for advancement
   D. Workplace atmosphere

II. *Job Y also offers some advantages.*
   A. Salary
   B. Fringe benefits
   C. Opportunity for advancement
   D. Workplace atmosphere

Model 7: Block organization—Type 2

In Type 2 block organization, you discuss all of the similarities of the items in one paragraph and all of their differences in a separate paragraph(s) or vice-versa. (See the essay "The T-Bird Versus the Rabbit" on page 107.)

Thesis Statement   One way to decide between two job offers is to evaluate what the similarities and differences are before making your final decision.

I. *The salary and fringe benefits of Job X and Job Y are almost the same.*
   A. Salary (Job X and Job Y).
   B. Fringe benefits (Job X and Job Y).

---

fringe benefits: employment benefits other than salary
(vacation time, health insurance, etc.)

II. *Although the salary and fringe benefits are equal, there are big differences in the areas of workplace atmosphere and opportunity for advancement.*
   A. Workplace atmosphere.
      1. Job X.
      2. Job Y.
   B. Opportunity for advancement.
      1. Job X.
      2. Job Y.

Note: When you have completed your discussion of the features of the first item or subject, use a comparison and contrast structure word, phrase or clause to refer to it and to introduce the second item or subject. Check the tables on pages 108 and 111 for more structure words.

Examples: *Like Job X, Job Y . . . .*
In contrast to Job X, Job Y . . . .
In spite of their similarities/differences . . . .

When you write about similarities and differences:

1. **Arrange your points of comparison and contrast in logical order. Use either point-by-point or block organization.**
2. **Use enough comparison and contrast structure vocabulary to make the points of comparison and contrast very clear.**

WRITING PRACTICE A

Pretend that you are the office manager of a small import-export company that needs to rent a duplicating machine. You have gathered information on two machines, the Quicko 33 and the Speedo 88. The information is given on the chart below.

Write a report to your boss in which you compare and contrast the two machines. Use whichever type of organization you think will work best.

Your conclusion should be a recommendation to your boss (who will make the final decision) as to which machine your company should rent. Consider the specific needs of your company: Does it need speed or flexibility? What are the advantages and disadvantages of free maintenance? How important is cost to your company?

Use an adequate number of transition signals and comparison and contrast structure words. If you write more than one paragraph, be sure to include between-paragraph linking expressions.

Check your report against the Essay Checklist on page 117 before you hand it in.

COMPARING TWO COPIERS

	QUICKO 33	SPEEDO 88
Size	Desk-top size	Desk-top size
Weight	155 pounds	160 pounds
Power requirements	Standard power plug	Standard power plug
Rental cost	$265 per month for 10,000 copies	$325 per month for 10,000 copies
Speed	First copy in four minutes; 30 copies per minute	First copy in three minutes; 50 copies per minute
Cost of supplies	Paper: $60 per month Chemicals: $10 per month (based on 10,000 copies/mo.)	Paper: $60 per month Chemicals: $10 per month (based on 10,000 copies/mo.)
Maintenance service	Immediate service; service contract at a cost of $30 per month	Service within 24 hours; free service
Flexibility	Copies flat documents only	Copies flat documents, books, and photographs

WRITING PRACTICE B

In this practice you will write comparison and contrast essays using point-by-point organization and block organization.

Choose your topics from the list below and think of three to five points on which the pairs of items or subjects may be compared and contrasted.

Write an outline for each essay. Include an introduction, topic sentences and conclusion to each outline.

Write each essay from your outlines.

Check your essay against the Essay Checklist on page 117 before you hand it in.

Topic Suggestions

A small private college and a large public university.

High school and college requirements.

Tennis and ping-pong (or racquetball and handball, skateboarding and roller-skating, snow skiing and waterskiing, etc.).

Courtship in two cultures.

Two television shows.

Living in a dormitory versus living at home (or living in a dormitory versus living in an apartment, living at home versus living in an apartment).

Essay Checklist

This checklist details all the things you have learned about writing paragraphs and essays. It is a good idea to keep this checklist in front of you when you are writing. It will remind you of all the essential elements of a good essay. After you have finished your first draft, check your essay for *every* item on the list. If anything is missing, add it before you write your final draft.

Essay Organization

Introduction

General statements ☐

Thesis statement ☐

Body

Logical and appropriate pattern of organization for the topic (chronological order, logical division, comparison-contrast, etc.) ☐

Between-paragraph transitions ☐

Conclusion

Summary of the main points or paraphrase of the thesis, and your final comments on the topic ☐

Paragraph Organization

Topic sentence for each paragraph ☐

Supporting Sentences

Concrete Support ☐

Unity ☐

Coherence (Transition Signals plus Logical Order) ☐

Concluding Sentence (if necessary) ☐

Part III

GRAMMAR AND PUNCTUATION

Chapter 9

SENTENCE STRUCTURE

The Sentence

A sentence is a group of words that you use to communicate your ideas in writing or in speech. It is a complete, independent unit of thought and consists of two main parts: a **subject** and a **predicate**.

Subject
The **subject** is the word or words that names the person, thing, or place that a sentence is about. It is usually a noun or pronoun.

Predicate
The **predicate** makes a statement about the subject. It consists of a verb and its modifiers or complements. The verb is the most important part of the predicate. It expresses action or a state of being.

A complement is a word or words used to complete the meaning of the verb.

Every sentence must have a subject and a verb. A sentence may be a statement, question, command, request, or exclamation. The first letter of a sentence must be capitalized, and the sentence must end with a final punctuation mark in the form of a period (.), a question mark (?), or an exclamation point (!).

The following are samples of different types of sentences.

1. *What is ecology?* Question
2. *Ecology is the science of the relationships between organisms and their environments.* Statement
3. *Save the environment!* Command
4. *Would you write a report on ecology and man?* Request
5. *What a polluted lake that is!* Exclamation

Note: In the third sentence, the subject is not included because it is understood to be "you."

THE CLAUSE

There are two kinds of clauses: **independent** (main) and **dependent** (subordinate).

An independent clause is a group of words that has a subject and verb. It is used as a part of a sentence but is grammatically independent and could therefore stand alone.

The following sentences show good examples of independent clauses:

I may declare my major now, but I can still change it later.

Foreign students suffer from culture shock when they come to the United States.

Because the cost of education has been rising rapidly, many students are having financial problems.

You will need certain qualifications if you choose a career in computer programming.

Note that each independent clause above is a complete sentence.

Independent Clause

An independent clause is formed with:
Subject + Verb + Complement

A dependent clause is introduced with a subordinator such as *when, while, if,* or *before.* It is followed by a subject, verb, and complement. It cannot stand alone because the subordinator signals the need for an independent clause to complete the meaning of the sentence.

When the semester was over . . .

. . . who was accepted by the university . . .

. . . if you leave your car unlocked.

Because I had a job interview . . .

Each of the above clauses is dependent since each of them expresses only a *part* of a complete thought and is therefore a fragment (an incomplete sentence). In order to form a grammatically complete sentence, each of the above clauses must be joined to an independent clause.

Dependent Clause

A dependent clause is formed with:
Subordinator + Subject + Verb + Complement

Kinds of Sentences

There are basically four kinds of sentences in English:

Simple
Compound
Complex
Compound-complex

The kind of sentence is determined by the kind of clauses used to form it.

A. A simple sentence is an independent clause.

   I enjoy playing tennis with my friends every weekend.
   I enjoy playing tennis and look forward to it every weekend.
   My friends and I play tennis and go bowling every weekend.

B. A compound sentence is two or more independent clauses joined together in any one of three ways.

   1. By a *coordinating conjunction.*
      I enjoy playing tennis, <u>but</u> I hate playing golf.

   2. By a *sentence connector:*
      I enjoy playing tennis; <u>however,</u> I hate playing golf.

   3. By a *semicolon:*
      I enjoy playing tennis<u>;</u> I hate playing golf.

C. A complex sentence is the combination of an independent clause and a dependent clause. The two clauses may be in either order.

   Although I enjoy playing tennis, I hate golf.
   I hate golf although I enjoy playing tennis.

D. A compound-complex sentence is a combination of two or more independent clauses and one or more dependent clauses.

   I hate playing golf, but I enjoy playing tennis even though I am not very good at it.

Clause Connectors

Three groups of words are used to connect clauses in order to form sentences that are both grammatical and logical. These three groups are coordinating conjunctions, sentence connectors, and subordinators.

Coordinating conjunctions and sentence connectors join independent clauses to form compound sentences.

Subordinators introduce dependent clauses, which are joined with independent clauses to then form complex sentences.

COMPOUND SENTENCES

Coordinating Conjunctions A compound sentence is made up of two or more independent clauses connected by a coordinating conjunction, such as *and, or, nor, but, for, so, yet.* Each clause in a compound sentence must have a subject and a verb, is of equal importance, and can stand alone. Punctuate the sentence by putting a comma (,) before the coordinating conjunction.

A compound sentence is formed with:
Independent Clause, + Coordinating Conjunction + Independent Clause

---

The following sample sentences indicate how coordinating conjunctions work to make compound sentences. In each sentence, the coordinating conjunction is underlined.

1. George has applied for a scholarship, <u>and</u> Diane has requested financial aid. (additional idea related to first idea)

2. Students may live in the dormitories, <u>or</u> they may live in off-campus housing. (choice of two possibilities)

3. Gerry has completed two math courses, <u>but</u> he must still take calculus. (contrast with first clause)

4. Ron completed his homework early, <u>so</u> he decided to go to the party. (result of first clause)

5. Foreign students must take English classes, <u>for</u> they must be able to communicate easily in speaking and writing. (reason for first clause)

6. I have taken two finals, <u>yet</u> I must take two more this week. (contrast to first clause)

7. Many students do not like to study for tests, <u>nor</u> do they like to write term papers. (negative choice in both clauses)

Note: In the last sentence, the word order after *nor* is that of a typical English question. This is standard practice for this conjunction.

Practice 1: Compound Sentences I

Choose the correct coordinator from the following selection and combine the two independent clauses in each pair in logical order. Rewrite the sentence and punctuate it correctly.

and, or, nor, but, for, so, yet

1. Are you applying for graduate school?
   Will you look for a job?

   _____

   _____

2. Geology is concerned with the structure of the earth. Astronomy is concerned with the physical universe beyond the earth.

   _____

   _____

3. The cost of installation is very high.
   Solar domestic heating systems are economical to operate.

   _____

   _____

4. Energy needs are not going to decrease.
   Energy sources are not going to increase. (use *nor*)

   _____

   _____

5. Our supplies will decrease.
   Consumers must conserve energy sensibly.

   _____

   _____

Practice 2: Compound Sentences II

Add another independent clause to the following independent clauses to form compound sentences. Circle the conjunctions and punctuate the sentences correctly.

Example   The college campus is located in the center of the city, (so) *it is very easy to do my shopping.*

1. Students can attend day classes and _____

   _____

2. Students may live in the dormitories or _____

   _____

3. I have completed my homework for tomorrow but _____

   _____

4. I have taken six units of classes in English as a second language yet _____

   _____

5. Foreign students must take ESL classes for _____

   _____

6. Some students do not like to write term papers nor _____

   _____

7. The professor was lecturing so _____

   _____

8. I had to write an essay for Friday yet _____

   _____

9. Mary returned the book to the library for _____

   _____

Practice 3: Compound Sentences in Paragraph Writing

Choose between A and B below.

A. Write seven compound sentences relating to your own experiences. Use each coordinating conjunction once. Circle the conjunction and punctuate correctly.

B. Write a paragraph about one of your classes. Circle the coordinating conjunctions.

Sentence Connectors   The independent clauses of a compound sentence can also be joined by a sentence connector such as *furthermore, however, otherwise,* and *therefore.* Sentence connectors are used frequently in formal writing to connect long clauses. Punctuate the sentence by placing a semicolon (;) after the first clause and a comma (,) after the sentence connector.

A compound sentence is also formed with:
Independent Clause; + Sentence Connector, + Independent Clause

---

The sentence connector used to link the ideas of the two independent clauses in a compound sentence shows a logical relationship between the idea expressed in the first clause and the idea expressed in the second clause. In the following compound sentence, for example, the first clause expresses an idea about bicycles as a form of transportation. The sentence connector *furthermore* tells the reader that an additional idea about transportation will be given in the second clause.

Some people are using bicycles for transportation; furthermore, others are joining carpools or taking public vehicles to get to their destinations.

Following are examples of sentence connectors that are used to connect compound sentences.

Junior colleges offer preparation for the professions, business, and industry; moreover, students may prepare for transfer to a university or college. (addition)

Many junior colleges do not provide dormitories; however, they provide housing referral services. (contrast)

Students must take the final exam; otherwise, they may be given the final grade of Incomplete. (choice)

You can receive individual guidance from your counselor; therefore, you should take advantage of this service. (result)

The following is a table of coordinating conjunctions and sentence connectors that are used to form compound sentences:

COORDINATORS AND CONNECTORS

Coordinating Conjunctions	Sentence Connectors	Meaning
and	furthermore, besides in addition, moreover, also	additional idea
but, yet	however, nevertheless, still in contrast	contrast idea
for		reason
or	otherwise	choice of two possibilities
so	consequently, therefore, thus accordingly	result
nor		negative choice

Practice 4: Adding Sentence Connectors

STEP 1 Add a sentence connector with the same meaning as the word in parentheses.

STEP 2 Insert the correct punctuation.

1. Advertising plays a significant part in American business _____ it has a tremendous impact on the nation's economy. (addition)

2. Without commercials, the public's favorite programs would not be shown _____ viewers must accept them as necessary. (result)

3. Many ads and commercials do give important information about products _____ some of them are merely humorous or foolish. (contrast)

4. Many consumers rely on advertisements _____ businesses maintain large sums of money for this expense. (result)

5. Careful consumers rely on good advertising _____ they would not buy products wisely. (or)

6. I dislike television commercials _____ I do not like direct mail advertising. (addition)

7. Some advertisers try to push mediocre products on the public _____ the consumer should beware. (result)

Practice 5: Writing Compound Sentences

Write a compound sentence about each of the following topics, using a different kind of sentence connector for each sentence. Punctuate the sentence correctly.

Example   *Watching television is an inexpensive form of entertainment; furthermore, it is a good way to learn English.*

1. (American students) _____

_____

2. (Examinations) _____

_____

3. (My major) _____

_____

4. (My family) _____

_____

5. (My native country) _____

_____

COMPLEX SENTENCES

A complex sentence is made up of an independent clause and one or more dependent clauses. The dependent clause is introduced with a subordinator, such as *when, while, where, who, because, as, if, even though, so that,* etc.

The dependent clause can come at the beginning or end of a complex sentence. When the dependent clause comes at the beginning, a comma (,) is placed before the independent clause.

In a complex sentence of two related ideas, one idea is generally more important than the other one. The more important idea is placed in the independent clause; the less important idea is placed in the dependent clause.

A complex sentence is formed with:

Independent Clause + Dependent Clause

or

Dependent Clause, + Independent Clause

Practice 6: Complex Sentences I

STEP 1 Underline the independent clause of each sentence with a straight line.
STEP 2 Underline the dependent clause with a wavy line.
STEP 3 Write SUB above the subordinator.

Example   *sub*
Because the cost of education is rising, many students must work part-time.

1. When foreign students come to the United States, they sometimes suffer from culture shock.

2. Because the cost of education has risen, many students are having financial problems.

3. Please tell me where the student union is.

4. Engineers, who have an aptitude for drafting and mathematics, must also be artistic and imaginative.

5. While the contractor follows the blueprint, the engineer checks the construction in progress.

6. Since the blueprint presents the details of the engineer's plans, it must be interpreted accurately by the contractor.

7. Students should declare a major by their junior year unless they have not made up their minds.

8. Even though I may declare my major now, I can still change it later.

Practice 7: Complex Sentences II

STEP 1 Add a logical independent clause to each of the following dependent clauses.
STEP 2 Punctuate the sentence correctly.

1. After I graduate _____

2. _____
   unless I take twelve units.

3. Although physical exercise is necessary for good health _____

   _____

4. _____
   before I sign up for the course.

5. Because I had to look for a job _____

6. _____ if you want
   to get to school on time.

7. While I waited in line to register for the new semester _____

   _____

8. _____ whom I met at the
   social club meeting last month.

Practice 8: Writing Complex Sentences

Write complex sentences about the following topics.

STEP 1 Use the given subordinator and the sentence pattern indicated in parentheses:

Pattern A = Independent Clause + Dependent Clause
Pattern B = Dependent Clause + Independent Clause

STEP 2 Underline the subjects once and the verbs twice in each clause.
STEP 3 Circle the subordinator and punctuate correctly.

Example (United States/even though/B) (Even though) I am enjoying the United States, I

still miss my country very much.

1. (Writing a paragraph/before/B) _____

_____

2. (My country/since/A) _____

_____

3. (Studying/until/B) _____

_____

4. (Public transportation/because/A) _____

_____

5. (Grades/even though/B) _____

_____

6. (English/unless/A) _____

_____

COMPOUND-COMPLEX SENTENCES

A compound-complex sentence is a combination of two or more independent
clauses and one or more dependent clauses:

*Many students drive their cars to the college, but others prefer to take public
transportation because free parking near the campus is unavailable.*

*If students wish to park in the campus parking lots, they must pay for a permit,
or the campus police will tag their cars.*

Coordination and Subordination

COORDINATION

You are the architect of your writing. You make your compositions interesting
or boring by the way you structure your sentences and by the words you choose.
Coordination in writing is the use of *and, or, but, for, so, yet,* and *nor* to form
compound sentences. Overcoordination, which results from the use of too many
compound sentences, produces an ineffective and boring writing style. A writer
who overuses this sentence structure is like an architect who designs identical
buildings. Overcoordination reveals a writer's lack of creativity or writing experience, just as designing too many similar buildings reveals an architect's lack of
imagination.

The following paragraph is an example of overcoordination, or writing with too many compound sentences.

Model 1: Overcoordination

1   John F. Kennedy was the 35th President of the United States, and he was born in Brookline, Massachusetts in 1917. His father was Ambassador to England, so he was exposed to politics at an early age. Kennedy decided to enter the political arena, so he ran for Congress from Massachusetts, and he was elected to the Senate in 1953. His

5   term ended in 1960, for he was elected President that same year at the age of 43. He was the first Roman Catholic, and he was the youngest man ever to occupy the presidency. He had planned to run again in the 1964 election year, but he was assassinated on November 22, 1963 in Dallas, Texas. Kennedy served America for such a short time, yet he inspired people all over the free world because of his youth, his spirit and his style.

The overuse of coordination in the above paragraph makes it both boring to read and difficult to focus on the ideas expressed. Note, however, that it is not necessary to completely avoid using compound sentences or even simple sentences. Compound sentences can be effective, and you should use them when you want to give equal emphasis to two ideas. Also, short sentences can add strength to your compositions. However, avoid overusing either of these kinds of sentences.

SUBORDINATION

Subordination is the use of complex sentences containing dependent clauses (and reductions of them), which are introduced by *because, although, while, when, if,* etc. In English, the use of subordination is considered a more mature, interesting and effective writing style. The writer who uses subordination is like an architect who designs unique buildings. The writing is more interesting to read, just as the buildings are more interesting to look at.

The following paragraph is an example of the effective use of subordination. Notice how the sentences have been combined.

Model 2: Subordination

1   John F. Kennedy, who was the 35th President of the United States, was born in Brookline, Massachusetts in 1917. Because his father was Ambassador to England, he was exposed to politics early in life. Deciding to enter the political arena, he ran for Congress from Massachusetts and was elected to the Senate in 1953. His term ended

5   in 1960 as he was elected President that same year at the age of 43. He was not only the first Roman Catholic but also the youngest man ever to occupy the presidency. He had planned to run again in the 1964 election year, but he was assassinated on November 22, 1963 in Dallas, Texas. Although Kennedy served America such a short time, he inspired people all over the free world because of his youth, his spirit and

10 his style.

Subordination involves two ideas, one of which is more important than the other. The more important idea is placed in the independent or main clause. Which of the following is the more important idea?

We were eating lunch.
We felt an earthquake tremor.

What happened in the second sentence is certainly more important than what happened in the first sentence. Therefore, "We felt an earthquake tremor" is placed in the independent clause. Since "We were eating lunch" is the less important idea, it becomes the subordinate, or dependent, clause. Now the sentences are in a more orderly arrangement, ready for connection:

We felt an earthquake tremor
we were eating lunch.

Next, a subordinator is needed to connect the independent clause to the subordinate clause. The logical joiner of these two clauses is *while*:

We felt an earthquake tremor <u>while</u> we were eating lunch.

When using subordination, you must be careful to avoid writing illogical sentences. Sometimes, depending upon the logical sequence of events, one idea *must* be subordinated to another. Avoid illogical subordination. For example:

I was blinded by the setting sun.
I drove through a boulevard stop sign.

Incorrect   *Because I drove through a boulevard stop sign, I was blinded by the sun.*

Correct   *I drove through a boulevard stop sign because I was blinded by the sun.*

               Because I was blinded by the sun, I drove through a boulevard stop sign.

Remember:

1. **The meaning of a sentence can change by emphasizing one of its ideas more than another.**
2. **The use of a subordinator automatically makes the clause that follows it less important.**
3. **To avoid illogical subordination, you must decide which part of a sentence is more important.**

Practice 9: Subordination

Rewrite the following compound sentences into complex sentences by subordinating one of the clauses.

STEP 1 Make one clause a dependent clause introduced by the given subordinator.
STEP 2 Name the kind of relationship that exists between the dependent and independent clauses.

Example   1. Nowadays, many American women work in full-time jobs, for they must help to support their families. (since) *Reason: Nowadays, many American women work in full-time jobs since they must help to support their families.*

2. Some women have become coal miners and construction workers, for there is less discrimination against them now. (because) _____

_____

_____

3. Many women in Third World countries want to work, for they are educated. (who) _____

_____

_____

4. Commercials are necessary for business, but they can be a nuisance to the public. (although) _____

_____

_____

5. Some people believe everything they see and hear on commercials, yet many of the advertisements give misinformation. (even though) _____

_____

_____

6. Many people will not buy a product, for they do not like the commercial. (if) _____

_____

_____

7. Camping in the mountains or on beaches is not very expensive, yet you must first buy a lot of essential equipment. (although) _____

_____

_____

8. Foreign travel is expensive, but it is worth a lot in new experiences and memories. (even though) _____

_____

_____

9. Travelers must know the tipping standards of foreign countries, or they might be embarrassed. (unless) _____

_____

_____

10. A three-minute phone call to New York City between 8 AM and 5 PM costs $1.68, but the same call between 5 PM and 8 AM costs $1.10. (whereas)

_____

_____

OTHER SUBORDINATE CLAUSES

As we stated earlier, subordination, the use of complex sentence structures, is the more desirable writing style in English. But there are many different ways to subordinate. You can subordinate by writing a relative (adjective) clause, an adverbial clause, a noun clause, or a participial phrase. For reference, a list of some of the most important subordinators follows. The subordinators are listed according to the types of dependent clauses they introduce.

TYPES OF SUBORDINATE CLAUSES

Relative Clause		
	Subordinator	Meaning
Relative Pronoun	who	person/people (subject)
	whom	person/people (object)
	whose + noun	person/people, thing(s)—possessive
	that	thing(s)—restrictive clauses only
	which	thing(s)
Relative Adverb	when	time
	where	place
	why	reason

Conditional Clause		
	if	suppose
	even if	
	unless	if . . . not
	when	in the event that . . .

Noun Clause		
Included Wh-Question	that	
	who	
	whoever	whatever person
	what	
	whatever	anything or everything
	where	
	wherever	anyplace
	when	
	how much (many, often, etc.)	
Included Yes/No Question	whether (or not)	
	if	

Adverbial Clause		
	Subordinator	Meaning
Time	when while as soon as after since as	a point in time/short duration longer duration of time immediately at or instantly after the time that subsequent to the time that from that time/moment while, when
Place	where wherever everywhere	a definite place anyplace
Distance/Frequency	as + adverb + as	
Manner	as	in the way or manner that
Reason	because as since	for the reason that
Result	so + adj. + that so + adv. + that such a(n) + noun phrase + that	
Purpose	so that in order that (in order to + verb†)	
Contrast/Concession	although even though though	in spite of the fact that

†*in order to* is not a subordinator because it is not followed by a clause. It is included in this list because of its usefulness in introducing a purpose:

We joined the demonstration <u>*in order to show*</u> *our support for the students.*

Chapter 10

PARALLELISM

In order to make the ideas in your sentences clear and understandable, words, phrases, and clauses should have **parallelism**—that is, the sentence structures should be grammatically balanced. Parallel construction is the repetition of grammatical patterns within a sentence or a series of sentences. By using similar grammatical forms to express equal ideas, your sentences will flow smoothly, and your writing style will improve.

Use similar grammatical structures to balance your writing. If the first structure is a noun, make all of the others nouns; if it is a phrase, make all of the others phrases; if it is a clause, make all of the others clauses.

Notice how the rule of parallelism is followed in the second set of sentences below. The first sentences are structurally unbalanced. The second sentences are correctly balanced: nouns with nouns, phrases with phrases, and clauses with clauses.

Incorrect	*A student needs textbooks, notebooks, and he needs pens.*
Correct	*A student needs textbooks, notebooks, and pens.*
Incorrect	*A student who does well in exams attends class, reads the textbook, and he reviews the notes.*
Correct	*A student who does well in exams attends class, reads the textbook, and reviews the notes.*
Incorrect	*The student wanted to know what the calculus problems were and the due date.*
Correct	*The student wanted to know what the calculus problems were assigned and when the due date was.*

Conjunctions—*And, Or, But*

Words, phrases, and clauses that are joined by *and*, *or*, and *but* are written in parallel form. Notice the parallel structures joined by conjunctions in the following sentences.

The Federal Air Pollution Control Administration regulates automobile exhausts, and the Federal Aviation Administration makes similar regulations for aircraft.

The states regulate the noise created by motor vehicles, <u>but</u> not by commercial aircraft.

Pesticides must be removed from the market if they present an adverse* effect on man <u>or</u> on the environment.

CORRELATIVE CONJUNCTIONS

Use parallel forms with the correlative conjunctions *both . . . and, either . . . or, neither . . . nor,* and *not only . . . but also.*

Correlative conjunctions are placed directly *before* the elements they join in the sentence. Notice the parallel structure in these clauses joined by correlative conjunctions:

Congress has provided the means for <u>both</u> regulating pesticides <u>and</u> ordering their removal if dangerous.

Air pollutants may come <u>either</u> from the ocean as natural contaminants given off by sea life <u>or</u> from the internal combustion engines of automobiles.

If <u>neither</u> industry <u>nor</u> the public works toward reducing pollution problems, future generations will suffer.

Many people are <u>neither</u> concerned about pollutants <u>nor</u> worried about their future impact.

At the present time, air pollution is controlled through laws passed <u>not only</u> to reduce the pollutants at their sources, <u>but also</u> to set up acceptable standards of air quality.

Practice 10: Parallelism I

Grammatical elements in the following sentences are written in parallel form.

STEP 1 Underline the words that are parallel.
STEP 2 In the parenthesis, write down the name of the grammatical class.

Example The ideal conditions for skiing are <u>sunshine</u>, powdery <u>snow</u>, and uncrowded <u>slopes</u>.   (nouns)

A. *Words*

1. The XYZ Corporation manufactures copiers, duplicators, and self-correcting typewriters.   (   )
2. The corporation gathers, edits and synthesizes information. (   )
3. The new personal computer is the most important, useful, and exciting electronic product of today.   (   )
4. The latest self-correcting typewriter works easily, speedily, and noiselessly.   (   )
5. The company's buyers sat in the conference room with the sales representative, both listening and talking.   (   )

B. *Phrases*

6. If you want to learn a foreign language well, you should try to think in the language and to speak the language as much as possible.   (   )

---

adverse: unfavorable

7. You must spend your time studying the vocabulary, listening to native speakers, and practicing new sentence structures. (   )

8. You can learn a foreign language in the classroom, at home, or in the foreign country where the language is spoken. (   )

C. *Clauses*

9. If the supply of oil drops and if the demand increases, alternative fuels will have to be found. (   )

10. At an international seminar, participating countries discussed who the major producers of oil were and how much they would export.(   )

11. It is a popular misconception that oil is found in vast underground pools and that it needs only to be pumped out. (   )

12. Americans are facing a fuel crisis, but according to statistics, they are driving their cars more often. (   )

13. Before the energy crisis began and before the government emphasized the need to save natural resources, Americans did not realize the seriousness of the situation. (   )

Not only . . . but also When you use the correlative conjunction *not only . . . but also* to join independent clauses, the word order sometimes causes problems. Here are some guidelines to help you.

If *not only* comes at the beginning of the first clause, use the question word order in that clause.

Not only does she come from a good family, but she is also very beautiful.

Not only can she cook well, but she is also a first-rate auto mechanic.

If *not only* doesn't come at the beginning of the first clause, use statement word order, and

1. place *not only* before main verbs, but
2. place *not only* after forms of the verb "to be" and after any auxiliary or modal verbs.

She not only comes from a good family, but she is also very beautiful.

She can not only cook well, but she is also a first-rate auto mechanic.

She is not only a first-rate auto mechanic, but she also plays the violin with the London Philharmonic.

She has not only learned to speak twelve languages, but she also enjoys mountain climbing.

When *but also* appears in a clause with a form of the verb "to be," or with auxiliaries or modals, the word *also* comes after the verb form.

She can not only play the violin well, but she can also sing like a nightingale.

She is not only a wonderful wife and mother, but she is also one of the top female astronauts in the United States.

She has not only taught herself to fly, but she has also taught her husband.

When *but also* appears in a clause with a simple present or simple past tense verb, the word *also* comes before the verb.

He not only works full-time, <u>but he also takes</u> a full course load at night school.
He not only made a million dollars, <u>but he also spent</u> it.

Practice 11: Parallelism II

Rewrite the following sentences in parallel form.

STEP 1   Underline the part of the sentence that is illogical and add the correct structure.

STEP 2   Circle the word or words that join the parallel structures.

Example   Attending the symphony or <u>to go</u> to the theater is what I enjoy the most.

Attending the symphony or going to the theater is what I enjoy the most.

1. Credit cards are accepted by department stores, airlines, and they can be used in some gas stations.

_____

_____

2. You do not need to risk carrying cash or to risk to pass up a sale.

_____

_____

3. With credit cards you can either pay your bill with one check, or you can stretch out your payments.

_____

_____

4. You can charge both at restaurants and when you stay at hotels.

_____

_____

5. Many people carry not only credit cards but also they carry cash.

_____

_____

6. Many people want neither to read a product's warranty nor sending it into a company.

_____

_____

7. Many warranties give comprehensive coverage, but some give coverage that is limited.

_____

_____

8. Getting a defective product fixed or to have it replaced is what a comprehensive warranty guarantees.

_____

_____

Review: Parallelism

These are the main points you should have learned from this chapter:

1. Words, phrases, or clauses that are joined by coordinating conjunctions and correlative conjunctions must be written in parallel form.
2. If the first structure is a noun, make all others nouns; if it is a prepositional phrase, make all the others prepositional phrases; if it is a dependent clause, make all the others dependent clauses.
3. All of the words in the first parallel structure do not have to be repeated in the second. You may repeat all or some of the words, depending upon what you wish to emphasize.

Example   *Before you write a paper or (before) (you) take a test, you must organize your thoughts.

"Before" and/or "you" may be deleted from the second parallel structure.

*Before you write a paper or take a test, you must organize your thoughts.

WRITING PRACTICE

Write eight original sentences in parallel form, using both coordinating conjunctions (_and, or, but_) and correlative conjunctions (_both . . . and, either . . . or, neither . . . nor, not only . . . but also_).

Chapter 11

NOUN CLAUSES

A **noun clause** is a dependent clause that functions as a noun. It can perform any function a noun can, for example, as subject, object, or subject complement. However, we will study the noun clause only as it is used as an object.

Because a noun clause is dependent, it must be connected to an independent clause to form a complex sentence. A noun clause used as an object is preceded by an independent clause that we call an introductory clause. The noun clause is the object of the introductory clause verb.

INTRODUCTORY CLAUSE		DEPENDENT NOUN CLAUSE
Subject	Verb	Object
I	know	that people have different opinions about capital punishment.

There are three types of dependent noun clauses:

> Included that–clauses
> Included wh-question clauses
> Included yes/no question clauses

A noun clause is composed of:
Subordinator + Subject + Verb + Complement

> (that)
> wh-question word
> whether (or not)
> if

The word order of most noun clauses is normal statement word order, as indicated in the following examples:

> *. . . (that) science courses require a laboratory period.*
> *. . . where the student union is.*
> *. . . whether our projects are due next week.*
> *. . . if lunch is being served.*

Note: One kind of noun clause has a slightly different pattern. In an included wh-question clause, the subordinator and the subject are the same word, so the pattern is:

Subject Subordinator + Verb + Complement

. . . who made the error.
. . .which team won the championship.

Types of Noun Clauses

There are three types of noun clauses: **included that–clauses, included wh-question clauses**, and **included yes/no question clauses**. The chart below shows the three types of noun clauses.

NOUN CLAUSES

Introductory Clause	Included That–Clause	
The bulletin stated	that	science courses require a laboratory period.
The credit department noted	that	Unusual Gift Shop's account was thirty days overdue.
	Included Wh-Question Clause	
Can you remember	who	made the error?
Do you know	where	the student union is?
The professor explained	how	shock waves are formed.
	Included Yes/No Question Clause	
I do not know	whether	our projects are due next week.
The engineer must determine	if	the given dimensions and tolerances are correct.

Punctuating noun clauses is fairly simple. No comma is used to separate the introductory clause from the noun clause. The introductory clause, which may be a statement or a question, determines the end-of-sentence punctuation. If the introductory clause is a question, a question mark is used:

I don't know when he called.
Do you know when he called?

Sequence of Tenses

Before you study each of the noun clause forms, you should learn the rules governing the sequence of tenses. The sequence of tenses refers to the verb tenses in different clauses of the same sentence. The verb tense in the independent clause determines the verb tense in the dependent clause.

When the verb in the introductory clause is in present tense, the verb in the dependent clause is in whatever tense expresses the intended meaning.

The president <u>agrees</u> that solar power <u>is</u> the answer to the energy crisis.

He <u>predicts</u> that solar power <u>is going to be</u> the energy source of the future.

He <u>believes</u> that solar energy companies <u>have expanded</u> operations since 1973.

A government source <u>estimates</u> that more than 200 solar firms <u>began</u> operations in the last five years.

The Solar Energy Industries <u>report</u> that homeowners <u>have to be convinced</u> of the effectiveness of solar energy.

Homeowners <u>think</u> that the cost of installing this equipment <u>may be increasing</u> too rapidly.

When the verb in the introductory clause is in past tense, the verb in the dependent clause must also be in a past form.

The president <u>agreed</u> that solar power <u>was</u> the answer to the energy crisis.

He <u>predicted</u> that solar power <u>was going to be</u> the energy source of the future.

He <u>believed</u> that solar energy companies <u>had expanded</u> operations since 1973.

A government source <u>estimated</u> that more than 200 solar firms <u>had begun</u> operations in the last five years.

The Solar Energy Industries <u>reported</u> that homeowners <u>had to be convinced</u> of the effectiveness of solar energy.

Homeowners <u>thought</u> that the cost of installing this equipment <u>might be increasing</u> too rapidly.

Note: The modals <u>should</u> and <u>must</u> do not have past forms.

INCLUDED THAT-CLAUSES

Included that–clauses are dependent noun clauses often introduced by the subordinator *that*. Since *that* is a subordinator with no grammatical function in the clause it introduces, it may sometimes be omitted.

An included that–clause is composed of
(That) + Subject + Verb + Complement

. . . (<u>that</u>) the study of the brain is fascinating.
. . . (<u>that</u>) the brain is the master control for both mind and body.
. . . (<u>that</u>) it controls sensations, moods, thoughts, and actions.

A complex sentence with an included that-clause is composed of an independent introductory clause and a dependent included that-clause:

I think (that) the study of the brain is fascinating.
The professor stated that the brain is the master control for both mind and body.
He further explained that it controls sensations, moods, thoughts, and actions.

The following is a list of some introductory clause verbs that are used to introduce included that–clauses.

INTRODUCTORY CLAUSE VERBS

Group I	Group II	Group III	Group IV
agree	explain (to + indirect object)	tell	write (to)
answer	admit	assure	promise
conclude	mention	convince	show
notice	point out	inform	teach
realize	reply	notify	warn
think		remind	

1. The verbs in Group I do not take an indirect object.

2. The verbs in Group II may or may not take an indirect object. However, if an indirect object follows one of these verbs, *to* must precede it.
   For example: suggested *to me*, pointed out *to the audience*

3. The verbs in Group III must be followed by an indirect object.
   For example: told *us*, convinced *the students*

4. The verbs in Group IV may or may not take an indirect object.
   For example: wrote (me), promised (the nation)

Practice 12: Included That-Clauses

STEP 1 Add a verb from the table to complete the introductory clause. Use a different verb in each sentence, and remember the sequence of tenses rule.

STEP 2 Add the subordinator *that*.

Example The president ___*pointed out that*___ coal was an increasingly important source of energy for the United States.

1. Industry _____ coal is regarded as energy's black gold.

2. The federal government _____ the country should double its coal use in ten years.

3. The speaker _____ the United States has the largest coal reserves in the world.

4. Environmentalists _____ new ways to burn coal cleanly must be found.

5. The Federal Energy Administration _____ only about 20 percent of energy used in the United States is from coal.

6. The Federal Energy Administration _____ technological advances will make converting coal into a synthetic natural gas more economical.

WRITING PRACTICE

Write six original sentences containing included that-clauses about a current news event. Use a different introductory clause verb in each sentence, and remember the sequence of tenses rule.

INCLUDED WH-QUESTION CLAUSES

An included wh-question clause is a dependent noun clause formed from a wh-question. A wh-question is first changed into a statement and then joined to an introductory clause to form a complex sentence.

An included wh-question clause can follow two patterns: the *subject pattern* or the *object pattern*. In the subject pattern, the wh-word is the subject of its own clause. In the object pattern the wh-word is only a subordinator; it is not the subject.

Subject Pattern

In the subject pattern, direct wh-questions become the dependent noun clause without any change in sentence structure. The following is a short list of direct wh-questions.

Who started the space race?
What happened in 1965?
How many astronauts have walked on the moon?
Which achievement was the most significant?
How much money was spent to put a man on the moon?

Below, these questions have been transformed into dependent noun clauses. Notice that there is no change in word order when you transform subject pattern direct wh-questions into included wh-question clauses.

INCLUDED WH-QUESTION CLAUSE WORD ORDER—THE SUBJECT PATTERN

Introductory Clause	Included Wh-Question Clause		
	Wh-question word	Verb	Complement
Do you know	who	started	the space race?
Can you tell us	what	happened	in 1965?
Does he remember	how many astronauts	have walked	on the moon?
The professor asked us	which achievement	was	the most significant.
Some people complain about	how much money	was spent	to put a man on the moon.

Practice 13: Included Wh-Question Clauses—Subject Pattern

Add the direct wh-question to the introductory clause to form a complex sentence.

Example Which companies offer the best opportunities in your field?

The job center can tell you *which companies offer the best opportunities in your field.*

1. Who is responsible for creating pollution and wasting resources?

   The ecologist* will explain _____

   _____

2. How many big cities have antipollution laws?

   The Environmental Protection Agency will tell you _____

   _____

ecologist: a scientist who studies the relationship between living things and their environments

3. Who is in charge of the Environmental Protection Agency?

   Does anyone know _____

   _____

4. What is required to solve the problem of air pollution?

   I would like to know _____

   _____

5. Which state has the most stringent* antipollution laws for automobiles?

   The E.P.A. has statistics showing _____

   _____

WRITING PRACTICE

Write six original complex sentences containing included wh-question clauses in the subject pattern.

STEP 1 Write six direct wh-questions in the subject pattern.

STEP 2 Connect each to an introductory clause. Remember the sequence of tenses rule, and punctuate your sentences correctly.

Object Pattern   In the object pattern, the word order changes when you transform a direct wh-question into an included wh-question clause. This pattern occurs when the wh-word is *not* the subject of its clause, and when you have questions containing the verb "to be" plus a subject complement. Study the following direct wh-questions.

Who are the hijackers?	(with *to be* plus a subject complement)
How can we end airplane hijackings?	(with modal verbs)
Where have they taken the hostages?	(with the auxiliaries *has/have*)
What do the hijackers want?	(with the auxiliaries *do/does/did*)

Notice what happens to the word order when you transform direct wh-questions into included wh-question clauses:

INCLUDED WH-QUESTION CLAUSE WORD ORDER—THE OBJECT PATTERN

Introductory Clause	Included Wh-Question Clause			
	Wh-word	Subject	Verb	Complement
No one seems to know	who	the hijackers	are.	
It's difficult to determine	how	we	can end	airplane hijackings.
The police won't reveal	where	they	have taken	the hostages.
The government wouldn't say	what	the hijackers	wanted.	

In the object pattern, included wh-question clauses use the statement word order, and the auxiliaries *do/does/did* are deleted.

---

stringent: strict

Practice 14: Included Wh-Question Clauses—Object Pattern

A. Change the direct wh-questions below into included wh-question clauses and connect them to the introductory clauses to form complex sentences. Remember the sequence of tenses rule, and punctuate your sentences correctly.

Example   How many hostages did the hijackers kill?

The newspapers haven't reported *how many hostages the hijackers killed.*

1. What language do the terrorists speak?

   No one seems to know _____

   _____

2. What country are they from?

   It is not known _____

3. How much ransom are the hijackers demanding?

   The government won't reveal _____

   _____

4. How did the hijackers get aboard the airplane with weapons?

   The police are trying to determine _____

   _____

5. Where have the hijackers been holding the hostages?

   Does anyone know _____

   _____

B. Change these direct wh-questions into included wh-question clauses and connect them to an introductory clause to form complex sentences.

Example   At which university did Albert Einstein teach?

I can't remember at which university Albert Einstein taught.

1. When did he receive the Nobel Prize?

   _____

   _____

2. For which theory did Einstein win the Nobel Prize?

   _____

   _____

3. What is Einstein's quantum explanation of the photoelectric effect?

_____

_____

4. How long has Einstein been dead?

_____

_____

5. How long will he be remembered?

_____

_____

WRITING PRACTICE

Write six original sentences containing included wh-question clauses in the object pattern. Use each of the four verb combinations given in the examples at least once.

STEP 1 Write six direct wh-questions in the object pattern.
STEP 2 Change them into included wh-question clauses and connect them to introductory clauses. Remember the sequence of tenses rule.

INCLUDED YES/NO QUESTION CLAUSES

Included yes/no question clauses are dependent noun clauses that are formed from yes/no questions. A yes/no question is changed into a statement by adding the subordinator _whether, whether or not,_ or _if._

Here are some direct yes/no questions:

Do final examinations begin next month?
Will the university accept late registration?
Was the notice posted on the bulletin board?
Has the quiz been postponed?

Notice how the structure of the above direct yes/no questions is changed when they are transformed into included yes/no question clauses, as they are in this table:

INCLUDED YES/NO QUESTION CLAUSE WORD ORDER

| | Included Yes/No Question Clause | |
Introductory Clause	Subordinator	Subject + Verb + Complement
Do you know	if	final examinations begin next month?
We would like to inquire	whether (or not)	the university will accept late registration.
The professor didn't know	if	the notice had been posted on the bulletin board.
Have you heard	if	the quiz has been postponed?

An included yes/no question clause is formed by:

1. changing the word order to statement form;
2. deleting the auxiliaries *do*, *does*, and *did*;
3. adding *if*, *whether* or *whether or not*.

Whether is formal, *if* is informal.
Whether and *if* may both occur alone.
    I don't know whether he is coming.
    I don't know if he is coming.
Whether or not may be written together at the beginning of the clause or may be separated.
    I don't know whether or not he is coming.
    I don't know whether he is coming or not.

Practice 15: Included Yes/No Question Clauses I

Change the following direct yes/no questions into included yes/no question clauses, adding the introductory clause given to form a complex sentence. Use any of the possible variations, which are shown in the chart.

Remember the sequence of tenses rule, and punctuate your sentence correctly.

Example   Are food additives safe?

   a. Does the public know   whether   food additives are safe?
   b. Does the public know   whether or not food additives are safe?
   c. Does the public know   whether   food additives are safe or not?
   d. Does the public know   if   food additives are safe?

1. Is the food industry concerned about the health of the people?

   The American public would like to know _____

   _____

2. Do food additives present health hazards?

   Will the Federal Drug Administration reveal _____

   _____

3. Has the safety of MSG*, which is frequently used in Chinese cooking, been thoroughly tested?

   Have you read _____

   _____

4. Does MSG cause cancer in humans?
   Many people have stopped using MSG until the FDA completes its tests to

   determine _____

5. Can food additives approved by the FDA be considered safe to eat?

   We need to ascertain _____

   _____

MSG: monosodium glutamate, a chemical compound
    used to enhance the flavor of food

Practice 16: Included Yes/No Question Clauses II

Add an independent clause and the subordinator: *whether, whether or not, whether . . . or not,* or *if* to introduce the dependent clause. Make sure your introductory clause is a question if there is a question mark at the end of the sentence.

Example   *Do you know whether or not* all food additives are fat soluble?

1. _____ toxicological phenomena can always be predicted with accuracy?

2. _____ toxicological phenomena can be explained on the basis of physical or chemical laws.

3. _____ this unpredictability of accurate results on additives establishes the need to perform tests on animals?

4. _____ the animals were fed different concentrations of the chemical and examined for signs of disease.

5. _____ the definition of food includes chewing gum and candy.

WRITING PRACTICE

Write six sentences with yes/no included question clauses. Use the subordinators *whether, whether or not, whether . . . or not,* or *if.*

Remember the sequence of tenses rule.

Practice 17: Review of Noun Clauses

Pretend you are going to graduate from the university and are now looking for a position in your field (business, accounting, engineering, medical technology, etc.). You could look in your local newspaper to see what job opportunities are available. The following are examples of help-wanted ads that you might find:

HELP WANTED

Do you have a BA or BS in accounting? No experience necessary. Training program in national firm. Inquiries welcomed. Write: Billings, Goodwill and Rush Accountancy Corp., 354 Waterfront Center, San Francisco, CA 94117.

Affirmative Action Employer

ENGINEERING GRADUATES

Must possess degree in electrical or mechanical engineering, physics or computer science. Job opportunities on West or East Coasts and in Middle East. Submit letters of inquiry to:

Frank Memry, Computech Corp., 475 Evanston Drive
Santa Clara, CA 94301.

An Equal Opportunity Employer M/F

a. If you are planning to become an accountant or engineer, you might answer either one of the above ads. If you are going into another field, however, look in your local newspaper for a help-wanted ad that answers your specific needs. Attach your ad to your assignment.

b. Write a letter of inquiry using noun clauses. Use that-clauses to state information which you already know. ("Your ad stated that your company was seeking . . ."); use wh-question and yes/no question clauses to ask for information. You might want to inquire about:

size of company	salary	vacation
number of employees	advancement	housing
training program	insurance program	recreational facilities

For example, if you are applying for a position in a foreign country, you would be interested in available housing, recreational facilities, etc. You are the applicant. Ask questions that you want answered by using noun clauses.

Letter of Inquiry

Heading
(your address)
(date)

777 Oak Avenue, Apt. 2-C
San Francisco, CA 94116
May 8, 19__

Inside Address

Mr. Frank Memry
Computech Corporation
475 Evanston Drive
Santa Clara, CA 94301

Salutation

Dear Mr. Memry:

Body

I would like to inquire about the positions for engineering graduates that were advertised in the *Metropolitan Tribune* of April 30, 19__. Please send me an application form. I would also like some more information about your company and its employment policies.

Would you please tell me how long your company has been in business?
I would also like to know whether your company has a training program.

Closing

Thank you for your attention.

Very truly yours,

Marvin Lemos

Signature
(handwritten
and typed)

Marvin Lemos

DIRECT AND INDIRECT SPEECH

When you give the exact words of a speaker or writer, it is called **direct speech** or quotation. When using direct speech, follow this rule for punctuation:

Place a comma (or under certain conditions, a colon) after the introductory clause, and put quotation marks before and after the actual words spoken.

The economics professor said, "The cost of living rose less rapidly last year than in the recent past."
John asked him, "Will the cost of living continue to decline?"
Mary asked him, "What should the people do to fight inflation?"

When direct speech is changed to indirect speech, the words of the speaker are reported (or given indirectly).

Notice how the direct speech sentences above are changed to indirect speech as follows:

The economics professor said that the cost of living had risen less rapidly last year than in the recent past.
John asked him if the cost of living would continue to decline.
Mary asked him what the people should do to fight inflation.

To change direct speech into indirect speech, follow these steps:

1. Write the introductory clause.
2. Introduce the noun clause with an appropriate subordinator: *that, if, whether (or not)*, or a *wh-question word*.
3. Do NOT use quotation marks.
4. Change the verb tenses if necessary.
5. Use statement word order in the dependent clause.
6. Change certain other words in order to keep the meaning of the sentence clear (for example, *my* to *her*).
7. If the introductory clause verb is past tense, change adverbs when necessary (*now* to *then*, *today* to *that day*, *tomorrow* to *the next day*, etc.)

Practice 18: Changing Direct Statements into Indirect Speech

STEP 1 Use the past tense form of the verb in parentheses in the introductory clause.
STEP 2 Change the direct quotation into a noun clause introduced by the subordinator *that*.
STEP 3 Underline the verbs. Follow the sequence of tenses rule.

Dean White of the American University Dental School said, "Many Americans are losing their teeth prematurely." (tell us)

Example   *Dean White of the American University Dental School told us that many Americans were losing their teeth prematurely.*

1. Dean White said, "Roughly speaking*, 98 percent of all Americans have tooth decay." (state)

_____

_____

2. He said, "People who brush and floss their teeth meticulously prevent cavities from forming." (emphasize)

_____

_____

3. Dean White said, "Fluoridated water can reduce tooth decay." (point out)

_____

_____

4. He said, "Repeated eating of sugar-rich snacks between meals may cause tooth surface damage." (warn)

_____

5. The Dean said, "School dental programs will teach children proper dental care." (announce)

_____

_____

6. He said, "Many school children are learning to brush their teeth properly." (inform us)

_____

_____

Practice 19: Changing Direct Questions into Indirect Speech

STEP 1 Use the introductory clause given in the direct question.
STEP 2 Change the direct quotation into a noun clause introduced with a subordinator, such as a *wh-question word*, *whether*, or *if*.
STEP 3 Underline the verbs. Remember the sequence of tenses rule.

Example Professor Watkins asked, "How many of you have invested in the stock market?"

Professor Watkins asked how many of us had invested in the stock market.

1. He asked us, "When did the New York Stock Exchange begin its business of trading?"

_____

_____

2. He asked us, "Do you know that you can still make money in stocks?"

_____

_____

---

roughly speaking: speaking in general

3. He asked us, "Do you know what stock dividends are?"

_____

_____

4. He asked us, "Do you know that there is always a risk* in stock ownership?"

_____

_____

5. I asked him, "Why have stocks failed to keep up with inflation in recent years?"

_____

_____

6. I asked him, "Where should one look for the latest reading of how a specific stock is doing?"

_____

_____

Practice 20: Recognizing Indirect Speech

Underline the verbs.
Circle the subordinators.

1   In my Business 40 class, Professor Watkins lectured on preferred stocks. He said
       that preferred stocks represented ownership in a company. He also stated that invest-
       ment in preferred stocks had both advantages and disadvantages. I asked him how often
       preferred stockholders were paid dividends. Furthermore, I asked him whether pre-
5   ferred or common stockholders would receive their dividends first if the company's
       assets were liquidated*. He said that preferred stockholders were paid dividends
       quarterly and that preferred stockholders would be the first to receive them. He asked
       us what would happen if a company had missed four quarterly dividend payments.
10   Finally, he said that we would visit the Stock Exchange next month.

WRITING PRACTICE

Use the above paragraph as a model, and write about a lecture given in one of your classes, using indirect speech.

---

risk: chance of loss or failure   **liquidation:** distribution of business assets after
                                                   payment of all debts

Chapter 12

ADVERBIAL CLAUSES

An **adverbial clause** is another type of dependent clause introduced by a subordinator. It is used to modify the verb of the noun clause, and it answers such questions as Where? When? Why? How? For what purpose?

The adverbial clause pattern is formed with:
Subordinator + Subject + Verb + Complement

Because scientists are interested in the planets...
After information is sent back to Earth...

Since the adverbial clause is a dependent clause, it cannot stand alone. It must be combined with an independent clause to form a complex sentence. The adverbial clause can come either before or after the independent clause. If it comes at the beginning of the sentence, a comma (,) is placed after it:

Because scientists are interested in the planets, they send spacecraft to orbit them.

Types of Adverbial Clauses

There are several different kinds of adverbial clauses including time clauses, place clauses, and reason clauses, among others. We will discuss each in turn.

TIME CLAUSES

An adverbial **time clause** tells *when* the action described by the main verb took place.

A time clause is introduced by such subordinators as *when, while, as soon as, after, since, whenever,* and *before.*

When people had to gather and hunt for food, they also had continuous moderate exercise.

American pioneers were consuming a great amount of protein and fat while they were living and working on farms.

After people moved to urban areas, they had less protein in their diet.

Our eating habits changed drastically <u>as soon as food processing methods improved</u>.

People have been eating more refined and processed foods <u>since modern technology has arrived</u>.

Practice 21: Time Clauses

STEP 1   Add a time subordinator to the appropriate sentence to form an adverbial clause.

STEP 2   Write a new sentence by combining the adverbial clause with the independent clause.

STEP 3   Circle the subordinator and punctuate the sentence if necessary.

Example   The United States is in the process of changing to the metric system.
Both the metric and English systems will be used.

(While) the United States is in the process of changing to the metric system, both the metric and English systems will be used.

1. American industries are slowly converting to the metric system. Many food products will indicate contents by ounces and kilograms.

_____

_____

2. It showed that more women were opposed to the metric system than men. A recent survey was taken.

_____

_____

3. U.S. soft drink companies have been using the 2-liter no-return bottle. Conversion to the metric system began in the 1970s.

_____

_____

4. The chemical industry converts from ounces to grams. All package chemicals to consumers will also be changed.

_____

_____

5. The United States converts to the metric system. Cooking recipes using the English system will have to be changed.

_____

_____

PLACE CLAUSES

An adverbial clause of place tells where the action described by the main verb took place.

Where (a definite place)
Wherever (any place)
Everywhere (any place)
Anywhere (any place)

a. *Most people prefer to shop <u>where they can be sure of quality</u>.*
b. *Consumers usually prefer to do business <u>wherever credit cards are accepted</u>.*
c. *<u>Everywhere</u> I shop, I use my credit cards.*
d. *I usually stop for lunch <u>anywhere that is handy</u>.*

Practice 22: Place Clauses

STEP 1 Add a place subordinator to the appropriate sentence of the pairs below to form an adverbial clause.

STEP 2 Write a new sentence by combining the adverbial clause with the independent clause.

STEP 3 Circle the subordinator and punctuate the sentence if necessary.

Example People prefer to shop.
Credit cards are accepted.

People prefer to shop (where) credit cards are accepted.

1. Consumers have a tendency to buy more.
   Credit cards are accepted for payment of the merchandise.

   _____

   _____

2. You can use credit cards.
   You can pay for your purchases after the monthly statement arrives.

   _____

   _____

3. Over 75 percent of American consumers use credit cards.
   They shop.

   _____

   _____

4. There is hardly any place of business.
   A credit card is not accepted.

   _____

   _____

5. They are acceptable.
   Americans can use credit cards in foreign countries.

   _____

   _____

MANNER, DISTANCE, AND FREQUENCY CLAUSES

Adverbial clauses of manner, distance, and frequency are introduced by:
as + adverb + as

1. *The students completed the experiment as quickly as they could.*   (manner)
2. *The students completed the experiment as their professor had instructed.*
                                                                        (manner)
3. *Pat jogs on the beach as often as she can.*   (frequency)

Practice 23: Manner, Distance, and Frequency Clauses

STEP 1 Write a manner, distance, or frequency subordinator in the blank to form
        an adverbial clause.
STEP 2 Form a new sentence by combining the adverbial clause with the indepen-
        dent clause.

The American people should try to conserve energy.

as often as they can (frequency)

The American people should try to conserve energy as often as they can.

1. The public must conserve energy.

   _____ the president has requested (manner)

   _____

   _____

2. Many Americans want to move.

   _____ they can from polluted cities (distance)

   _____

   _____

3. We should not consume our natural resources.

   _____ we have in the past (manner)

   _____

   _____

4. Citizens should make a strong effort to conserve all natural resources.

   _____ the government has advised (manner)

   _____

   _____

5. The Environmental Protection Agency must remind people.
   _____ they can about the dangers of pollution (frequency)

   _____

   _____

6. All nations should work together.

   _____ they can to share their knowledge (frequency)

   _____

   _____

REASON CLAUSES

An adverbial **reason clause** answers the question Why? A reason clause is introduced by the subordinators *because*, *since*, and *as*.

a. *Some women are choosing coal mining as a job because modern technology has improved working conditions*.
b. *Since coal production will more than double by the 1990s*, the work force will also have to increase.
c. *As a tremendous quantity of coal deposits is deep underground*, miners must bring it up.

Practice 24: Reason Clauses

STEP 1 Add a reason subordinator (*as*, *because*, or *since*) to the appropriate sentence to form an adverbial clause.

STEP 2 Write a new sentence by combining the adverbial clause with the independent clause. Do *not* use a pronoun in the first clause.

STEP 3 Circle the subordinator and punctuate the sentence if necessary.

Example   They need them to fight the crops' natural enemies.
~~Farmers rely on chemicals for their crops~~

Farmers rely on chemicals for their crops (because) they need them to fight the crops' natural enemies.

1. Chemical preservatives for crops are necessary.
   They help to protect against spoilage, disease, and pests.

   _____

   _____

2. Chemicals improve nutrition and quality.
   They are used in agriculture.

   _____

   _____

3. Many drugs are synthesized* in the laboratory.
   Natural materials are scarce.

   _____

   _____

4. Chemicals have become an important part of our lives.
   The chemical industry has developed tremendously.

   _____

   _____

5. Millions of people work in the chemical industry.
   The industry has grown rapidly.

   _____

   _____

synthesized: produced by artificial (especially chemical) means

RESULT CLAUSES

An adverbial **result clause** expresses the outcome of the main clause statement. The result clause is introduced by:

so + adjective/adverb + that, or by
such a(an) + adjective + noun + that.

a. *New textbooks are so expensive that many students buy used ones.*
b. *The cost of education is rising so rapidly that students are looking for ways to cut expenses.*
c. *The library is such a big place that I could not find the book I needed.*

Practice 25: Result Clauses

STEP 1 Add a result subordinator to the first sentence in the following pairs to form an adverbial clause.

STEP 2 Write a new sentence by combining the adverbial clause with the independent clause.

STEP 3 Circle both parts of the subordinator and punctuate the sentence if necessary.

Example Oil plays an important part in engine protection.
It must be changed regularly.

Oil plays (such an) important part in engine protection (that) it must be changed regularly.

1. Changing the oil and filter in a car is easy.
   Anyone can do the job.

   _____

   _____

2. Changing the oil is an easy job.
   An understanding of automotive mechanics is not necessary.

   _____

   _____

3. The oil can be changed with little effort.
   The job can be completed in about twenty minutes.

   _____

   _____

4. Oil contamination* occurs rapidly.
   It is important to change the oil every 2,000 to 3,000 miles.

   _____

   _____

5. The viscosity* of the oil is critical*.
   Using the right weight of oil is important for proper engine performance.

   _____

   _____

contamination: to make impure   **critical:** extremely important
viscosity: thickness

PURPOSE CLAUSES

An adverbial **purpose clause** states the purpose of the action in the main clause. The purpose clause is introduced by:

so that or
in order that.

Farmers are using chemical pesticides <u>*so that they can grow bigger harvests*</u>.

Farmers spray their fields <u>*in order that*</u> *any pests may be killed before the crops are destroyed.*

Practice 26: Purpose Clauses

STEP 1 Add a purpose subordinator—either *so that* or *in order that*—to the appropriate sentence in order to form an adverbial clause.

STEP 2 Write a new sentence by combining the adverbial clause with the independent clause.

STEP 3 Circle the subordinator and punctuate the sentence if necessary.

Example Chemists are constantly creating new products in the laboratory.
People can have substitutes for scarce or unavailable products.

Chemists are constantly creating new products in the laboratory (so that) people can have substitutes for scarce or unavailable products

1. Chemicals are used in many food products.
   They will stay fresh longer.

   _____

   _____

2. Farmers use chemical fertilizers and pesticides.
   They can increase food crops.

   _____

   _____

3. The Clean Air Act was adopted.
   Public health would be protected.

   _____

   _____

4. Environmentalists endorse the Clean Air Act.
   Air quality in the United States would improve.

   _____

   _____

5. Environmentalists want strong antipollution laws.
   Less damage to lakes and fish will occur.

   _____

   _____

CONCESSION CLAUSES

Adverbial clauses of **concession** place limits on the statement of the main clause. The information in the independent clause indicates a **concession** or unexpected result of information in the dependent clause. The adverbial clauses of concession are introduced with *although, even though,* and *though.*

Although most students dislike English courses, they must take them in order to graduate.

Andrew is going to sail his boat in the race although a storm is due.

Practice 27: Concession Adverbial Clauses

STEP 1 Add a concession subordinator to the appropriate sentence in order to form an adverbial clause.

STEP 2 Write a new sentence by combining the adverbial clause with the independent clause.

STEP 3 Circle the subordinator and punctuate the sentence if necessary.

Example   Chemicals are beneficial to man.
They also cause risks.

Although chemicals are beneficial to man, they also cause risks.

1. Scientists do not agree about the safe levels of chemical exposure.
   They do agree that everyone must be protected from unnecessary risks.

   _____

   _____

2. Government regulations may be strict.
   All risks cannot be eliminated entirely.

   _____

   _____

3. Chemicals may not be 100 percent safe.
   Their benefits are significant.

   _____

   _____

4. The insecticide DDT was once considered an important aid to pest control.
   It was later considered dangerous.

   _____

   _____

5. Natural vitamins are preferable.
   Laboratory manufactured ones are almost as good for you.

   _____

   _____

STRONG CONTRAST ADVERBIAL CLAUSES

In adverbial contrast clauses, the information in the first clause of the sentence is in strong contrast or in complete opposition to the information in the sentence's second clause. In such a sentence, either clause can be introduced by the subordinator *while*. In addition, the second clause may also be introduced by the subordinator *whereas*. Place a comma between the contrast clauses.

San Francisco is very cool during the summer, whereas Los Angeles is extremely hot.

While Los Angeles is extremely hot, San Francisco is very cool during the summer.

Ron is a playboy, whereas his brother is a serious student.

Whereas Ron is a playboy, his brother is a serious student.

Practice 28: Strong Contrast Adverbial Clauses I

STEP 1 Add contrast subordinator *while* or *whereas* to the first or second clause.
STEP 2 Write a new sentence by combining the adverbial clause with the independent clause.
STEP 3 Circle the subordinator and punctuate the sentence.

1. The West Coast suffered a severe drought.
   The East Coast had heavy rainfall.

   _____

   _____

2. The Northwest rainfall averages hundreds of inches annually.
   The Southwest averages less than twelve inches annually.

   _____

   _____

3. The air is polluted in industrial areas.
   The air is clean in many rural areas.

   _____

   _____

4. Smokers claim the right to smoke in public places.
   Nonsmokers claim the right to clean air.

   _____

   _____

5. College graduates with engineering and business degrees are in demand.
   Graduates with liberal arts degrees are not.

   _____

   _____

6. The space shuttle Columbia landed in the desert.
   The Apollo spacecrafts splashed down in the ocean.

   _____

   _____

Practice 29: Strong Contrast Adverbial Clauses II

STEP 1 Complete the following sentences with an opposite idea.
STEP 2 Circle the subordinator and punctuate the sentence.

1. While Americans usually drink coffee for breakfast _____

_____

2. My English professor is witty and stimulating _____

_____

3. While Helen understands calculus _____

_____

4. San Francisco has many hilly streets _____

_____

5. My uncle is wealthy _____

_____

6. Living alone is expensive _____

_____

7. Eating at home is economical _____

_____

Review: Adverbial Clauses

These are the main points you should have learned from this chapter:

The adverbial clause is a dependent clause that modifies the verb of the main clause or an adjective or adverb. It answers such questions as Where? When? Why? How? For what purpose?

The adverbial clause can come either before or after the independent clause. If it comes at the beginning of the sentence, it is separated by a comma.

There are several types of adverbial clauses, each with its own subordinating conjunctions. They are:

1. *Time Clause* - While, When, Since, As soon as, After, etc.

   While the drought was going on, many people took fewer showers and baths.

2. *Place Clause* - Where, Wherever, Everywhere

   Everywhere that people went to dine, they drank beer, wine and soft drinks instead of water.

3. *Manner, Distance, Frequency Clauses* - As, As + Adverb + As

   People conserved water as public officials had requested.
   People conserved water as often as they could.

4. *Reason Clause* - Because, Since, As

   Californians still practice conservation because they remember the distressful years of the water shortage.

5. *Result Clause* - So + Adjective/Adverb + That
Such (a) + Adjective + Noun + That

Rainfall was so plentiful that streams, lakes, and reservoirs were filled at the end of the rainy season.

The drought was such a depressing experience that Californians will remember it for a long time.

6. *Purpose Clause* - So That, In Order That

Concerned citizens are still conserving water, however, so that they will not have to suffer so extremely again.

7. *Contrast, Concession Clause* - Although, Even Though, Though

Although the farmers needed the rain, the sudden downpour ruined their crops.

The people were delighted with the change in the weather pattern even though the rain was excessive.

8. *Strong Contrast Clause* - While, Whereas

While Californians were having a severe drought, Easterners were having record snowfalls.

Easterners were having record snowfalls, whereas Californians were having a severe drought.

Practice 30: Adverbial Clauses I

Complete the following sentences by adding adverbial clauses as indicated in the parentheses.

STEP 1 Circle the subordinator and punctuate the sentence if necessary.

STEP 2 Remember the sequence of tenses rule:

a) When the verb in the independent clause is in the present tense, the verb in the dependent clause is in whatever tense expresses the desired meaning.

b) When the verb in the independent clause is in the past tense, the verb in the dependent clause is also in a past tense form.

Example I reviewed my class notes (before) I took the final exam. (time)

1. I bought all of my textbooks _____

_____ (time)

2. Washington, D.C. is _____

_____ (place)

3. Tom rode on the subway _____

_____ (distance)

4. _____

_____ the company hired me. (reason)

5. I study in the library _____

_____ (purpose)

6. _____

_____ I will study for a master's degree. (time)

7. I registered for my classes early _____

_____ (purpose)

8. A serious student spends time studying _____

_____ (reason)

9. Tom wanted to become a doctor _____

_____ (concession)

10. _____

_____ many young couples prefer living together. (concession)

11. Many people drove big gas-consuming cars _____

_____ (time)

12. Pollution becomes a problem _____

_____ (place)

13. City living is stressful _____

_____ (strong contrast)

14. A single person leads a carefree life _____

_____ (strong contrast)

Practice 31: Adverbial Clauses II

STEP 1 Fill in the blanks with the correct adverbial subordinators.
STEP 2 Punctuate the sentences correctly.

Several years ago _____ (time) I was driving toward San Francisco from Marin County a tire on my old Volkswagen blew out. _____ (time phrase) I realized my problem I brought my car to a stop on the side of the highway. _____ (time) I was checking the damaged tire a man stopped his car. _____ (contrast) he could not help me I was glad he was there. _____ (time) he left he told me that he would notify the highway patrol. _____ (time) he left I felt nervous again _____ (reason) it was dark foggy and windy. _____ (at any time) I saw a car approaching I thought it was someone coming to help me. _____ (time) an hour had passed I heard the sirens of a tow truck and my heart sang songs of joy. _____ (time) the driver would tow my car to San Francisco I had to pay him _____ (reason) I didn't carry insurance. Now _____ (any place) I decide to go I doublecheck my car _____ (time) I leave. _____ (contrast) I carry insurance I still don't want to have such a frightening experience again.

WRITING PRACTICE

Using the above paragraph as a model, write an original description of a personal experience, such as an accident, a live concert, a fire, or a wedding. Use as many adverbial clauses as you can and underline the subordinators.

Chapter 13

RELATIVE CLAUSES

Relative Pronouns and Adverbs

A **relative**, or **adjective**, **clause** is a dependent clause introduced by a relative pronoun or relative adverb. It functions as an adjective; that is, it modifies or describes a noun in the independent clause.

A relative pronoun replaces a noun phrase or pronoun in the dependent clause. A relative adverb replaces a prepositional phrase in the dependent clause.

> ... *which is located in the Pacific Ocean*
> ... *that is causing a major problem in the auto industry*
> ... *who ran for mayor of our city last year*
> ... *whose main office is in Chicago*
> ... *whom I told you about*
> ... *where we shop for groceries*

The relative pronouns are *who, whom, which, that,* and *whose + noun.*
The relative adverbs are *where, when* and *why.*

Who refers only to people and is a subject pronoun.
Whom refers only to people and is an object pronoun.
Which refers to things and is a subject or object pronoun.
That refers to things or people and is a subject or object pronoun in restrictive clauses only.
Whose + noun refers to things or people and is a possessive.
Where refers to a place.
When refers to a time.
Why refers to a reason.

Since the relative clause is a dependent clause, it must be combined with an independent clause to form a complex sentence. The relative clause comes right after the noun phrase it modifies (the antecedent).

Guam Island, which is located in the Pacific Ocean, was a strategic military base during World War II.

A situation that is causing a major problem in the auto industry is the popularity of Japanese imports.

Tom Brown, who ran for mayor of our city last year, is a friend of my brother.

He went to work for Computex Corporation, whose main offices are in Chicago.

She is the wonderful counselor whom I told you about.

The store where we shop for groceries is closed for vacation.

PUNCTUATION OF RELATIVE CLAUSES

Relative clauses are classified as *restrictive* or *nonrestrictive*. The information in a restrictive clause is necessary to identify the noun phrase it modifies. Do not use a comma to separate the restrictive clause from the independent clause.

The information in a nonrestrictive relative clause is not necessary to identify the noun phrase it modifies; it merely provides additional information. Use a comma to separate the nonrestrictive clause from the independent clause.

Restrictive   *The attorney who represented Mrs. Gaines in her medical lawsuit received a fee of $550,000.*

A body of land that is surrounded on three sides by water is called a peninsula.

Nonrestrictive   *Mr. Walter Winter, who represented Mrs. Gaines in her medical lawsuit, received a fee of $550,000.*

San Francisco, which is surrounded on three sides by water, is a peninsula.

A restrictive clause is not separated from the main clause by any punctuation.

A nonrestrictive clause *is* separated from the main clause by commas.

Practice 32: Restrictive and Nonrestrictive Clauses

STEP 1   Underline the relative clause or clauses. (Some sentences have two.)

STEP 2   Write R for a restrictive and NR for a nonrestrictive clause in the parentheses.

STEP 3   Add commas to the nonrestrictive clauses.

Example (**R**) The senator whose family was politically active in Massachusetts visited China.

 (**NR**) Senator Kennedy, whose family was politically active in Massachusetts, visited China.

(   ) 1. The sun which in forty minutes can produce enough solar energy to meet man's needs for a year is one of the earth's potential sources of power.

(   ) 2. All tobacco companies whose goal is to get the public to buy their cigarettes claim that their particular brands have the lowest nicotine and tar content.

(   ) 3. According to an article which the professor cited we are at the door of the medical computer revolution.

(   ) 4. The machine that analyzes and delivers laboratory test and electrocardiogram results is a medical computer.

(   ) 5. Laser beams which are useful in both medicine and industry were first predicted in science fiction stories thirty years ago.

(   ) 6. Physicians who feed patient symptoms into the computer receive a list of diseases that fit the symptoms of their patients.

(   )   7. The country that has the highest per capita* income is not the United States which is only in third place.

(   )   8. Kuwait which is a small country in the Middle East is in first place.

(   )   9. It was a thrilling experience to meet the author of the book that we had been reading all semester.

(   ) 10. The public is highly suspicious of the oil industry whose profits have been increasing in spite of the energy crisis.

(   ) 11. Carbohydrates which are composed of carbon, hydrogen and oxygen are organic compounds.

(   ) 12. Foreigners who do not understand American "body language" may become confused when they talk to Americans.

(   ) 13. People who use body language to express themselves are interesting to watch.

(   ) 14. Italian people who use their hands a lot when they are talking are especially well-known body-language practitioners.

(   ) 15. The man whom my sister married is Italian; he uses his hands almost continually when he is carrying on a conversation.

(   ) 16. First National Bank where we have our savings account recently raised its interest rates, so we are now earning more on our savings.

(   ) 17. The president gave several reasons why he didn't want to sign the bill, but his opponents didn't believe any of them.

(   ) 18. Americans celebrate their Independence Day on July 4th which is the day when the Declaration of Independence was signed; it is not the day when the United States actually achieved independence.

(   ) 19. All businesses are closed on Christmas Day when Christians celebrate the birth of Jesus Christ.

(   ) 20. Professor Rosenbaum whose courses are highly popular with the students was given an award for outstanding teaching.

RELATIVE PRONOUNS AS SUBJECTS

The relative pronoun may be the subject of its own clause.

A relative clause in the subject pattern is formed with
Who
Which   +   **VERB**   +   **COMPLEMENT**
That

In the examples below, notice how sentences a and b are combined to form a new sentence c, which contains a relative clause:

a. People want to save time and energy.

b. They use microwave ovens.

c. People who use microwave ovens want to save time and energy.

a. Ovens use microwave energy.

b. They are capable of cooking foods quickly.

c. Ovens that are capable of cooking foods quickly use microwave energy.

---

per capita: per person (literally, "per head" in Latin)

a. An electron tube produces microwaves.

b. Microwaves cook foods quickly.

c. An electron tube produces microwaves, <u>which cook foods quickly</u>.

a. Microwave ovens have push-button controls.

b. They defrost and cook food automatically.

c. Microwave ovens, <u>which defrost and cook foods automatically</u>, have pushbutton controls.

Practice 33: Relative Pronouns as Subjects

STEP 1 Look for nouns and pronouns that are the same in both sentences.
STEP 2 Change the noun or pronoun in the second sentence to a relative pronoun to make a relative clause. Use *that* wherever possible.
STEP 3 Combine it with the first sentence to make a complex sentence containing a relative clause. Remember to put the relative clause immediately after the noun it modifies.
STEP 4 Add commas if the relative clause is nonrestrictive.

Example   Mr. Lawson passed the bar examination*.
Mr. Lawson teaches political science.

Mr. Lawson, who teaches political science, passed the bar examination.

1. John Fish explained the tapeworm's complex structure.
   He is a research biologist.

   _____

   _____

2. While he lectured, he showed us a slide.
   The slide diagrammed the various parts of the tapeworm's structure.

   _____

   _____

3. Words in English are often difficult for foreigners to pronounce.
   They begin with the consonants *th*.

   _____

   _____

4. Foreigners also have difficulty with English spelling.
   English spelling is not always logical.

   _____

   _____

5. The drugs have the same effects on human beings.
   They are used on experimental animals.

   _____

   _____

bar examination: the examination that law
students must pass in order to
practice law

6. Scientists must experiment on animals.
They closely duplicate the functions of the human body.

_____

_____

7. A person must be able to work logically.
A person wants to be a computer programmer.

_____

_____

8. The thyroid is an endocrine gland.
It controls our growth.

_____

_____

WRITING PRACTICE

Write six sentences about your major subject or future career. Three should contain restrictive relative clauses, and three should contain nonrestrictive relative clauses.

In the relative clauses, use *who*, *which*, or *that* in the subject position. The relative clause may modify any noun in the independent clause.

RELATIVE PRONOUNS AS OBJECTS

The relative pronoun is the object of its own clause.

A relative clause in the object pattern is formed with:
Whom
Which + **SUBJECT** + **VERB** + **COMPLEMENT**
That

Note: The relative pronoun may be omitted in the object pattern in restrictive clauses only.

In the examples that follow, notice how sentences a and b are combined to form a new sentence c containing a relative clause.

Restrictive
a. The science magazine is published in England.
b. The professor discussed the science magazine.
c. The science magazine that the professor discussed is published in England.
  The science magazine   the professor discussed is published in England.

a. The professor is Dr. White.
b. You should see Dr. White.
c. The professor whom you should see is Dr. White.
  The professor   that you should see is Dr. White.
  The professor   you should see is Dr. White.

Nonrestrictive
a. Dr. White is an ecologist.
b. You met Dr. White in my office.
c. Dr. White, whom you met in my office, is an ecologist.

a. The Space Museum in Washington, D.C. has many fascinating displays.

b. Our science class visited the Space Museum during Easter vacation.

c. The Space Museum in Washington, D.C., <u>which our science class visited during Easter vacation</u>, has many fascinating displays.

Practice 34: Relative Pronouns as Objects

STEP 1 Change the second sentence into a relative clause.
STEP 2 Combine it with the first sentence and add punctuation if it is nonrestrictive.
STEP 3 Write restrictive relative clauses with and without a relative pronoun.

1. This is the geology book.
   The professor recommended it.

   _____

   _____

   _____

2. Geologists are searching for uranium.
   Our nation needs uranium.

   _____

   _____

   _____

3. Uranium is an important source of energy.
   Nuclear power plants use uranium.

   _____

   _____

   _____

4. My Aunt Bess had open-heart surgery last week.
   We had all considered Aunt Bess "a goner*."

   _____

   _____

   _____

5. Dr. Andrew Hunter is a world-famous heart surgeon.
   We consulted Dr. Hunter.

   _____

   _____

   _____

"a goner": slang for someone who is dead or dying

6. We wanted to see a doctor.
   Our family physician had recommended him.

   _____

   _____

   _____

7. We didn't want Dr. Hunter because of his high fees.
   We couldn't afford his high fees.

   _____

   _____

   _____

8. We finally hired Dr. Hunter anyway, and he recommended immediate open-heart surgery.
   Aunt Bess had hoped to avoid open-heart surgery.

   _____

   _____

   _____

9. The operation was a success.
   Dr. Hunter performed the operation yesterday.

   _____

   _____

   _____

WRITING PRACTICE

Write six sentences using relative clauses in the object pattern. (Remember your two choices with restrictive clauses using *that* or dropping the pronoun.)

POSSESSIVE RELATIVE CLAUSES

These clauses are used to show possession. As with other relative clauses, they may be used as subjects or as objects. When used as a subject, the *whose* + *noun* phrase is the subject of its clause.

A relative clause in the subject pattern is formed with:
   Whose + NOUN   +   VERB   +   COMPLEMENT
The relative pronoun *whose* replaces a possessive word.

In the sentences below, notice how sentences a and b are combined to form a new sentence c which contains a relative possessive clause in the subject pattern:

Possessive—Subject Pattern

a. Opportunities for college graduates may be on the upswing.

b. College graduates' degrees are in business and engineering.

c. Opportunities for college graduates whose degrees are in business and engineering may be on the upswing.

a. A meteorologist cannot forecast conditions a month in advance.

b. A meteorologist's job is to make weather predictions.

c. A meteorologist, <u>whose job is to make weather predictions</u>, cannot forecast conditions a month in advance.

a. A population of between 252 and 373 million people for the year 2025 is predicted by the U.S. Census Bureau.

b. The U.S. Census Bureau's figures take into consideration projected births, deaths, and immigration.

c. A population of between 252 and 373 million people for the year 2025 is predicted by the U.S. Census Bureau, <u>whose figures take into consideration projected births, deaths, and immigration</u>.

Practice 35: Possessive Clauses—Subject Pattern

STEP 1 Change the second sentence into a relative clause.
STEP 2 Combine it with the first sentence and add punctuation if it is nonrestrictive.

1. Denver still has dirty air problems.
   Denver's pollution is not considered serious.

   _____

   _____

2. Securities Corporation's president is Mr. Mann.
   His expertise on financial investments is well known.

   _____

   _____

3. Large corporations can afford costly research and development.
   Large corporations' investments lead to new manufacturing techniques.

   _____

   _____

4. Companies that manufacture products usually spend large sums of money for advertising to attract consumers.
   Consumers' business is necessary for profits.

   _____

   _____

5. A manufacturer can sell to consumers at lower prices.
   A manufacturer's costs are lower because of mass production.

   _____

   _____

6. Stockholders are not responsible for a corporation's debts.
   Stockholders' financial liability is limited.

   _____

   _____

7. First Space Bank publishes a brochure for women investors.
   The bank's president is a woman.

   _____

   _____

Possessive relative clauses can also be in the object pattern. In that case, the relative pronoun phrase (*whose* + a noun) is the object of the verb or main statement of the relative clause.

A possessive relative clause in the object pattern is formed with:
Whose + NOUN + SUBJECT + VERB + COMPLEMENT

Again, notice how sentences a and b are combined to form a new sentence c which contains a relative possessive clause.

Possessive—Object Pattern

a. Farmers depend on meteorologists.

b. They need meteorologists' accurate forecasts for successful agricultural planning.

c. Farmers depend on meteorologists, whose accurate forecasts they need for successful agricultural planning.

a. Independent research laboratories test many new products on the market.

b. Consumers trust their evaluations.

c. Independent research laboratories, whose evaluations consumers trust, test many new products on the market.

a. The young woman traveled 1700 miles across Australia's western wilderness.

b. I read her article in *National Geographic*.

c. The young woman whose article I read in *National Geographic* traveled 1700 miles across Australia's western wilderness.

Practice 36: Possessive Clauses—Object Pattern

STEP 1 Change the second sentence into a relative clause.
STEP 2 Combine it with the first sentence and add punctuation if it is nonrestrictive.

1. The community college offers vocational training.
   I received the college's bulletin in the mail.

   _____

   _____

2. Bay View City College is popular with many students in the city.
   My brother took the college's computer programming class last summer.

   _____

   _____

3. The King of Xanadu was deposed by a revolution.
   The United States had supported his government.

   _____

   _____

4. The author of this poem died penniless and heartbroken.
   The world never recognized his talent.

   _____

   _____

5. Mr. French is the state's budget director.
   The newspaper published his report yesterday.

   _____

   _____

6. There are several women claiming to be Princess Anastasia of Russia.
   The revolutionaries executed her entire family in 1918.

   _____

   _____

7. The actress has played in several successful films.
   I can't remember her name right now.

   _____

   _____

WRITING PRACTICE

Write six sentences containing possessive relative clauses introduced with the relative pronoun *whose* + noun. Try to write three sentences in the subject pattern and three in the object pattern.

RELATIVE PRONOUNS AS OBJECTS OF PREPOSITIONS

A relative pronoun can be the object of a preposition in its own clause.

A relative clause in the object of preposition pattern is formed in two ways:

                    Whom
Preposition +   **Which**   + SUBJECT + VERB + COMPLEMENT
                    Whose + NOUN

Whom
Which
That   + SUBJECT + VERB + COMPLEMENT + PREPOSITION
Whose + NOUN

The first pattern is more formal than the second pattern.

The relative pronoun *that* can only be used in the informal pattern (preposition at the end of the clause) in restrictive clauses.

Notice how, in these sets, sentences a and b are combined to form a new sentence c, which contains a relative clause.

a. The total environment includes the geosphere, the biosphere, and the sociosphere.

b. Scientists are interested in the total environment.

c. The total environment, in which scientists are interested, includes the geosphere, the biosphere, and the sociosphere.

   The total environment, which scientists are interested in, includes the geosphere, the biosphere, and the sociosphere.

a. The candidate didn't win the election.

b. I voted for the candidate.

c. The candidate <u>for whom I voted</u> didn't win the election.
The candidate <u>whom I voted for</u> didn't win the election.
The candidate <u>that I voted for</u> didn't win the election.

a. The names of the victims are unknown.

b. This monument was built in the victims' memory.

c. The names of the victims <u>in whose memory this monument was built</u> are unknown.

Practice 37: Relative Pronouns as Objects of Prepositions

STEP 1 Change the second sentence into a relative clause.
STEP 2 Combine it with the first sentence and punctuate it if it is nonrestrictive.
STEP 3 Write each new sentence twice: once in the formal pattern and once in an informal pattern.

1. Finding reasonably priced housing is becoming a major problem.
Many young couples are concerned about the problem.

   _____

   _____

   _____

   _____

2. Single-family homes are becoming harder to find.
Buyers must pay high prices for single-family homes.

   _____

   _____

   _____

   _____

3. There are many young people.
Such homes would be ideal for many young people, yet they can't afford them.

   _____

   _____

   _____

   _____

4. One solution may be condominiums.
Many families occupy single units in condominiums.

   _____

   _____

   _____

   _____

5. Many former apartment buildings are being converted into "condos."
   Buyers must still pay high prices in addition to monthly maintenance fees for
   them.

   _____

   _____

   _____

   _____

6. Another type of housing is the two-master-bedroom dwelling.
   Two couples live in this dwelling.

   _____

   _____

   _____

   _____

7. One problem with this type of housing is choosing the people.
   You are going to share living space with these people.

   _____

   _____

   _____

   _____

8. You must get along well with the people.
   You are going to live with these people.

   _____

   _____

   _____

   _____

9. Since you will be sharing a kitchen and a living room, a strict time schedule
   will have to be observed.
   Both couples must work around this time schedule.

   _____

   _____

   _____

   _____

WRITING PRACTICE

Write six sentences about your house or apartment, or about your family. Each
should contain a relative clause in the object of preposition pattern.

RELATIVE PRONOUNS IN PHRASES OF QUANTITY

A relative pronoun is also often the object of a phrase of quantity: *some of which, one of whom, each of whom, all of whom,* etc. These clauses may be in the subject or object pattern.

A relative clause in the prepositional phrase pattern is formed with:

Some of which ⎱
One of which ⎰ + SUBJECT + VERB + COMPLEMENT
All of whom ⎱ +   VERB + COMPLEMENT
Each of whom ⎰
      etc.

All such clauses are nonrestrictive.

In the following sample sets, notice how sentences a and b are combined to form a new sentence c, which contains a relative clause:

a. The members of the special commission on crime meet weekly.

b. Some of them were appointed by the mayor.

c. The members of the special commission on crime, some of whom were appointed by the mayor, meet weekly.

a. A witness to the crime has to identify the suspect by viewing a line-up of people.

b. One of those people is the accused person.

c. A witness to the crime has to identify the suspect by viewing a line-up of people, one of whom is the accused person.

a. As an experiment, the television station decided to show only movies.

b. I had already seen most of the movies.

c. As an experiment, the television station decided to show only movies, most of which I had already seen.

Practice 38: Relative Pronouns in Phrases of Quantity

STEP 1 Change the second sentence to a relative clause.
STEP 2 Combine it with the first sentence and punctuate it, following the examples above.

1. The students wrote a letter of protest to the Dean.
   Half of the students had received a failing grade in chemistry.

   _____

   _____

2. The State of Nevada has very little agriculture.
   Most of the state is desert land.

   _____

   _____

3. My three older sisters are living abroad.
   Each of them attends a different university.

   _____

   _____

4. At our school's annual international fair, I ate a lot of native foods.
   I had not tasted some of the foods before.

   _____

   _____

5. Medical researchers have tested thousands of drugs on cancer victims.
   Most of the drugs prove to be useless.

   _____

   _____

6. Humphrey Bogart made many films.
   One of the films was *Casablanca*.

   _____

   _____

7. She has seven brothers and two sisters.
   One of her brothers is the head of the family.

   _____

   _____

WRITING PRACTICE:

Write six sentences of your own that contain relative pronouns in prepositional phrases of quantity.

Relative Adverbial Clauses

Relative clauses may also be introduced by the relative adverbs *where*, *when* and *why*.

Where replaces a prepositional phrase of place.
When replaces a prepositional phrase of time.
Where and *when* relative clauses may be restrictive or nonrestrictive.
Why introduces a reason and is always restrictive. (*That* may be used in place of *why*.)

Notice how sentences a and b can be combined to form a new sentence c, which contains a relative clause.

a. The village was destroyed by an earthquake.
b. My mother was born in the village.
c. The village where my mother was born was destroyed by an earthquake.

a. Kyoto is famous for its many beautiful temples and shrines.

b. My mother was born in Kyoto.

c. Kyoto, <u>where my mother was born</u>, is famous for its many beautiful temples and shrines.

a. December 25 is the day.

b. Christians celebrate the birth of Jesus Christ on that day.

c. December 25 is the day <u>when Christians celebrate the birth of Jesus Christ.</u>

a. Many people exchange gifts on December 25.

b. Christians celebrate the birth of Jesus Christ on December 25.

c. Many people exchange gifts on December 25, <u>when Christians celebrate the birth of Jesus Christ.</u>

a. The slavery issue was only one reason.

b. The northern and southern states fought against each other during the Civil War for a reason.

c. The slavery issue was only one reason <u>why (that) the northern and southern states fought against each other during the Civil War.</u>

Practice 39: Relative Adverbial Clauses

STEP 1 Change the second sentence to a relative clause introduced by *where*, *when*, or *why*.

STEP 2 Combine it with the first sentence and punctuate it if it is nonrestrictive.

1. 1849 was the year.
   Gold was discovered in California in that year.

   _____

   _____

2. By 1850, thousands of people had joined the "California Gold Rush."
   California became a state in 1850.

   _____

   _____

3. Many large cities contain ethnic neighborhoods.
   Members of the different ethnic groups live in those neighborhoods.

   _____

   _____

4. San Francisco, for example, has a very large "Chinatown."
   Thousands of Chinese people live in Chinatown.

   _____

   _____

5. One reason may be that they can find familiar food.
   People like to live together with their own people for a reason.

   _____

   _____

6. Another reason may be that people can communicate more easily in their native language.
Ethnic neighborhoods develop in large cities for a reason.

_____

_____

7. No one can predict the day.
A strong earthquake will strike California on a day.

_____

_____

8. Most people remember what they were doing on the day.
President Kennedy was assassinated on that day.

_____

_____

9. Most people remember what they were doing on November 22, 1963.
President Kennedy was assassinated on that day.

_____

_____

10. We may never know the real reason.
President Kennedy was assassinated for a reason.

_____

_____

WRITING PRACTICE

Write six sentences of your own. Use each of the relative adverbs *where, when,* and *why* twice.

Summary of Relative Clause Patterns

Relative Pronouns

Who   Subject pattern
Refers only to people, both singular and plural.

> *The instructor who teaches intermediate accounting is a senior analyst with Banking Investments, Inc.*
>
> *Instructors who teach only night classes do not usually hold regular office hours.*

Whom   Object pattern
Refers only to people, both singular and plural.

> *My physics professor, whom the students respect, is retiring at the end of this semester.*
>
> *My mother and father, whom I haven't seen in a year, are coming to visit me during vacation.*
>
> *The person whom I look up to the most is my father.*
>
> *The English teachers, most of whom have Ph.D. degrees, are on strike for higher salaries and smaller classes.*

Which Subject and object pattern
Refers to things, both singular and plural. Used in nonrestrictive clauses.

> *Electrical Engineering 455, which is a review course, is offered during the summer session.*
>
> *Electrical Engineering 455, which I signed up for last summer, was very helpful.*
>
> *You must maintain at least a B average in your major courses, all of which must be taken at this college.*

That Subject and object pattern
Refers to things or people, both singular and plural.

That can be substituted for *who, whom* and *which* in restrictive clauses only.

> *The course that reviews mechanical engineering is Engineering 456.*
>
> *The course that I signed up for has been cancelled.*
>
> *The person that I look up to the most is my father.*

Whose + noun Subject and object pattern
Shows possession and refers to people or things, both singular and plural.

> *College students, whose incomes are usually fixed, may have a hard time in an inflationary period.*
>
> *I don't remember the name of the music teacher whose course I took last semester.*

Relative Adverbs

Where Refers to a place.

> *The city where I live is the capital of my country.*
>
> *Riyadh, where I live, is the capital of my country.*

When Refers to a time.

> *I can't remember a night when I didn't have a mountain of homework to do.*
>
> *Last night, when I couldn't sleep, I read an entire novel.*

Why Refers to a reason.

> *There are several reasons why I didn't call you last night.*

The Relative Clause

1. The relative clause is a dependent clause introduced by a relative pronoun or adverb subordinator: *who, whom, which, that, whose, where, when, why.*

2. The relative clause is used as an adjective and modifies a noun or noun phrase in the independent clause.

   > *The woman that is giving the lecture tomorrow is a meteorologist.*
   >
   > *Ms. Brown, whom we will hear tomorrow, is a meteorologist.*

3. When the relative clause gives identifying information about the noun phrase it modifies, it is *restrictive* and is not set off with commas.

   > *The experts who predict future global climate are called climatologists.*

4. When the relative clause gives additional but unnecessary information about the noun phrase it modifies, it is *nonrestrictive* and is set off with commas.

   > *Earthquakes, which are among the most destructive natural disasters, cannot be predicted with any accuracy.*

Practice 40: Reviewing Relative Clauses

Insert relative clauses into the following short essay.

STEP 1 Change the sentences in parentheses into relative clauses and write them in the blanks provided.

STEP 2 Add commas if necessary.

A Day in Central Park

1   Yesterday was a beautiful spring day, so Mei-Ling _____
                                                              (Mei-Ling comes from China)

and Maryam _____ decided to go
                              (Maryam is from Iran)

sightseeing. The subway _____ made
                                           (They rode in a subway)

several stops before they arrived at their destination. The Central Park Station

5   _____ was crowded with people
    (They got off at the Central Park Station)

_____. Unfortunately, Mei-Ling and
(The people were waiting for their trains)

Maryam lost each other in the crowd, but after some anxious moments, they saw

each other on the escalator _____.
                                           (They rode on the escalator up to the street level)

Arriving at the park, they decided to stroll around for a while. They strolled on the

10   paths _____ and watched the people
              (The paths were bordered by beautiful flowers)

_____

(Some of the people were relaxing on the grass and some of the people were

_____. An hour later, Mei-Ling and Maryam decided to leave. As
playing games)

they were crossing the street, they saw a crowd of people _____
                                                                              (The people were

_____. Squeezing themselves through the crowd, they saw a funny
laughing and applauding)

15   man dressed in a black tuxedo, a top hat and white gloves. He had an unusual face

_____. He also had brightly painted
(The face was painted white)

red lips and black makeup around his eyes _____
                                                              (The black makeup around his eyes

_____. Maryam asked a bystander
made him look like a clown)

who this odd-looking fellow was. The woman said that he was a mime. She further

20   explained that a mime is an actor _____.
                                                      (A mime acts out situations without speaking)

He makes only body movements and gestures _____

(The body movements and gestures

_____. While Mei-Ling and Maryam

are stiff and mechanical)

were listening to the woman, the mime began to mimic a woman _____

(A woman was

_____. The mime followed stiffly behind the unsuspecting woman

walking by)

25   to the entrance of a nearby store _____

(She disappeared into the store)

_____. The audience laughed as he returned to the center of his

sidewalk stage _____ much to the

(He continued his act on the sidewalk stage)

delight of the crowd. He continued to do other clownish acts such as walking up an

imaginary ladder and walking on a tightrope. After the mime had completed his

30   performance, he passed around his top hat _____

(The audience dropped money into his

Mei-Ling and Maryam really enjoyed seeing a different form

top hat)

of entertainment _____

(They decided to tell their classmates about the different form

_____.

of entertainment in their next conversation class)

WRITING PRACTICE

Using the above paragraph as a model, choose one of the following topics and write

A. A description of an interesting place you have visited such as Disneyland, Marine World, Liberty Island, a national or state park, etc.

B. A description of an interesting city or town in the United States that you have visited.

Use as many adjectives clauses as you can, and underline the subordinators.

Chapter 14

PASSIVE SENTENCES

Sentences are written in either active or passive voice. In **active sentences** the subject performs the action of the verb.

ACTIVE VOICE STRUCTURE

Subject	Verb	Direct Object	Complement
The management	will prosecute	shoplifters.	
Everyone	may purchase	tickets	at the box office.
People	use	computers	in modern industry.
Meteorologists	gave	hurricanes	feminine names until recently.
You	should take	the medicine	three times a day.

In **passive sentences** the subject *receives* the action of the verb. The direct object of the active sentence becomes the subject of the passive sentence. Because every sentence in English must have a subject, passive sentences can be formed only from *transitive verbs*, which can take direct objects.

Hence, you cannot say "He was died," because *die* is an intransitive verb. In this instance, you would have to use the verb *kill* to make a passive sentence: "He was killed."

PASSIVE VOICE STRUCTURE

Subject	Verb	Complement
Shoplifters	will be prosecuted.	
Tickets	may be purchased	at the box office.
Computers	are used	in modern industry.
Hurricanes	were given	feminine names until recently.
The medicine	should be taken	three times a day.

FORMATION OF PASSIVE SENTENCES

A passive sentence is composed of the following parts:
SUBJECT + some tense of BE + PAST PARTICIPLE + AGENT

---

1. The object of an active sentence becomes the subject of the passive sentence.
2. The tense is carried by *BE*.
3. The subject of the active sentence becomes the agent of the passive sentence.
4. The agent may sometimes be omitted.

Verb Tenses in Passive Sentences

PRESENT TENSES

Simple Present	*Big cars are bought by status-conscious people.*
Present Continuous	*Big cars are being bought by Americans even though they consume a lot of fuel.*
Present Perfect	*Car manufacturers have been advised to build smaller cars.*
Present Modals	*Steps must be taken to educate the public about the economy of smaller cars.*

PAST TENSES

Simple Past	*Detroit's new fuel-efficient cars were shown in dealer showrooms throughout the country.*
Past Continuous	*Until recently, fuel-efficient cars were not being designed by Detroit car manufacturers.*
Past Perfect	*American cars had always been designed primarily for comfort until the price of gas started to rise.*
Perfect Modals	*Car manufacturers might not have been required by the government to design fuel-efficient cars if there hadn't been a gasoline shortage.*

FUTURE TENSES

"Will"	*Non-military satellites will be used to assist scientists in mapping and forecasting weather conditions.*
"Going to"	*Factories, laboratories and cities are going to be built in space in the future.*
Future Perfect	*By the 1990s, the space shuttle will have been put into regular use as a cargo carrier.*

The Agent in Passive Sentences

A passive sentence can be written in two ways: with the agent or without the agent.

With the Agent

The agent in passive sentences answers the question *by whom* or *by what* the action was performed.

The agent is named if it is important or necessary to complete the meaning or understanding of the sentence.

The accident was caused <u>by pilot error</u>.
The woman was murdered <u>by her husband</u>.
Noise is produced <u>by the irregular vibration of some nearby object</u>.

Without the Agent

The agent in a passive sentence is not named under certain conditions:

---

1. When the identity of the agent is understood and does not have to be mentioned.
   The governor has been re-elected to another term (by the voters).
   Spanish is spoken in many countries of the world (by people).

2. When the identity of the agent is unimportant.
   Television newscasts are translated into both Spanish and Chinese in cities with large numbers of Spanish and Chinese speakers (by someone).
   After the metal had been heated to 1,250 degrees (by someone), *it was plunged into boiling water* (by someone).

3. When the identity of the agent is unknown:
   My car was stolen last night (by someone).
   An error has been made in the computer input data (by someone).

USES OF PASSIVE

It is usually better to write sentences with active verbs because active verbs are more direct, but there are two circumstances in which the passive voice is preferred:

When you want to give your writing an objective and impersonal tone, use the passive.

Because the "doer" of an action may be omitted in passive sentences, the tone is more objective. For this reason, passive is often used in scientific and business writing, as well as in newspaper reports.

For example, suppose you had to write a report describing a scientific experiment that you had performed. You should try to maintain an objective and impersonal tone in your report and avoid using either *I* or *you* as subject pronouns.

Poor   *I submerged a length of copper wire in a vegetable oil bath. I varied the temperature of the bath, and then I measured the current and voltage acting on the wire.*

Better   *A length of copper wire was submerged in a vegetable oil bath. The temperature of the bath was varied, and then the current and voltage acting on the wire were measured.*

When you want to focus attention on the "receiver" of an action, use the passive.

For example, if you were writing a paper about the discovery of the X-ray, you might write passive sentences such as:

This para- *The X-ray was discovered quite by accident. It was discovered by*
graph is   *a young German scientist named Wilhelm Roentgen in 1895. It was*
focused on *named "X-ray" because the letter "x" means "unknown" in mathe-*
the X-ray   *matics and science—and the mysterious ray discovered by Roentgen*
              was indeed unknown.

If you were to write the same information with active verbs, the reader might think your paper was about Wilhelm Roentgen, not about the X-ray.

This para- *Someone discovered the X-ray quite by accident. A young German*
graph is   *scientist named Wilhelm Roentgen discovered it in 1895. He named*
focused on *it "X-ray" because the letter "x" means "unknown" in mathematics*
Wilhelm   *and science—and indeed no one knew the mysterious ray that*
Roentgen   *Roentgen had discovered.*

The first paragraph, using the more objective-sounding passive voice, puts the emphasis in the proper place.

Practice 41: Passive Verb Forms I

Underline the passive verbs in the following paragraph.

This procedure is followed for the determination of the concentration of an exoenzyme that is produced by streptococcus. Before use, a simple serum sample must be diluted to a series of different concentrations (i.e., serial dilutions). Then, one drop of each dilution is placed in a separate and labeled tube. To each of these tubes, add two drops of enzyme reagent. These tubes are mixed gently and then are incubated for two minutes at 37 degrees Centigrade. The tubes are then removed from the incubator. While the tubes are being mixed, one drop of a 3 percent type O red-blood cell suspension is added to each tube, and the tubes are placed back into the incubator at 37 degrees Centigrade for one hour. The tubes are then examined for the presence or absence of the lyses of the red blood cells.

Practice 42: Passive Verb Forms II

Fill in the correct form of the passive verb in each blank by changing the active verb form into the passive verb form. Use present tenses.

A.

1   Forecasts _____ (make) in businesses regularly. They _____ (use) by many large companies and corporations as a preliminary step to outlining sales strategies*. Accurate predictions _____ (must make) because the future of a business depends on its sales. For example, Computex Corporation

5   manufactures pocket-size computers. The marketing manager depends on forecasts to plan marketing actions for their products. These forecasts _____

---

strategies: tactics, operations

(can make) by marketing strategists* for as large a territorial area as the East and

West Coasts or for each state or city. Furthermore, sales _____

(can forecast) for various time periods, ranging from as long as a year to a short

10   specific buying season such as Christmas. From the pertinent information that

_____ (has given) to the marketing manager, sales strategies for

the company's products _____ (will make) as accurately as possible.

B.

1   Laser light _____ (can use) for transmitting* power. Electrical

power _____ (translates) to laser light. At the end of the distant

beam, the reverse process takes place. Because fog or rain would interfere with

transmissions on earth, lasers _____ (must beam) through evacu-

5   ated* pipelines to prevent power loss. These pipelines _____ (must

make) perfectly straight in order to accommodate the arrow-like laser beam.

Mirrors _____ (require) to allow the beams to change directions

and go around corners.

Practice 43. Passive Sentences 1

Change the following active sentences to passive sentences.

STEP 1 Use the correct passive verb tense and underline it twice. Remember to
watch subject and verb agreement.

STEP 2 Add the agent if it is necessary and circle it.

Example   The Food and Drug Administration has outlined the rules for food labels.

The rules for food labels have been outlined by the (Food and Drug Administration.)

1. The Food and Drug Administration has ordered manufacturers to list the
ingredients of canned and packaged foods in decreasing order by weight.

_____

_____

2. Manufacturers must show the name of the product and the net contents on all
food labels.

_____

_____

3. Consumer groups are constantly reminding shoppers to read these labels
carefully.

_____

_____

_____

strategist: one who plans campaigns or   **evacuated:** emptied
operations
transmitting: sending

4. Many markets sell artificial foods such as imitation ice cream, mayonnaise, and maple syrup.

   _____

   _____

5. Many of these imitation foods might affect your health.

   _____

   _____

6. Health food stores do not sell imitation foods.

   _____

7. Many health-conscious people are buying natural foods.

   _____

8. Wise shoppers will consider both quality and economy when they shop.

   _____

   _____

9. Busy people will still buy frozen dinners regardless of cost.

   _____

   _____

10. People are going to spend less money on gourmet foods as food prices continue to rise.

   _____

   _____

Practice 44: Passive Sentences II

Write passive sentences about the given topics.

STEP 1 Use the passive verb form in the given tense.
STEP 2 Add an agent if necessary.

Example   The letter _____ (send/past)

The letter was sent by airmail to the company.

1. The book _____ (translate/present perfect)

   _____

   _____

2. Women _____ (liberate/present continuous)

   _____

   _____

3. Accountants _____ (train/present modal)

   _____

   _____

4. Engineers _____ (employ/present)

_____

_____

5. The letter _____ (write/future)

_____

_____

6. My homework _____ (correct/past perfect)

_____

_____

7. The club's meeting _____ (call off/perfect modal)

_____

_____

8. Our flight _____ (delay/future)

_____

9. His money _____ (not find/past)

_____

10. The new engine _____ (test/past continuous)

_____

_____

WRITING PRACTICE

Write six sentences in paragraph form about a topic with which you are familiar. Use the passive verb form.

Chapter 15

PARTICIPIAL PHRASES

A **participle** is a word formed from a verb that is used to modify nouns. Notice how an active voice verb is changed to a **present participle** by adding the suffix *-ing* to the verb.

CHANGING ACTIVE VERBS TO PARTICIPLES

Verbs	Present Participles
The custom *fascinates* me.	*fascinating*
The woman *jogged* in the park.	*jogging*
The hostages *will return* soon.	*returning*

An active voice verb (present, past, or future tense) becomes a present participle.

Now notice how a passive voice verb becomes a **past participle**.

CHANGING PASSIVE VERBS TO PARTICIPLES

Verbs	Past Participles
The movie *is rated* "X."	*X-rated*
The steak *was burned*.	*burned*
My heart *was broken*.	*broken*

A passive voice verb (present or past tense) becomes a past participle.

Note: The terms present and past participle are misleading because these forms have nothing to do with present tense or past tense. Rather, they are based on active or passive voice. The present participle comes from an active voice verb, and the past participle comes from a passive voice verb.

There are also perfect and continuous forms of participles, as shown on the following chart.

SUMMARY OF PARTICIPIAL PHRASE FORMS†

Forms	Active	Passive
The *general forms* do not indicate time: time is determined by the main clause verb	*Verb + ing* opening	*Verb + ed, en, t, d* opened bought taken sold
The *continuous form* emphasizes action going on *right now*; may also express future time		*Being + Past Participle* being opened
The *perfect form* emphasize that the action happened before the time of the main verb action	*Having + Past Participle* having opened	*Having Been + Past Participle* having been opened

†There is a sixth participle form, the perfect continuous active:

Having been opening jars all morning, my hand has become cramped.

It is not included here because it is not commonly used.

PARTICIPIAL PHRASES

A **participial phrase** is a reduction of a relative (adjective) clause or an adverbial clause. A participial phrase is:

PARTICIPLE + OBJECTS/COMPLEMENTS + MODIFIERS

> . . . *the fascinating Chinese custom*
> . . . *an extremely well-written paragraph*
> . . . *not knowing the correct answer*
> . . . *being too young to get married*
> . . . *wounded in his right hand*

PARTICIPIAL PHRASES FROM RELATIVE CLAUSES

Participial phrases may be formed by reducing subject-pattern relative clauses. To do this, delete the relative pronouns (*who, which,* or *that*) and change the verb to a participle.

Just like relative clauses, participial phrases can be restrictive or nonrestrictive. If the original relative clause was restrictive, the participial phrase formed from it will be also. Conversely, if the original clause was nonrestrictive, so will the phrase be. Participial phrases are made negative by placing the word *not* in front of the participle.

GENERAL FORMS IN THE ACTIVE VOICE

In the following sets of sentences, the relative clause in the first sentence has been changed to a participial phrase in the second. Notice that the general form in the active voice can be made from a present, past, or future tense verb. Also notice the similar punctuation of restrictive and nonrestrictive clauses and phrases.

a. Many students <u>who study at this university</u> are from foreign countries.

b. Many students <u>studying at this university</u> are from foreign countries.

a. Many students <u>who are studying at this university</u> are from foreign countries.

b. Many students <u>studying at this university</u> are from foreign countries.

a. The president's wife, <u>who looked tired after the long trip</u>, could hardly smile at the cheering crowd.

b. The president's wife, <u>looking tired after the long trip</u>, could hardly smile at the cheering crowd.

a. Commercial airliners <u>that were arriving at the same time as the president's plane</u> couldn't land immediately.

b. Commercial airliners <u>arriving at the same time as the president's plane</u> couldn't land immediately.

a. Everyone <u>who will go on our field trip next weekend</u> must sign up now.

b. Everyone <u>going on our field trip next weekend</u> must sign up now.

a. Linda, <u>who did not understand physics</u>, failed the course.

b. Linda, <u>not understanding physics</u>, failed the course.

Practice 45: Participial Phrases: Active Voice

STEP 1 Rewrite each sentence, changing the relative clause to a participial phrase.
STEP 2 Use the same punctuation as in the original sentence.

1. The expression "test tube baby," which refers to a baby whose existence began outside its mother's body, is misleading.

_____

_____

_____

2. The doctors who developed the procedure called it "in vitro fertilization."

_____

_____

3. In the future, the process of in vitro fertilization will be perfected, which will allow hundreds of childless couples to become parents.

_____

_____

_____

4. Doctors in the United States, who are just now learning about the procedure, haven't fully mastered the technique.

_____

_____

5. In early 1981, doctors in the United States performed the procedure on a woman who wanted to have a child.

_____

_____

6. The woman's physicians, who didn't know if they would be successful, would not release her name to the press.

_____

_____

GENERAL FORMS IN THE PASSIVE VOICE

The next sets of sentences show the general participial forms in the passive voice. Again, the relative clause in sentence a has been changed to a participial phrase in sentence b.

Notice that the general form in the passive can be formed from present or past tense verbs.

a. Children under the age of sixteen may not be admitted to movies that are rated X by the Film Censorship Board.

b. Children under the age of sixteen may not be admitted to movies rated X by the Film Censorship Board.

a. The president, who was surrounded by bodyguards, was only slightly wounded in the assassin's attack.

b. The president, surrounded by bodyguards, was only slightly wounded in the assassin's attack.

THE CONTINUOUS FORM

The continuous form emphasizes that the action is happening now (and, less frequently, in the future). It uses only one form of the verb "to be" as an auxiliary: *being*. Notice in these sentences how relative clauses have been changed to the passive continuous form of the participial phrase.

a. The law that is currently being debated is about abortion.

b. The law currently being debated is about abortion.

a. The circulars that were being distributed on campus support a woman's right to have an abortion.

b. The circulars being distributed on campus support a woman's right to have an abortion.

a. The movie that will be shown tomorrow was made by an anti-abortion group.

b. The movie being shown tomorrow was made by an anti-abortion group.

Practice 46: Participial Phrases: Passive Voice

STEP 1 Rewrite each sentence, changing the relative clause to a participial phrase.
STEP 2 Use the same punctuation as in the original sentence.
STEP 3 Use the continuous form to express action in the participle that is occurring *right now*; otherwise, use the general form.

1. The technique of in vitro fertilization, which was developed by a team of British physicians, is very complex.

_____

_____

2. An egg that is removed from the woman's ovary is fertilized by sperm in a laboratory dish.

_____

_____

3. The procedure of in vitro fertilization, which is now being tried out in the United States, has created considerable controversy.

_____

_____

4. Ethical questions that are being raised concern the increasing power of scientists to manipulate life.

_____

_____

5. Louise Brown, who was born in England, is the world's first test tube baby.

_____

_____

PERFECT FORMS

Remember that the perfect forms, whether active or passive, emphasize the completion of that action before the action of the main verb.

a. The secrets of the universe, <u>which have fascinated men for centuries</u>, are slowly being revealed.

b. The secrets of the universe, <u>having fascinated men for centuries</u>, are slowly being revealed.   (present perfect, active)

a. The film, <u>which had been shown too often in movie theaters</u>, did not attract a large audience when it was aired on television.

b. The film, <u>having been shown too often in movie theaters</u>, did not attract a large audience when it was aired on television.   (past perfect, passive)

Practice 47: Participial Phrases—The Perfect Forms

STEP 1 Rewrite each sentence, changing the relative clause to a participial phrase, as in the examples above.

STEP 2 Use the same punctuation as in the original sentence.

1. The parents of Louise Brown, who had long given up hope of having a child, do not care about the moral question posed by their daughter's birth.

   _____

   _____

2. Doctors, who have always had the responsibility to prolong life, are now able to create it.

   _____

   _____

3. In vitro fertilization, which has been performed only a few times since Louise Brown's birth, is still highly controversial.

   _____

   _____

4. Hundreds of childless couples, who have read about Louise Brown's birth, have written to the British doctors.

   _____

   _____

5. The creation of life in a laboratory, which has been accomplished once, will probably become less sensational as time goes on.

   _____

   _____

PUNCTUATING PARTICIPIAL PHRASES

Punctuating participial phrases is the same as for relative clauses—that is, it depends on whether the participial phrase is restrictive or nonrestrictive.

A *restrictive* participial phrase is not set off with commas because it is necessary to correctly identify the noun phrase it modifies.

A person belonging to the Sierra Club can participate in many outdoor activities.
Students hoping to graduate next semester must file petitions for graduation now.

A *nonrestrictive* participial phrase is set off by commas because it gives unnecessary additional information about the noun it modifies.

The Browns, belonging to the Sierra Club, participate in many outdoor activities.
Bob, hoping to graduate next semester, filed his petition for graduation today.

The position of the participial phrase depends on whether it is restrictive or nonrestrictive.

A restrictive participial phrase follows the word it modifies.

The computer science course <u>offered this semester</u> is COBOL.
The instructor <u>teaching the course</u> is a systems specialist.

A nonrestrictive participial phrase may be in the following positions:

1. **At the beginning of a sentence, before the noun it modifies.**
2. **In the middle of a sentence, after the noun it modifies.**
3. **At the end of a sentence if it modifies the entire sentence.**

Beginning of sentence:

> *<u>Working on computers for cars</u>, the American car industry will soon put electronic controls into every new automobile.*

Middle of sentence:

> *These future cars, <u>using safer fuels</u>, will pollute the air less.*

End of sentence:

> *The jury's verdict* was guilty, <u>shocking the defendant*</u>.*

Practice 48: Participial Phrases I —Mixed Forms

STEP 1 Rewrite the following sentences, changing the relative clauses to participial phrases.

STEP 2 Use the same punctuation (commas or no commas) as in the original sentence.

STEP 3 Use the appropriate participle form (active or passive—general, continuous, or perfect).

STEP 4 *If it is possible*, write each sentence twice: once with the participial phrase after the noun it modifies, and once with the participial phrase at the beginning of the sentence.

Example Alaska, which was purchased from Russia in 1867, became the 49th state of the United States in 1959.

a. Alaska, purchased from Russia in 1867, became the 49th state of the United States in 1959.

b. Purchased from Russia in 1867, Alaska became the 49th state of the United States in 1959.

---

verdict: decision, especially in a trial
defendant: a person on trial

1. The purchase of Alaska, which was negotiated by Secretary of State William Seward, became a good investment.

   a. _____

   _____

   b. _____

   _____

2. The people of the United States, who did not understand the value of the purchase, called it "Seward's Folly*."

   a. _____

   _____

   b. _____

   _____

3. The state, which was once connected to Russia by a land bridge, is now separated from it by only a few miles of water.

   a. _____

   _____

   b. _____

   _____

4. The native inhabitants of Alaska, who had migrated across this land bridge from Asia, can be considered distant cousins of modern Asians.

   a. _____

   _____

   b. _____

   _____

5. The Eskimos, who have lived in Alaska for millions of years, have adapted well to their harsh environment.

   a. _____

   _____

   b. _____

   _____

6. The Eskimos have to live in cold and darkness most of the year, which causes them to develop a lively sense of humor and a hospitable* attitude.

   a. _____

   _____

   b. _____

   _____

folly: silly act, foolishness
hospitable: welcoming, friendly toward strangers

7. The Eskimos, who had been hunters and fishermen before the arrival of the white man, are experiencing a difficult time adapting to modern ways.

a. _____

_____

b. _____

_____

8. A problem that is being discussed in the Alaskan government concerns the rights of Alaska's natives.

a. _____

_____

b. _____

_____

9. Those Eskimos who want to preserve their traditional way of life do not care about the modern world.

a. _____

_____

b. _____

_____

10. On the other hand, Eskimos who want to improve their standard of living hope that they can combine both worlds—old and new.

a. _____

_____

b. _____

_____

Practice 49: Participial Phrases II—Mixed Forms

Rewrite the following sentences, using participial phrases.

STEP 1 Change the relative clause into a participial phrase.
STEP 2 Combine the participial phrase with the independent clause.
Use different positions for the nonrestrictive participial phrases.
STEP 3 Punctuate the participial phrase if necessary.

Example   Thousands of people work with everyday issues and problems.
(who are currently employed as computer programmers)

Thousands of people currently employed as computer programmers work with everyday issues and problems.

1. A new computer is for household use.
(that is being advertised)

_____

_____

2. A home computer can perform many time-consuming tasks.
   (which will free individuals to do other things)

   _____

   _____

   _____

3. Some people do not want one in their homes.
   (who are frightened by the complexity of the computer)

   _____

   _____

   _____

4. They may be afraid that the computer will take control of their lives.
   (who have seen the movie *2001*)

   _____

   _____

   _____

5. They may be right, for computerized robots are already being used in many
   factories. (which are programmed to perform complex functions)

   _____

   _____

   _____

6. In addition, many aspects of business can be computerized.
   (which include accounting systems, inventory control and statistics)

   _____

   _____

   _____

7. In the schools, computers can teach students many subjects.
   (which will replace the need for personal contact with a tutor)

   _____

   _____

   _____

8. A big breakthrough in computer technology was the microprocessor, or "computer chip." (that was developed in the 1970s)

   _____

   _____

   _____

9. Information can now be put into a piece of silicon* no larger than the head of a
   nail. (which formerly required miles of computer tape)

   _____

   _____

   _____

silicon: a very hard, nonmetallic element

10. Furthermore, the price of computers will be even less in the future.
    (which has fallen for a number of years)

_____

_____

_____

WRITING PRACTICE

Write ten original sentences containing participial phrases. Use each participle form twice.

First, write ten sentences that contain relative clauses. Then, change the relative clause to a participial phrase and recopy your sentence.

Your paper should include both sentences, or a total of twenty sentences.

Participial Phrases from Adverbial Clauses

Participial phrases can also be formed from certain adverbial clauses, but only from those dealing with time and reason (see the section on adverbial clauses, page 155).

PARTICIPIAL PHRASES FROM TIME CLAUSES

Adverbial clauses introduced by the time subordinators *after*, *while*, *when*, *before*, *since*, and *as* may be reduced to participial phrases if the subjects of the adverbial clause and the independent clause are the same. One of those subordinators must be removed from the phrase; others must be removed in certain situations.

To change a time adverbial clause into a participial phrase:

1. Make sure that the subjects of the adverbial clause and the independent clause are the same.
2. Transfer the subject to the independent clause.
3. Change the verb form.
4. Delete or retain the subordinator according to the following rules:
   a. *Before* and *since* must be retained.
   b. *As* must be deleted.
   c. *After*, *while*, and *when* must be retained if the participial phrase follows the independent clause; otherwise, they may be omitted.

A participial phrase reduced from an adverbial clause may occupy several positions in a sentence. If it precedes the independent clause, it must be followed by a comma. If it follows the independent clause, no comma is necessary. Also, the subordinator is usually retained.

It is also possible to place a participial phrase formed from an adverbial clause immediately after the subject noun phrase. In this position, it acts as a participial phrase formed from an adjective clause. It is separated from the independent clause by commas, and it follows the rules for deletion or retention of the subordinator given above.

The samples below show how a time adverbial clause can be changed into a participial phrase.

1. While the president was traveling in Europe, he met many important political leaders.

   a. *While traveling in Europe, the president met many important political leaders.*

   b. *Traveling in Europe, the president met many important political leaders.*

   c. *The president met many important political leaders while traveling in Europe.*

   d. *The president, while traveling in Europe, met many important political leaders.*

   e. *The president, traveling in Europe, met many important political leaders.*

2. After the president had visited Europe, he flew on to the Middle East.

   a. *After having visited Europe, the president flew on to the Middle East.*

   (Also possible: *After visiting Europe, the president flew on to the Middle East.* The general form of the participle is possible here as long as the time subordinator *after* is retained. Because *after* already indicates the correct time relationship, the perfect participle form is not needed.)

   b. *Having visited Europe, the president flew on to the Middle East.*

   c. *The president flew on to the Middle East after having visited Europe.*

3. When the president's plane landed in Cairo, it lost a wheel and almost crashed.

   a. *When landing in Cairo, the president's plane lost a wheel and almost crashed.*

   b. *Landing in Cairo, the president's plane lost a wheel and almost crashed.*

   c. *The president's plane lost a wheel and almost crashed when landing in Cairo.*

4. As the First Lady was stepping off the plane, she stumbled and almost fell.

   a. *Stepping off the plane, the First Lady stumbled and almost fell.*

   b. *The First Lady stumbled and almost fell stepping off the plane.*

   (*Note:* The subordinator *as* must be deleted even when the participial phrase follows the independent clause.)

5. Before they were driven away in a limousine, the president and his wife were greeted by a group of government officials.

   a. *Before being driven away in a limousine, the president and his wife were greeted by a group of government officials.*

   (*Note:* The continuous form of the participle seems to be preferred when it is derived from a passive verb in time clauses. Additional examples: after I was asked = after being asked; before they were served = before being served; after they are born = after being born.)

   b. *The president and his wife were greeted by a group of government officials before being driven away in a limousine.*

6. Since the president left Washington, he had traveled more than 50,000 miles.

   a. *Since leaving Washington, the president has traveled more than 50,000 miles.*

   b. *The president has traveled more than 50,000 miles since leaving Washington.*

Practice 50: Participial Phrases from Time Clauses

STEP 1 Rewrite the following sentences, changing the adverbial time clauses to participial phrases.

STEP 2 Write each new sentence in as many ways as possible, following the examples above, and punctuate them correctly.

1. While people were watching the launch of the space shuttle Columbia on television, they felt as tense and excited as the spectators at Cape Canaveral.

a. _____

_____

_____

b. _____

_____

_____

c. _____

_____

_____

2. Since the Americans landed on the moon in 1969, they have been steadily losing the "space race" to the Russians.

a. _____

_____

_____

b. _____

_____

_____

c. _____

_____

_____

3. As the space shuttle Columbia orbited the globe every 90 minutes, it followed an almost circular path.

a. _____

_____

_____

b. _____

_____

_____

c. _____

_____

_____

4. Before the astronauts returned to earth, they had been busy testing fire control rockets at regular intervals.

   a. _____

   _____

   _____

   b. _____

   _____

   _____

   c. _____

   _____

   _____

5. After many world leaders had witnessed America's success in space, they sent messages of congratulations.

   a. _____

   _____

   _____

   b. _____

   _____

   _____

   c. _____

   _____

   _____

6. When we saw the Columbia coming in for a landing in the California desert, we celebrated with a bottle of champagne.

   a. _____

   _____

   _____

   b. _____

   _____

   _____

   c. _____

   _____

   _____

WRITING PRACTICE

STEP 1 Write six sentences containing adverbial clauses of time. Use each of the following time subordinators once: *before*, *after*, *while*, *when*, *since*, and *as*.

STEP 2 Change the adverbial clause into a participial phrase and rewrite the sentence in at least two ways.

PARTICIPIAL PHRASES FROM REASON CLAUSES

Reason adverbial clauses introduced by the subordinators *because, since* and *as* may also be reduced to participial phrases. Here, however, the subordinator *must* be deleted.

To change an adverbial clause of reason to a participial phrase:

1. **Make sure that the subjects of the adverbial clause and the independent clause are the same.**
2. **Transfer the subject to the independent clause.**
3. **Change the verb form.**
4. **Delete the subordinator.**

A reason participial phrase may come before or after the independent clause. However, putting the phrase *before* the independent clause is preferred. In both positions, it is separated by a comma. See how this is done in the examples below.

1. Because Carlos had only recently arrived in this country, he didn't speak English fluently.

   a. *Having only recently arrived in this country, Carlos didn't speak English fluently.*

   b. *Carlos didn't speak English fluently, having only recently arrived in this country.*

2. As he had never been away from home before, he was a little homesick at first.

   a. *Never having been away from home before, he was a little homesick at first.*

   b. *He was a little homesick at first, never having been away from home before.*

3. Since he didn't know anything about the area, he decided to live in a college dormitory for a while.

   a. *Not knowing anything about the area, he decided to live in a college dormitory for a while.*

   b. *He decided to live in a college dormitory for a while, not knowing anything about the area.*

Practice 51: Participial Phrases from Reason Clauses

Rewrite the following sentences, changing the adverbial reason clauses to participial phrases. Write each sentence only once, with the participial phrase in front of the independent clause.

1. Because Carlos came from a very conservative family, he was shocked at the American system of coed dormitories.

   _____

   _____

   _____

2. As he had never shared living space with people outside his family, he felt very strange at first.

_____

_____

_____

3. Carlos didn't understand the American students' attitude toward coed living since he came from a different culture.

_____

_____

_____

WRITING PRACTICE

STEP 1 Write three sentences with reason adverbial clauses on a topic of your choice, using each of the reason subordinators once.
STEP 2 Change the adverbial clause to a participial phrase and rewrite the sentence.
STEP 3 Place the participial phrase in front of the adverbial clause.

Practice 52: Time and Reason Participial Phrases

Rewrite the following sentences using participial phrases of time or reason.

STEP 1 Change the adverbial clause into a participial phrase.
STEP 2 Move the noun phrase in the adverbial clause to the subject position in the independent clause.
STEP 3 Combine the participial phrase with the independent clause, deleting the subordinator and adding commas if necessary.

Example As the students were listening intently to the professor's lecture, they took notes rapidly.

Listening intently to the professor's lecture, the students took notes rapidly.

1. As the scientist spoke about solar power satellites of the future, he showed many slides.

_____

_____

2. Since the federal government disclosed the hazards of an energy shortage, it has been working closely with industry.

_____

_____

3. As people are excited about new space technology, they enjoy seeing spectacular movies about adventures in space.

_____

_____

4. As we are approaching the twenty-first century, we are facing many more exciting technological challenges.

_____

_____

5. People wasted a tremendous amount of natural resources because they did not realize that a serious shortage would result.

_____

_____

6. Since the public realized the problems of the gas shortage, it has made every effort to stop unnecessary waste.

_____

_____

Practice 53: Participial Phrases from Relative and Adverbial Clauses

Read the following sentences and underline the participial phrases. In the blank space, name the origin of the participial phrase—adverbial clause or relative (adjective) clause.

Example   Although NASA engineers have spent ten years on the development of the tiles used on the Columbia space shuttle, they must still work out some imperfections.

Relative clause

1. Spectators waiting for the launching of the Columbia for hours screamed with joy as the space shuttle blasted off into space. _____

2. After traveling through space for two and one half days, the Columbia ended its flight in the California desert. _____

3. While crossing the California coast and coming in for a landing, the Columbia's course was being watched by the flight controllers on video display screens.

_____

4. After watching the landing of the Columbia on television, the president sent a congratulatory message to the astronauts. _____

5. The space shuttle Columbia, launched from Florida's Cape Canaveral on April 12 and November 12, 1981, was termed a 100 percent success.

_____

6. Having returned safely, the spaceplane is going to be prepared for several more missions. _____

Participial Phrases from Simple Sentences

You have learned that participial phrases can be formed from relative clauses and adverbial clauses. Participial phrases can also be used to combine simple sentences that have the same subject. Here is a group of sample sentences.

a. Laser-light shows were shown at many concerts. They produced exciting designs with colored lights.

b. Laser-light shows, producing exciting designs with colored lights, were shown at many concerts.

a. Lasers can blister and burn the retina of the eyes. They produce intense beams of light.

b. Lasers, producing intense beams of light, can blister and burn the retina of the eyes.

a. Laser beams can cause instant and permanent damage. They are directed or reflected into the human eye.

b. Laser beams directed or reflected into the human eye can cause instant and permanent damage.

Practice 54: Participial Phrases from Simple Sentences

Rewrite the following sentences by using participial phrases.

STEP 1 Change one sentence into a participial phrase.
STEP 2 Combine the participial phrase with the independent clause.
STEP 3 Punctuate the sentence if necessary.

Example   The beams of light must be aimed far above the spectators' heads. They are bright and dangerous.

The beams of light, being bright and dangerous, must be aimed far above the spectators' heads.

OR

Being bright and dangerous, the beams of light must be aimed far above the spectators' heads.

1. The laser beam is useful in surveying.
   It is straight.

   _____

   _____

2. Doctors have discovered countless medical and surgical uses for lasers.
   Doctors have experimented for several years with lasers.

   _____

   _____

   _____

3. A laser beam requires mirrors to send it around corners.
   A laser beam is straight.

   _____

   _____

   _____

4. Astronauts placed laser reflectors on the moon.
They wanted to measure the exact distance between the earth and the moon.

_____

_____

_____

5. Lasers are very intense and concentrated.
They are used by eye surgeons to put detached retinas back into place without surgery.

_____

_____

_____

Practice 55: Using Participial Phrases

The following paragraphs contain simple sentences and complex sentences with relative clauses and adverbial clauses; however, they do not contain any participial phrases. Your task is to rewrite the paragraphs, adding participial phrases.

STEP 1 Rewrite sentence 1, making the relative clause a participial phrase.
STEP 2 Combine sentences 2 and 3, making sentence 2 a participial phrase.
STEP 3 Combine sentences 4 and 5, making sentence 4 a participial phrase.
STEP 4 Rewrite sentences 6, 7, 8, and 9, changing the dependent clause in each.
STEP 5 Combine sentences 10 and 11, making sentence 11 a participial phrase.

(1) Pioneer Venus 1, which was launched several years ago, will arrive at and orbit Venus before Pioneer Venus 2. (2) The Venus 1 spacecraft is destined for a long life. (3) It will orbit Venus for eight months or more. (4) It will carry out observations with various instruments. (5) It will send important information back to Earth.

(6) Venus' evolution took place in the same part of the solar system as Earth's although it has been completely different from that of our planet. (7) Its atmosphere, which is thought to be mostly carbon dioxide, contains little if any oxygen or water vapor. (8) Its atmosphere is much denser than Earth's, which creates a pressure nearly 100 times that of Earth at the surface. (9) Heat that is trapped by the atmosphere produces a temperature of about 900 degrees day or night. (10) Even at the poles it is only about 10 degrees colder. (11) This suggests that heat is spread evenly.

Practice 56: Writing Participial Phrases

STEP 1 Rewrite the statements in parentheses as participial phrases; add subordinators where possible.
STEP 2 Punctuate the sentences correctly.

I had an extraordinary dream last week. In my dream, I was a stewardess on a

plane _____. The flight attendants
(that was flying over the Pacific Ocean to Hawaii.)

and I were going up and down the aisle _____
(We were making sure the passengers

_____. Suddenly, two gunmen appeared out of nowhere. One of

were comfortable.)

them went to the back of the plane while the other one _____
                                                          (who rushed up to the front)
ordered everyone to freeze*. _____
                                      (Because some of the passengers were terrified and
_____ some of the passengers began
shaken by the gunmen's sudden appearance)
screaming. _____ I waited for a
              (While I tried to calm them down)
chance to grab one of the gunmen's weapons. _____
                                                  (Because I saw one gunman go into
_____ I decided to bring the other one a cup of coffee. _____
the pilot's cabin)   (While I was
_____ I was smiling. _____
approaching him with the coffee)   (He thought that I had brought
_____ he smiled back. At that moment, I threw the hot coffee in his
the coffee for him)
face. _____ the flight attendants
         (When the flight attendants saw what I had done)
quickly jumped on him _____.
                         (They grabbed his gun.)

     Then, I quickly ran into the pilot's cabin with the gun in my hand.
_____ I saw the gunman _____
(When I opened the door)   (who was holding his weapon to the
_____. "Drop your gun!" I demanded. _____ he
pilot's head.)   (He was surprised.)
quickly turned around. _____ the
                         (Before he dropped his gun)
gunman shot me in the arm and tried to shoot me again. But I returned his fire
first, and he dropped his gun to the floor. _____
                                              (Because we were wounded by the
_____ both the gunman and I were bleeding. The gunman _____
gunfire)   (who was
_____ gave up without a struggle.
quickly overtaken by the co-pilot)

     While the plane was landing at the Honolulu airport, I heard Hawaiian music.
Just then, I woke up. I heard my clock radio _____
                                               (which was playing the same song)
I had heard in my exciting dream.

---

freeze: slang expression for "Don't move!"

WRITING PRACTICE

Write one or two paragraphs, using as many participial phrases as you can. Choose your topic from the selection below.

1. Write your autobiography. Include some interesting comments about yourself; don't just state the bare facts.

   Being an only child, I became very spoiled at an early age.

   Having finished high school with excellent grades, I was sent to continue my studies at an American university.

2. Write about a frightening or exciting experience, real or imaginary.

   Suddenly realizing that a burglar was in my apartment, I started screaming, hoping that the neighbors would hear me.

Chapter 16

CONDITIONAL SENTENCES

A **conditional sentence** is formed by joining an independent clause to a special kind of adverbial clause—a **conditional clause**.

The conditional clause is formed with:

If
Unless | SUBJECT + VERB | COMPLEMENT

If it rains tomorrow...
If the weather doesn't clear up...
Unless the sun shines...

In a **conditional sentence**, the *if* or *unless* clause states the condition, and the independent clause states the result.

Unless means *if... not*, as shown in these clauses:

Unless the weather clears up tomorrow...
If the weather doesn't clear up tomorrow...

Unless you study harder...
If you don't study harder...

The dependent clause can come before the independent clause. If it comes before, it is followed by a comma; if it comes after, no comma is needed as in the sentences below:

I can graduate next semester if I complete sixteen units.
I would major in computer science if I were you.
We might have sent you a postcard if we had known your address.

Types of Conditional Sentences

There are four possible types of conditional sentences: **real**, **future possible**, **present unreal**, and **past unreal**. These types determine the time (future, present, or past) of the condition, and whether the condition is real, merely possible, or completely unreal. Some conditional sentences use special combinations of verb forms to indicate all of these factors.

Real conditions	*If I have a headache, I usually take aspirin.*
	If I had a problem, I went to my advisor.
	(*When* could replace *if* in these sentences.)
Future possible conditions	*If I complete sixteen units, I will graduate next semester.*
Present unreal conditions	*If I were you, I would major in computer science.*
Past unreal conditions	*If we had known your address, we would have sent you a postcard.*

In this unit, we will study only the last three types of conditional sentences because they involve special verb forms. In the first type, real conditions, the verb forms are not unusual.

FUTURE POSSIBLE

A future possible conditional sentence describes a situation in which the result of an action becomes possible if a condition is met. The most common patterns are the *simple/future*, *simple/imperative*, and the *modal/simple*.

IF/CLAUSE VERB FORM	INDEPENDENT CLAUSE VERB FORM
	Future Form—*will* or *going to*
Simple Present Tense	Imperative Form
	Modal (*may, can, must*) + Simple Form

Simple Present/ Future

If you learn the rules, you will write correct conditional sentences.
If you spend more time studying, you are going to get better grades.
You will have enough money for presents if you start saving right now.

Simple Present/ Imperative

If you are in a car during an earthquake, stop in the safest available place.
Watch out for falling things if you are indoors.
Unless you are sure there are no gas leaks, don't light any matches.

Simple Present/ Modal

If an earthquake occurs, you may not know what to do.
You can risk your life if you panic.
If you are in a crowded area, you must not panic.

Practice 57: Future Possible Conditional Sentences

Combine the following sentences to form future possible conditional sentences.

A. Use the simple/future pattern.

STEP 1 Add *if* to the logical dependent clause.
STEP 2 Change the verb form in the independent clause.
STEP 3 Punctuate the sentence if necessary.

Example You choose a career in computer programming.
You need certain qualifications.

If you choose a career in computer programming, you will need certain qualifications.

1. The programmer puts the correct formula into the computer.
   The mathematical calculations come out correctly.

   _____

   _____

2. I need to understand this complex machine.
   I hope to master the control and use of the computer.

   _____

   _____

3. You find that they belong to the general family of desk calculators.
   You look up the history of electronic computers.

   _____

   _____

4. You make an acronym* of "*c*ommon *b*usiness *o*riented *l*anguage."
   You coin the word COBOL.

   _____

   _____

5. A student majors in computer science.
   He needs to take systems programming.

   _____

   _____

B. Use the simple present + imperative pattern.

STEP 1 Add *if* to the logical dependent clause.
STEP 2 Punctuate the sentence if necessary.

Reduce the car's speed immediately.
You see danger ahead.

If you see danger ahead, reduce the car's speed immediately.

acronym: a word formed by combining
initial letters of words

1. Use your windshield washers before you turn your wipers on.
   You drive in the rain.

   _____

   _____

2. You come to a yield sign.
   Stop to allow the car in front of you to pass.

   _____

   _____

3. You see a pedestrian in the crosswalk.
   Stop immediately.

   _____

   _____

4. Slow down and come to a full stop.
   The signal light turns yellow.

   _____

   _____

5. Observe all traffic laws.
   You want to be a safe driver.

   _____

   _____

C. Use the modal/simple pattern in this set of sentences.

STEP 1 Add *if* to the logical dependent clause.

STEP 2 Change the verb tense in the independent clause to include a modal. Do not use *will*.

STEP 3 Underline the verbs in both clauses and punctuate the sentence if necessary.

Example   We continue to use energy at the present rate.
           We face a worse energy crisis in the 1990s.

           If we <u>continue</u> to use energy at the present rate, we <u>may</u>
           <u>face</u> a worse energy crisis in the 1990s.

1. Prices double or triple within a short time.
   The energy crisis continues.

   _____

   _____

2. They control the use of oil.
   Americans want to prevent this disaster.

   _____

   _____

3. You look at statistics.
   You see that we use a third of all energy used in the world.

   _____

   _____

4. We are in danger.
   We do not reduce our take of the world's oil.

   _____

   _____

5. We have a serious problem in the future.
   We do not conserve oil now.

   _____

   _____

Practice 58: Future Possible Conditional Clauses—Unless

Rewrite each sentence, using *unless* in place of *if . . . not.*

Example   If you don't quit smoking, you may develop lung cancer.

Unless you quit smoking, you may develop lung cancer.

1. If it doesn't rain soon, the food crops will be lost.

   _____

   _____

2. If the food-producing nations of the world don't send immediate aid, thousands
   of people in the drought region will perish.

   _____

   _____

3. You will have to suffer the consequences if you don't obey the rules.

   _____

   _____

4. Peace in the world will remain only a dream if the major powers don't stop the
   arms* race.

   _____

   _____

5. Don't park here if you don't want to get a ticket.

   _____

   _____

arms: weapons

PRESENT UNREAL

A present unreal conditional sentence describes a situation or condition that does not exist and is not likely to happen. The verb forms that show this unreal situation follow this pattern:

IF/CLAUSE VERB FORM	INDEPENDENT CLAUSE VERB FORM
SIMPLE PAST TENSE	WOULD COULD + SIMPLE FORM MIGHT

If I had time, I would take a leisurely trip around the world.
You could get better grades if you studied harder.
If you left right now, you might still catch your plane.

Note: In formal written English, the verb "to be" has a special form in present unreal conditional clauses. The form *were* is preferred for *all* persons and numbers.

If I   were a millionaire ...
If you were a millionaire ...
If he   were a millionaire ...
If we   were millionaires ...
If you were millionaires ...
If they were millionaires ...

Practice 59: Present Unreal Conditional Sentences

A. Complete the blanks in the following present unreal conditional sentences.

STEP 1 Add the past tense form of the verb in parentheses to the *if* clause.
STEP 2 Add a modal (*could, would,* or *might*) to the independent clause.
STEP 3 Punctuate the sentence if necessary.

Example   If the bank ___*lent*___ (lend) me money, they ___*would*___ ask me for interest on the loan.

1. If everybody _____ (decide) to walk and use public transportation the car industry _____ collapse.

2. Legislators _____ prohibit smoking in all public places if they _____ _____ (want to).

3. If I _____ (make) a thousand dollars on the stock market the Internal Revenue Service _____ tax me.

4. The federal government _____ abolish income taxes if the people _____ (protest.)

5. If I _____ (want) to buy an airplane I _____ pay cash.

B. The sentences in this part give you practice in using the special form of "to be" in present unreal conditional clauses.

STEP 1 Add the verb *were* to the dependent *if* clause.
STEP 2 Add *would, could,* or *might* to the independent clause.
STEP 3 Punctuate the sentence if necessary.

Example If the price of real estate ___*were*___ low, I ___*might*___ buy an apartment building.

1. If I _____ an engineering expert I _____ solve the malfunctioning of the company's equipment.

2. If you _____ a certified public accountant you _____ be a professional business adviser.

3. If John _____ the personnel manager he _____ hire me.

4. The new business _____ succeed if the salespersons _____ more pleasant.

5. I _____ try to make a point of familiarizing myself with departmental functions if I _____ the corporation president.

WRITING PRACTICE

Write a series of eight sentences describing what would happen if you were a millionaire, a movie star, an astronaut, or anything else you would like to be. Try to write your sentences in a chain, as in the example below.

Example If I were a millionaire, I would take a trip around the world.
If I took a trip around the world, I would visit China.
If I visited China, I might go to Peking.
If I went to Peking, I . . . .

PAST UNREAL

A past unreal conditional sentence describes a situation or condition in the past that is unreal and really did not happen at all. The condition is stated in the *if* clause, and the response to the condition is stated in the independent clause.

The verb forms that show this unreal condition in the past follow this pattern:

IF-CLAUSE VERB FORM	INDEPENDENT CLAUSE VERB FORM
Past Perfect Tense (*had* + Past Participle)	WOULD COULD + HAVE + PAST PARTICIPLE MIGHT

If I had received a letter of recommendation from my previous employer, I could have gotten the job.

I might have earned a higher grade if I had written a better term paper.

If I had been with Neil Armstrong in 1969, I would have been the second human to walk on the moon.

Practice 60: Past Unreal Conditional Sentences

Complete the blanks in the following past unreal conditional sentences.

STEP 1 Use the past perfect tense of the verb in parentheses in the *if* clause.

STEP 2 Use a modal (*could, would,* or *might*) plus *have* and the past participle of the main verb in the independent clause.

STEP 3 Punctuate the sentence if necessary.

Example If the company ____*had flooded*____ (flood) the market with attractive advertising, the gismo gadget ____*would have been*____ (be) a huge success.

1. If X-Cel Corporation _____ (hire) a new sales manager sales of the gismo gadget _____ (increase) ten-fold.

2. The sales promotion _____ (include) special sales and coupon offers if the promotion staff _____ (have) a little imagination.

3. If the public relations department _____ (ask) for more funds, the president _____ (give) it to them.

4. The company's marketing analyst _____ (be) more accurate if she _____ (spend) more time surveying the potential market.

5. The marketing analyst _____ (anticipate) problems if she _____ (realize) the impact of new competitors*.

6. If the accounting, production, and marketing experts _____ (come up) with more accurate cost comparisons of the two largest populated areas, the gismo gadget sales _____ (show) a greater profit.

WRITING PRACTICE

Write a series of eight sentences, describing what would have happened if you had been some historical person in the past. Again, try to write your sentences in a chain.

If I had been Napoleon, I wouldn't have lost the Russian Campaign.
If I had conquered Russia, I would not have been defeated at Waterloo.
If I had won at Waterloo, I . . . .

---

competitors: others with the same goal; in business, other firms in the same field

Conditional Sentences with Mixed Verb Patterns

The patterns you have just practiced for conditional clauses are the most common ones; however, they are not the *only* possible combinations of verb forms. You might, for example, have a past condition and a present result:

If I had been born in France, I would speak French.
If I hadn't failed chemistry last semester, I wouldn't be in summer school now.

Also, you might have a present condition and a past result:

If I were smarter, I wouldn't have failed chemistry.
If my car were running, I could have picked you up at the airport.

Alternatively, the continuous tenses might be more appropriate in certain situations:

If his father weren't the president of the company, he wouldn't be working here.

The present perfect tense might also be appropriate in conditional sentences:

If I have offended you, I apologize.
If I have offended you, I will apologize.

There are, in other words, many possible combinations of verb forms in conditional sentences. You should combine the patterns to fit the meaning of your sentences.

Review of Conditional Sentences

These are the important points you should have learned in this chapter:

1. A conditional sentence is composed of a dependent conditional clause and an independent clause.
2. The subordinators *if* and *unless* (the negative of *if*) introduce the conditional clause.
3. The verb tenses in both clauses depend on the time (present, past, or future) and on the reality, possibility, or unreality of the situation.

There are four basic types of conditional sentences:

	IF-CLAUSE		INDEPENDENT CLAUSE
Real Conditions, Present or Past Time	Present Tense Past Tense	+ +	Present Tense Past Tense
	*If (when) he *makes* a mistake, he always *apologizes*. *If (when) he *made* a mistake, he always *apologized*.		
Possible Conditions, Future Time	Present Tense	+	Future Tense ("will" or "going to") Simple (imperative) Form Modal + Simple Form
	*Unless you *leave* now, I *will call* the police. *If you *want* to stop smoking, *take* my advice. *If you *want* to live longer, you *must stop* smoking.		
Unreal Conditions, Present Time	Past Tense	+	Would Could + Simple Form Might
Exception: Instead of *was* (past tense of BE), always use *were* in an if-clause.			
	*If I *knew* Russian, I *could become* a translator. *If he *weren't* *coming*, he *would call* us.		
Unreal Conditions, Past Time	Past Perfect Tense +		Would Could + Have + Past Might Participle
	*If he *hadn't lied* during the interview, he *would have gotten* the job.		

As with most complex sentences, the order of the clauses may be reversed. Don't use a comma if the independent clause comes first.

I will call the police unless you leave now.
Unless you leave now, I will call the police.

Chapter 17

PUNCTUATION

Commas

Commas function in four ways:

1. as *introducers*,
2. as *coordinators* in compound sentences,
3. as *inserters*, and
4. as *linkers*.

Let's start by analyzing how commas relate to the main clause of a sentence. Notice below how the additional words, phrases, or clauses modify the main clause.

Introducer

INTRODUCER	MAIN CLAUSE
Recently,	*the legislature banned smoking in public places.*

Coordinator

MAIN CLAUSE	COORDINATING CONJUNCTION	MAIN CLAUSE
Many people opposed the new law,	*but*	*it finally passed.*

Inserter

MAIN	INSERTER	CLAUSE
Smallpox,	*once a widespread disease,*	*is under control.*

Linker

MAIN CLAUSE	LINKER
My beloved pet dog died,	*(in spite of my efforts to save her).*

INTRODUCERS

A comma is used after introductory words, phrases and clauses.

Words	*However, the new law was largely ignored by the public.*
Phrases	*As a result, an even stricter law was proposed.*
	After a long vacation, he returned to work.
	Having studied very hard, she passed the exam easily.
Clauses	*Because he had missed so many classes, he had to drop the course.*
Appositives	*An old man, my grandfather can barely walk.*

Our thanks to Anne Katz of San Francisco State University for permission to adapt her presentation of comma rules.

COORDINATORS

A comma is used between two independent clauses joined by the coordinating conjunctions *and, but, yet, or, for, nor,* and *so* to form compound sentences.

And   *The exam was quite easy, and most students passed.*

But   *The exam was quite easy, but most students failed.*

Yet   *The experiment was considered successful, yet the results were disappointing.*

Or   *Will you write your thesis this semester, or will you wait until next semester?*

For   *Your decision is important, for our future plans depend on it.*

Nor   *He didn't come to class during the last three weeks, nor did he take the final exam.*

So   *He didn't study, so he didn't pass the course.*

Note: Nor is a troublemaker. It is a negative word, and it signals inverted word order. The verb must come before the subject. Also, do not confuse compound sentences with simple sentences that have two verbs. A compound sentence has two subjects and two verbs:

She asked the question, and she answered it in the same breath.

A simple sentence can also have two verbs, but it has only one subject:

She asked the question and answered it in the same breath.

INSERTERS

A comma is used before and after words, phrases and clauses that are inserted into the middle of a main clause.

Transitions   *The new law, however, was largely ignored by the public.*

The students, on the other hand, felt that the test was unfair.

The computer, for example, has both positive and negative uses.

Appositives   *My grandfather, an old man, can barely walk.*

Dr. Danielson, a professor in the English Department, has written several books.

Dr. William Porter, a professor of medicine at the University of California, suggested in his article, "The Effects of Marijuana on Motor Responses," that potsmokers' reactions are slower.

Nonrestrictive   *Income taxes, which all people who receive an income*
Clauses   *must pay, are due on April 15 every year.*

My husband, who used to smoke three packs of cigarettes a day, has stopped smoking.

Mary Baker Eddy, who founded Christian Science, lived in New England.

LINKERS

A comma is used (a) when adding words and phrases at the end of a sentence, and (b) when linking items in a series.

Transitions

The new law was largely ignored by the public, however.

The students felt that the test was unfair, of course.

Items in a series

Cholera, smallpox, yellow fever, and diphtheria are some of the diseases that have been conquered in this century.

A nurse has to be willing to work at night, on weekends, and on holidays.

We ran into the airport, checked our luggage, raced to the boarding area, gave the attendant our tickets, and collapsed in our seats.

Practice 61: Using Commas

STEP 1 Add commas wherever they are necessary. (Not all sentences need them.)

STEP 2 Name the function of each comma (introducer, coordinator, inserter, or linker).

FUNCTION

_____ 1. The advertising industry which is one of the largest industries in the United States employs millions of people and spends billions of dollars.

_____ 2. A company that wants to be successful must spend a great deal of money to advertise its products.

_____ 3. Advertising is essential to the free enterprise system yet it can sometimes be very annoying.

_____ 4. Every minute of the day and night people are exposed to ads on television on billboards in the newspapers and in magazines.

_____ 5. You can't even avoid advertising in the privacy of your own car or your own home for advertisers have begun selling their products in those places too.

_____ 6. In the last few years advertising agencies have started to hire young people to hand out circulars on street-corners and in parking lots.

_____ 7. You can often find these circulars stuck on your windshield thrust through the open windows of your car stuffed in your mailbox or simply scattered on your front doorstep.

_____ 8. Because Americans are exposed to so much advertising they have become immune* to it.

_____ 9. As a result advertisers have to make louder commercials use brighter colors and hire sexier models to catch the public's attention.

_____ 10. Many people object especially to commercials that use sex as a sales strategy.

_____ 11. Sexy commercials that sell everything from toothpaste to automobiles seem to imply that you will become sexier if you buy the product.

_____ 12. Sex is used in many cigarette and liquor ads for example.

_____ 13. The women in such ads are often dressed in revealing clothes and are surrounded by handsome men and the men in such ads are always extremely handsome and virile.

_____ 14. As everyone knows smoking and drinking do not make you sexy or virile.

_____ 15. On the contrary drinking makes you fat and smoking makes you sick.

_____ 16. The government is considering a ban on sex in cigarette and liquor ads because of their potentially harmful effect on teenagers.

_____ 17. The government is considering a ban but no action has been taken yet.

_____ 18. If such action is taken my boyfriend the Marlboro man will be out of a job.

_____ 19. Catherine Deneuve who sells automobiles and perfume would lose some work too.

_____ 20. On the other hand it is more pleasant to look at beautiful women and handsome men than at ugly people.

---

immune: cannot be affected

Semicolons

Using **semicolons** is not difficult if you remember that a semicolon (;) is more like a period (.) than a comma. It is a very strong punctuation mark. Semicolons are used in three places:

1. Between two sentences that are closely connected in idea.
2. Before sentence connectors and some transitional phrases.
3. Between items in a series.

BETWEEN SENTENCES

Use a semicolon at the end of a sentence when the following sentence is closely connected in meaning. You could also use a period, but when the sentences are connected in meaning, it is better to use a semicolon.

INDEPENDENT CLAUSE	;	INDEPENDENT CLAUSE
Alice is going to Harvard;		*she isn't going to M.I.T.*
Computer use is increasing;		*computer crime is, too.*
The committee adjourned at dawn;		*nothing had been accomplished.*
SENTENCE	;	SENTENCE

BEFORE CONNECTORS

Use a semicolon before connectors such as *however, therefore, nevertheless, moreover*, and *furthermore*. You may also use a semicolon before some transitional phrases such as *for example, as a result, that is, in fact*, etc.

	CONNECTOR		
INDEPENDENT CLAUSE	; TRANSITION	,	INDEPENDENT CLAUSE
	PHRASE		

Skiing is dangerous; nevertheless, hundreds of people ski.

Chris Evert is a great tennis player; moreover, she is attractive.

Jimmy Conners played well; however, Bjorn Borg beat him.

He had smoked all his life; as a result, he died of lung cancer.

I have never been to Southern California; in fact, I have never been to San Jose.

BETWEEN ITEMS IN A SERIES

Semicolons may be used as well to separate items in a series, as long as some of the items already contain commas.

I cannot decide which car I like best: the Ferrari, with its quick acceleration and ease of handling; the small, conventional Datsun, with its reclining bucket seats; or the uncomfortable Volkswagen, with its economical fuel consumption.

Practice 62: Using Semicolons and Commas I

STEP 1 The following sentences need semicolons and commas; add the correct punctuation in the appropriate places.

STEP 2 In the space provided at left, state whether the semicolon is:

1. between two closely connected sentences,
2. before a sentence connector, or
3. between items in a series.

Example   __2__   Professor Smith is at a conference; however, Dr. Jones, who is the department chairman, will be glad to see you.

_____ 1. Grace works for a prestigious law firm she is their top criminal lawyer.

_____ 2. My favorite leisure-time activities are going to movies especially musicals reading novels* especially stories of love and adventure listening to music both rock and classical and participating in sports particularly tennis and volleyball.

_____ 3. The future of our wild animals is uncertain for example illegal shooting and chemical poisoning threaten the bald eagle*.

_____ 4. Homework is boring therefore I never do it.

_____ 5. The freeways are always crowded during the busy rush hours nevertheless people refuse to take public transportation.

_____ 6. I like the following foods: ice cream sundaes with lots of hot fudge pizza with garlic and mushrooms and waffles with lots of melted butter and syrup.

_____ 7. The Smiths' marriage should succeed they share the same interests.

_____ 8. Hoping that he would pass the course he stayed up all night studying for the final exam unfortunately he overslept and missed the test.

_____ 9. In general I enjoy my English class the amount of homework our teacher assigns is definitely not enjoyable however.

_____ 10. If you are a college student, an average day is filled with challenges: you have to avoid running into Professor Jones whose class you missed because you overslept you have to race across the campus at high speed to reach your next class which is always at the other side of the campus and you have to secretly prepare your homework assignment during class hoping all the time that the teacher won't catch you.

Practice 63: Using Semicolons and Commas II

Punctuate the following sentences by adding semicolons and commas. Use semicolons wherever possible.

1. My bus was late therefore I missed my first class.

2. The politician was discovered accepting bribes as a result his political career was ruined.

3. My father never cries in fact he never shows any emotion at all.

4. The restaurant was closed consequently we went home to eat.

---

novels: fiction books
bald eagle: a large bird of prey, symbol of the United States

5. Some people feel that grades are unnecessary on the other hand some people feel that grades motivate students.

6. Technology is changing our lives in insidious* ways for example the computer is replacing human contact.

7. The computer dehumanizes business nevertheless it has some real advantages.

8. Writing essays is easy it just takes a little practice.

9. Americans love pets every family seems to have at least one dog or cat.

10. The life expectancy of Americans is increasing for example the life expectancy of a man born today is 77.2 years which is an increase of 26.12 years since 1900.

11. Your proposal is a good one however I do not completely agree with your final suggestion.

12. Efficiency is a highly prized quality among Americans it has almost attained the status of a moral attribute.

WRITING PRACTICE

Write three original sentences for each of the three rules for using semicolons:

1. Between closely connected sentences.
2. Before connectors and some transitional phrases.
3. Between items in a series.

Colons

A **colon** (:) can be used in five ways:

LISTS

Use a colon to introduce a list.

Libraries have two kinds of periodicals: bound periodicals and current periodicals.

I need the following groceries: eggs, milk, and coffee.

The causes of the Civil War were as follows: the economic domination of the North, the slavery issue, and the issue of states' rights versus federal intervention.

Note: Do *not* use a colon to introduce a list after the verb "to be" unless you add *the following* or *as follows.*

The causes of the Civil War were the economic domination of the North, the slavery issue, and the issue of states' rights versus federal intervention.

To me, the most important things in life are health, happiness, good friends and a lot of money.

BUT *To me, the most important things in life are the following: health, happiness, good friends, and a lot of money.*

---

insidious: harmful but seductive

LONG QUOTATIONS

Use a colon to introduce a long quotation, that is, a quotation longer than three lines. This type of quote is indented on both sides, and no quotation marks are used.

As Albert C. Baugh and Thomas Cable state in their book, The History of the English Language:

> *There is no such thing as uniformity in language. Not only does the speech of one community differ from that of another, but the speech of different individuals of a single community, even different members of the same family, is marked by individual peculiarities.*

SUBTITLES

Use a colon between the main title and the subtitle of a book, article or play.

A popular book on nonverbal communication is Samovar and Porter's Intercultural Communication: A Reader.

The name of an article from The New York Times *is "Space Stations: Dream or Reality?"*

TIME

Use a colon between the numbers for hours and minutes when indicating the time of day.

Helen left the class at 12:30.
Our plane arrived at 1:40, six hours late.

FORMAL SALUTATIONS

Use a colon after the salutation of a formal letter.

Dear Professor Danielson:
Dear Sir:
Gentlemen:
Dear Mrs. Smith:
To Whom It May Concern:

In informal letters, a comma is more appropriate.

Dear Mom,
Darling,
Dear Mark,

Practice 64: Using Punctuation Marks

Add commas, semicolons and colons to the following.

1. The library offers many special services the Student Learning Center where students can receive special tutoring the phonorecord library where you can listen to records and tapes and group study rooms.

2. Dear Dr. Patterson
   Dear Alice
   Dear Mr. Carter

3. To check a book out of the library you should follow this procedure write down the call number of the book find the book bring it to the circulation desk fill out the card and show your student I.D.

4. The principal sources of air pollution in our cities are factories airplanes and automobiles.

5. I have a dental appointment at 330 today. Please pick me up at 315.

6. Write a sentence in which you list two pieces of advice that you have received from your parents. Use a colon to direct attention to them.

   _____

   _____

   _____

   _____

   _____

7. Write the title and subtitle of the following book correctly. Remember to underline the full title.
   (Title) San Francisco   (Subtitle) A Visitor's Guide to Restaurants

   _____

   _____

Quotation Marks

Quotation marks ["..."] have three basic functions:

DIRECT QUOTE

Use quotation marks to enclose a direct quotation that is shorter than three lines. A direct quotation states the *exact* words of a speaker. Do not use quotation marks with indirect speech.

Punctuation with quotation marks can be a little tricky. Here are some rules to follow:

Periods and commas go *inside* quotation marks.

   "I thought he was responsible," he said, "but he isn't."

Colons and semicolons go *outside* quotation marks.

   "Give me liberty or give me death": these are immortal words.

Exclamation points (!) and question marks (?) go inside quotation marks if they are a part of the quotation; otherwise, they go outside.

   "Is it eight o'clock?" she asked.
   Did she say, "It's eight o'clock"?

When a quoted sentence is divided into two parts, the second part begins with a small letter unless it is a new sentence.

   "I thought he was responsible," he said, "but he isn't."
   "I think he is responsible," he said. "Look at his fine work."

Use single quotation marks ('...') to enclose a quotation within a quotation.

   As John F. Kennedy reminded us in his inaugural address, "We should never forget the words of Martin Luther King, Jr., who said, 'I have a dream.'"

UNUSUAL WORDS

Use quotation marks to enclose foreign words or words that are used in a special or uncommon way.

A lot of people talk about "machismo" these days, but no one really knows what it means.

The "banquet" turned out to be no more than hot dogs and soft drinks.

TITLES

Use quotation marks to enclose the titles of (a) articles from periodical journals, magazines, and newspapers; (b) chapters of books; (c) short stories; (d) poems; and (e) songs.

In the article "The Future of Space," published in the July 19, 1974 issue of <u>Scientific American</u>, *the authors explore the possibility of manned space stations.*

The <u>New York Times</u> *recently published an article entitled "Space Stations: Dream or Reality?" in which the potential of space cities in orbit was discussed.*

Note: The titles of books, journals, magazines, newspapers, and movies should be underlined.

Practice 65: Using Quotation Marks

Get a copy of any newspaper and write a paragraph about any article. Copy five quotations from the article. Mention the name of the newspaper and the article in your sentence and include the name of the speaker.

Chapter 18
SENTENCE PROBLEMS

Sentence Fragments

Sentence fragments are incomplete sentences or parts of sentences. Remember that in order to be complete, a sentence must contain (a) at least one main or independent clause, and/or (b) contain at least one main subject and one main verb.

Study the following four examples of sentence fragments and the suggested methods for correcting them.

FRAGMENTS

1. Because some students have part-time jobs in addition to going to school.
2. For example, the increase in the cost of renting an apartment.
3. Having no money and being lonely in the big city.
4. Many people who get married before they are mature enough.

Problem	1. This is a subordinate clause.
To correct	Attach it to an independent clause.
Complete Sentence	*Because some students have part-time jobs in addition to full-time classwork, they have very little free time.*
Problem	2. No main verb.
To correct	Rewrite the sentence so that it has a subject and a verb.
Complete Sentence	*For example, the cost of renting an apartment has increased.*
Problem	3. This is a participial phrase. It has no subject or verb.
To correct	(a) Rewrite the phrase to include a subject and a verb.
	(b) Attach the phrase to an independent clause.
Complete Sentences	(a) *She had no money and was lonely in the big city.*
	(b) *Having no money and being lonely in the big city, the woman committed suicide.*

Fragment	*Many people who get married before they are mature enough.*
Problem	This is a subordinate (adjective) clause.
Solution	Rewrite the clause by eliminating the adjective clause aspect.
Complete Sentence	*Many people get married before they are mature enough.*

Practice 66: Rewriting Sentence Fragments

Read the following sentences. Mark them FRAG if they are sentence fragments, or SENT if they are complete sentences. Rewrite each fragment to make complete sentences.

_____ 1. The desire of all mankind to live in peace and freedom, for example.

_____ 2. Second, the fact that men are physically stronger than women.

_____ 3. The best movie that I saw last year.

_____ 4. *Star Wars* was the best movie that I saw last year.

_____ 5. For example, many students have part-time jobs.

_____ 6. Although people want to believe that all men are created equal.

_____ 7. Finding a suitable marriage partner is a challenging task.

_____ 8. Many of my friends who didn't have the opportunity to go to college.

_____ 9. Working during the morning and attending classes during the afternoon.

_____ 10. Because I don't feel that grades in college have any value.

WRITING PRACTICE

Read the following short essay. Put brackets [ ] around any sentence fragments that you find and mark them *FRAG*. Then correct all fragments. Rewrite the entire essay.

Women Drivers

1   Male chauvinism extends even into the area of automobile driving, it seems. Believing that they are far better drivers than women. Men consider women drivers incompetent, inattentive, and even dangerous behind the wheel.

However, statistics prove that women are, in fact, safer drivers than men. For
5   example, insurance rates. Insurance rates for women are 20% lower than for men. Another proof is that more accidents are caused by male drivers between the ages of 18 and 25 than by any other group. Also the greater percentage of accidents involving deaths caused by men. Although women are criticized for being too cautious. They are really just being safe drivers.

10   The reasons for women drivers' safer driving habits can perhaps be found in the differing attitudes of the sexes toward automobiles. On the one hand, women drivers who regard the automobile as a convenience. Like a washing machine. On the other hand, men regard the automobile as an extension of their egos. Using it as a weapon when they feel particularly aggressive. Or using it as a status symbol.

15   In conclusion, women are safer drivers. Because of their attitude. Men can learn to become safe drivers. If they adopt the attitude that an automobile is merely a convenience.

Note: Always check your own writing for sentence fragments! Pay particular attention to your sentences beginning with subordinating conjunctions (*Although, Since, Because, If, Before,* etc.). These are DANGER WORDS! Make sure that every subordinate clause beginning with these words is attached to an independent clause.

Choppy Sentences

Choppy sentences are sentences that are too short. They are the result of using too many simple sentences, like those that follow. Although simple sentences are quite effective sometimes, overuse of them is considered poor style in academic writing.

Choppy
We must find new sources of energy. The earth's natural sources of energy are dwindling. Solar energy is a promising new source of energy. Solar energy is energy from the sun's radiation.

Choppy
Government and industry are spending huge sums of money to develop solar energy. Research scientists are working hard to develop economical means of converting the sun's rays into usable energy.

Choppy sentences are easy to correct. Just combine two or three simple sentences to make one compound or complex sentence. Your decision to make a compound or a complex sentence should be based on whether the ideas in the simple sentences are equal, or whether one sentence is dependent on the other.

---

1. If the simple sentences are equal, make a compound sentence, using a coordinating conjunction (*and, or, but, so, yet, nor, for*) or a sentence connector (*moreover, otherwise, however, therefore,* etc.)

2. If one sentence depends on the other, make a complex sentence, using a subordinating conjunction (*who, which, when, although, because, since, if,* etc.).

Compound
Government and industry are spending huge sums of money to develop solar energy, and research scientists are working hard to develop economical means of converting the sun's rays into usable energy.

Complex
We must find new sources of energy, because the earth's natural energy sources are dwindling. Solar energy, which is energy from the sun's radiation, is a promising new source of energy.

Examine your own writing carefully. Do you use too many simple sentences? If you do, practice combining them.

Practice 67: Rewriting Choppy Sentences

Improve the following choppy sentences by combining them to make either compound or complex sentences.

1. Gasoline is becoming expensive. Automobile manufacturers are producing smaller cars. Smaller cars use less gasoline.

   _____

   _____

   _____

2. The computer has undoubtedly benefited humanity. The computer has also created problems for humanity.

   _____

   _____

   _____

3. Government and private agencies have spent billions of dollars advertising the dangers of smoking. The number of smokers is still increasing.

   _____

   _____

   _____

4. Some students go to college to get a degree. Some students go to college to get an education.

   _____

   _____

   _____

5. The grading system at our college should be abolished. The students don't like getting grades. The instructors don't enjoy giving grades.

   _____

   _____

   _____

Run-Together Sentences

A **run-together sentence** is a sentence in which two or more independent clauses are incorrectly joined by a comma without a coordinating conjunction or sentence connector. This kind of error is also called a *run-on sentence* or a *comma splice.*

Run-together Sentences	*Getting married is easy, staying married is a different matter.*
	A foreign student faces many problems, for example, he has to cope with a new culture.
	San Francisco is a very cosmopolitan city, there are people from many cultures and ethnic groups living there.

A comma alone cannot join two independent clauses.

Correcting this problem is easy. The hardest part is simply *recognizing* a run-together sentence. Learn to check your sentences for this error by substituting a period for the comma. If the sentence reads correctly, the comma should be changed.

A run-together sentence can be corrected in four ways. By adding:

1. *a period:*

   Getting married is easy. Staying married is a different matter.

2. *a semicolon:*
   Getting married is easy; staying married is a different matter.

3. *a coordinating conjunction:*
   Getting married is easy, <u>but</u> staying married is a different matter.

4. *a subordinating conjunction:*
   Getting married is easy <u>although</u> staying married is a different matter.

Practice 68: Run-Together Sentences—I

Correct the following run-together sentences using the method indicated.

1. A foreign student faces many problems, for example, he has to cope with a new culture.

   a. (Add a period) _____

   _____

   b. (Add a semicolon) _____

   _____

2. San Francisco is a very cosmopolitan city, there are people from many cultures and ethnic groups living there.

   a. (Add a period) _____

   _____

   b. (Add a semicolon) _____

   _____

   c. (Add a subordinating conjunction) _____

   _____

   d. (Add a coordinating conjunction) _____

   _____

3. Learning a new language is like learning to swim, it takes a lot of practice.

   a. (Add a coordinating conjunction) _____

   _____

4. Ask for assistance at the reference desk in the library, there is always a librarian on duty.

   a. (Add a semicolon) _____

   _____

5. Hang-gliding is a dangerous sport, you can easily break your leg.

   a. (Add a subordinating conjunction) _____

   _____

Practice 69: Recognizing Run-Together Sentences—II

Some of the following sentences are run together and some are correct. Check each sentence by substituting a period for the comma. If it is a run-together sentence, write *RTS* in the space at the left and circle the comma. If the sentence is correct, leave the space blank.

Example   **RTS**   Two letters arrived on Monday⊙a third one came on Wednesday.

_____ 1. An encyclopedia is a valuable source of information, it contains summaries of every area of knowledge.

_____ 2. Because of the rapid expansion of human knowledge, it is difficult to keep encyclopedias current.

_____ 3. Almost as soon as an encyclopedia is published, it becomes obsolete.

_____ 4. Home editions of encyclopedias are shorter and more concise than library editions, they don't contain as much detailed information.

_____ 5. Articles in encyclopedias are written by experts in each subject, who are often university professors.

_____ 6. An editor of an encyclopedia doesn't write articles, he only collects and edits articles written by other experts.

_____ 7. To find a book on a certain subject, you should look in the card catalog, but to find a magazine article on a subject, you should look in a periodical index.

_____ 8. A periodical index, which is also called a periodical guide, does not contain any articles, it merely gives a list of articles and tells you where to find them.

_____ 9. The reference room of the library has several periodical indexes, one is the *Reader's Guide to Periodical Literature.*

_____ 10. If you can't find any information on a subject, you can always ask a librarian to help you, they are paid to assist students.

WRITING PRACTICE

On a separate sheet of paper, correct all of the run-together sentences in Practice 69.

Practice 70: Correcting Run-Together Sentences—III

Locate the run-together sentences in the following paragraphs. Mark them by circling the comma and writing RTS above it. Then, on a separate sheet of paper, rewrite both paragraphs, correcting the run-together sentences that you found.

Grade Inflation

1   Teachers at Stone Mountain State College give higher grades than teachers at twelve of the nineteen other colleges in the state college system, according to a recent report from the State Institutional Research Committee. This report showed that more than one-third of the undergraduate grades awarded in the spring semester, 1977, were
5   A's, only 1.1 percent were F's. The percentage of A's awarded to graduate students was even higher, almost two-thirds were A's.

While students may be happy to receive high grades, there is evidence that this trend is having negative consequences. Investigation of the admissions criteria* of some graduate and professional schools indicates that the admissions offices of these

10   schools are discounting high grades on the transcripts of SMSC students, this means that an A from SMSC is not equal to an A from other universities. Grade inflation may, therefore, hurt a student from Stone Mountain State College who intends to apply to a graduate or professional school, he or she may not be accepted despite a high grade point average.

Stringy Sentences

Another type of problem that students sometimes create is the **stringy sentence**. This is a sentence in which too many clauses are connected, usually with *and, but, so,* and *because,* forming one very long sentence. The result is a sentence that seems endless.

Stringy Sentences	My roommate, Bill, goes to college and from the beginning of this semester until last week, he hadn't studied at all and the reason was because he had no exams during that period. But the day before yesterday, I was astonished because I saw him studying and later on, he told me he had studied all day long and the reason was because he was going to have an exam the next day and he wanted to get a good grade in the exam so he decided to study.

This example contains far too many clauses.

There are several ways to correct a stringy sentence:

Stringy Sentence	*Many students attend classes all morning and they work all afternoon and then they have to study at night so they are usually exhausted by the weekend.*
Divide	*Many students attend classes all morning and work all afternoon. Then, they have to study at night. As a result, they are usually exhausted by the weekend.*
Subordinate	*Many students, after they attend classes all morning, also work in the afternoon. Because they also have to study at night, they are usually exhausted by the weekend.*
Subordinate and Combine	*Many students, who attend classes all morning, work all afternoon, and also have to study at night, are exhausted by the weekend.*
Participial Phrases	*After attending classes all morning, working all afternoon, and studying at night, many students are exhausted by the weekend.*

Practice 71: Correcting Stringy Sentences

Improve these stringy sentences. Use any method or combination of methods.

1. He enrolled in an advanced calculus class, but he found it too difficult, so he dropped it.

_____

_____

_____

criteria: standards by which a judgment is made

2. The tidal wave ruined the crops, and it destroyed several villages, and it caused many deaths, so it was a real disaster.

_____

_____

_____

3. The analysts worked many hours on the computer program, but they couldn't find the cause of the problem, so they finally gave up, and they went home.

_____

_____

_____

4. Junk food is bad for your health, and it also contains no vitamins, and it damages your stomach, so people shouldn't eat it.

_____

_____

_____

5. The lack of rainfall in Northern California has caused a severe water shortage, so people have to conserve water every day, and they also have to think of new ways to re-use water, but the situation is improving.

_____

_____

_____

APPENDIX A:
SUMMARY OF VERB FORMS

INTRODUCTION

When you are deciding which verb form, or tense, to use, you should make certain that you do not confuse the words *tense* and *time*. Tense refers to the *form* of a verb, as in is eating, has eaten, will eat. *Time* is not a grammatical form; it is a concept existing in the mind of the speaker or writer. There are only three "times"—past, present, and future—but there are many tenses in English. These tenses express the relationships between time and other factors, such as whether the action is completed or still in progress and whether the sentence states a true fact or only a wish.

For example, the verb forms (or tenses) in the four sentences below all express different relationships to present time:

Present Continuous

He is working for his brother while his brother is in the hospital.

By using the present continuous form, the writer is emphasizing that the action is taking place *now*—during the time that his brother is unable to work—and that it is only a temporary activity.

Simple Present

He studies during the day and works at night.

By using the simple present form, the writer is telling us that this is a habitual activity which has happened in the past, is happening in the present, and will probably continue to happen in the future.

Present Perfect

He has lived in the apartment for ten years.

By using the present perfect form, the writer is indicating that the person still lives there now. If the person no longer lived there, the writer would have used the simple past form.

Past

He lived in the same apartment for ten years.

From these examples, you can see that verb tense and time are not the same thing. Many factors determine the correct verb tense.

THE PRESENT TENSES

Simple Present   SIMPLE FORM   I go
                        SIMPLE FORM + S   He goes

States general truths. The time is unimportant.

Heavy rainfall <u>accompanies</u> a hurricane except in the eye*, which <u>remains</u> relatively calm.
The sun <u>rises</u> in the east and <u>sets</u> in the west.

It also describes repeated or habitual actions. In this case, an adverb of frequency (*always, often, sometimes, occasionally, seldom, never,* etc.) or other time expressions (*every day, every weekend, daily,* etc.) are often added to indicate the frequency of repetition.

John <u>attends</u> classes three times a week.
Businessmen usually <u>fly</u> to save time.

In addition, the simple present is used with certain non-activity verbs to describe feelings, perceptions and conditions at the moment of speaking. These verbs are not normally used in the present continuous:

I <u>love you</u>.   *Do you <u>believe</u> in God?*
I <u>don't understand</u> you.   *They <u>need</u> a loan.*
He <u>knows</u> the answer.   *They <u>want</u> to get married.*

Present Continuous   AM   I am going
                        IS + VERB + ING   He is going
                        ARE   We are going

Describes a temporary action or condition that is actually taking place at the moment of speaking:

The students <u>are taking</u> a grammar quiz now.
They <u>are writing</u> as fast as they can.

The present continuous also describes an action or condition that is currently in progress even if not actually at the moment of speaking:

Scientists <u>are investigating</u> the ocean for new sources of food.
The cost of living <u>is</u> still <u>climbing</u>.

Present Perfect   HAS   I have gone
                        HAVE   + PAST PARTICIPLE   He has gone

It links the present and the past. It *must* be used for actions and conditions that began in the past and still exist in the present.

I <u>have lived</u> in the same apartment for two years.
They <u>have been</u> married since 1975.

---

eye: the center of a hurricane

In addition, it *may* be used when the action began in the past and (1) is somehow still important in the present (in the mind of the speaker), (2) happened in the very recent past, or (3) is a recurring action in the past. The simple past may also be used in these three cases.

You <u>have worked</u> very hard this semester.
He <u>has</u> just <u>finished</u> his term paper.
We <u>have moved</u> three times in the past year.

| Present Perfect Continuous | HAS / HAVE | BEEN + VERB + ING | I have been going / He has been going |

This tense *must* be used to combine a point-in-time action with a period-of-time time expression:

He <u>has been writing</u> this book for a year.
(Not: He has written this book for a year.)
I <u>have been catching</u> a cold for several days.
(Not: I have caught a cold for several days.)

The present perfect continuous *may* be used instead of the present perfect to emphasize the continuous or incomplete nature of an action.

(continuous action)
The price of gas <u>has been rising</u> steadily since the Arab oil embargo precipitated* the energy crisis.
It <u>has been raining</u> all morning.

(incomplete activity)
I <u>have been reading</u> Shogun for several weeks.
(but I haven't finished it yet)
He <u>has been smoking</u> my cigarettes.
(but there are still some left in the package)

THE PAST TENSES

| Simple Past | SIMPLE FORM + ED / IRREGULAR PAST FORMS | He worked / He went |

The simple past describes an action or event that took place *and was completed* at a definite time in the past. Expression of past time such as a *week/month/year ago*, *yesterday*, and *last year*, etc. indicate the simple past:

I <u>saw</u> the opera "Othello" on television last night.
The store <u>installed</u> a small XYZ computer a month ago.
The company <u>doubled</u> its profits in 1977.

| Past Continuous | WAS / WERE + VERB + ING | He was going / We were going |

This tense describes an incomplete or temporary past action:

The president <u>was talking</u> on the way to the White House.
The little girl <u>was dancing</u>.

---

precipitate: to cause to happen suddenly

In two-clause sentences, it also describes a temporary action that was in progress when a second action took place. The second action can either happen at the same time, or it can interrupt the first action:

Use *while* + past continuous for the action in progress.
Use *when* + simple past for the interrupting action.

> *His wife was working to support him while he was attending medical school.*
> *The president was smiling and waving to the crowd when the band struck up.*
> *While the president was smiling and waving to the crowd, the band struck up.*
> *We were driving across the bridge when it collapsed.*
> *While we were driving across the bridge, it collapsed.*

Past Perfect   HAD + PAST PARTICIPLE   He had gone

It expresses one past time before another past time. The more recent past time may be either expressed or understood. If the more recent action is expressed, it is usually in the simple past tense:

> *Until last year, the government had not concerned itself with the problem of illegal aliens.*
> *He drove his car to school because he had missed the bus.*
> *The president did not begin the news conference until the room had become quiet.*

Past Perfect Continuous   HAD + BEEN + VERB + ING   He had been going

Like the past perfect, it expresses one past time before another past time. However, the continuous tense emphasizes the duration of the earlier action:

> *We had been waiting for an hour before we were told that the concert had been cancelled.*
> *The president had been speaking for almost two hours when the protesters arrived.*
> *Because he had been working too hard, he was nervous and irritable.*

THE FUTURE TENSES

"Will"   WILL + SIMPLE FORM   He will go

This is the most neutral way to express future time:

> *The government will raise income taxes next year.*
> *The sun will set at exactly 6:48 p.m. tomorrow.*

"Going to"   IS
                          ARE + GOING TO + VERB   He is going to go

This form is also used to express future time, especially when the idea of intention or inevitability is involved:

> *I am going to change my major.* (intention)
> *She is going to have a baby next month.* (inevitability)

	AM	
"Present Continuous"	IS + VERB + ING	He is going (tomorrow)
Future Time —	ARE	

The present continuous tense is also used to express future time. Normally, a future time expression ("*tomorrow*," "*next week*," "*this evening*") is necessary to convey the future meaning.

> We *are leaving* on our vacation tomorrow.
> I *am meeting* my advisor at 2:15 this afternoon.

"Simple Present"	SIMPLE FORM	He leaves (tomorrow)
Future Time —	SIMPLE FORM + S	

The simple present tense may also be used to describe future actions in the following three situations:

(a) with verbs like *come, go, arrive, depart, leave* and a future time expression:

> The president *leaves* on his goodwill trip to South America tomorrow.

(b) in time clauses introduced by a time subordinator (*after, before, until,* etc.):

> After the president *delivers* his speech, he will leave for the airport.
> I will not receive my degree until I complete my master's thesis.

Note: The present perfect tense may also be used in these time clauses to express future time.

> After the president *has delivered* his speech, he will leave for the airport.
> I will not receive my degree until I *have completed* my master's thesis.

(c) in conditional clauses:

> If we *finish* the project before the end of the term, we won't have to work on it during the summer vacation.

Future Continuous   WILL + BE + VERB + ING   He will be going

Describes a future action that will be in progress at a specific time or times in the future.

> I *will be working* on my term paper for the next several weekends.
> The children *will be sleeping* by the time we get home.

Future Perfect   WILL + HAVE + PAST PARTICIPLE   He will have gone

Describes a future action that precedes another future action.

> He *will have become* a millionaire by the time he is twenty.
> The movie *will have* already *started* before we get to the theater.

| Future Perfect Continuous | WILL + HAVE + BEEN + VERB + ING | He will have been working |

Is used to emphasize the *duration* of a future action that occurs before another future action. Usually occurs with a "for + period of time" expression.

The movie will have been playing for thirty minutes by the time we get to the theater.

APPENDIX B:
USING THE LIBRARY

Time is the biggest problem of most students. It becomes particularly difficult when you have to do library research for a term paper or report. Finding information in the library can take so much time that many students avoid it until the last possible minute.

Library research does not have to be very time-consuming. If you learn to use a library efficiently, you can save yourself a great deal of time. The exercises in this section are designed to familiarize you with the library so that you can find the information you need *quickly*.

The first and most important thing to know about a library is that when you can't find something,

Ask a librarian for help

Librarians are usually very helpful people. They are paid not just to shelve books, but to provide information and assistance. The most helpful librarians are usually those who work in the *reference room*. They will help you get started on a term paper and even help you find material.

There are two basic places to begin looking for information: the card catalog and the various periodical indexes. The *Card Catalog* is a list of all the *books* in the library. A *Periodical Index* is a list of all the *magazine and journal articles* written on any subject.

If you need to find a *book*, look in the card catalog.

If you need to find a *magazine article*, look in a periodical index.

In the next few pages, we will study both of these sources of information.

The Card Catalog

The card catalog is a catalog of all the books in the library. Every book has at least three cards: an *author* card, a *title* card, and one or more *subject* cards. If you need a book by a particular author, look in the author catalog. If you know the title of the book you need, look in the title catalog. If you need a book on a particular subject, look in the subject catalog.

READING THE CARDS

Every card contains a lot of basic information about the book such as the topics covered. If you learn to read the cards, you won't waste time looking for books that you can't use. Read the card carefully and completely to get all the information possible from the card *before* you start to look for the book.

The most important thing to look for on the card is the date of publication. An engineering book published in 1898 is probably not worth finding. Next, look at the bottom of the card for the subjects under which the book is catalogued. Do they seem relevant to your topic? Now look for the total number of pages in the book. The length may help you decide whether it is worth your time to find the book and read it. Finally, look for the word *Bibliography*, often abbreviated *Bibliog.* on the card. If a book is relevant to your subject and contains a bibliography, it is worth checking. The bibliography will lead you quickly to other relevant sources of information.

If you find a book in the card catalog that you think will contain the information you need, your next step is to write down three things:

1. the call number (from the upper left-hand corner of the card);
2. the author's name; and
3. the title of the book.

All books are shelved by their call number. Be sure you copy it down accurately and completely. The call number is the key to locating a book on the library shelves.

Some cards have the abbreviation *Ref.* typed above the call number. This means that the book is a *reference book*. A reference book may be shelved alphabetically by call number, but it may also be in a special area, the reference room. You will have to look for it in both places.

You may also notice cards that have a plastic cover imprinted with the words *Reserve Book* or *Reserve Room*. These books are not shelved alphabetically with all the other books, but are kept in the reserve room of the library. They can be checked out only for limited periods of time (usually two hours or two days, depending on the book).

Library Assignment 1: The Card Catalog

A. Study the two library cards below. On a separate sheet of paper, give the following information from both cards.

Ref. KOREANS IN HAWAII -
 Z BIBLIOGRAPHY
 4708
 K6 Gardner, Arthur L.
 G33   The Koreans in Hawaii: an
     annotated bibliography by
     Arthur L. Gardner. Hono-
     lulu, Social Science Re-
     search Institute, University
     of Hawaii, 1970.
 	
     83 p. 28 cm. (Hawaii
     series, no. 2)
 	
   1. Koreans in Hawaii.
   2. Hawaii - population.
	PJ
	 7695 Manzalaoui, Mahmoud, ed.
	 E8 Arabic Writing Today; the
	 M3 short story. Cairo, Ameri-
	     can Research Center in
	     Egypt, 1968
	   407 p. 22 cm.
	
	 Bibliog: p. 403–407.
	
	 1. Short stories, Arabic-
	 translations into English.
	 2. Short stories, English-
	 translations from Arabic.

1. Type of card (subject, author, or title)
2. Call number.
3. Author's name.
4. Title of book.
5. Date of publication.
6. Number of pages.
7. Size of book.
8. Name of publisher.

B.

1. What are the other subjects under which this book is listed?
2. Does this book contain a bibliography? (Is the book a bibliography itself?)
3. Where can this book be found in the library?

Periodical Indexes

Periodical indexes are books that contain lists of all articles published in magazines and academic journals on every subject. These indexes do not contain the actual articles; they simply tell you where to find the articles you need in other magazines and journals. Periodical indexes are probably more helpful than the card catalog because they tell you where to find short magazine articles on your term paper topic. Isn't it easier to read a 20-page article than a 200-page book?

Periodical indexes are organized just like the card catalog. Every article is listed in at least two places: by the author's name and under one or more subjects. However, they are not listed by title.

There are several different indexes in the library. The most general and largest is the *Reader's Guide to Periodical Literature*. In addition, many fields of study have their own special indexes, such as the *Reader's Guide to the Social Sciences*, the *Education Index*, the *Business Periodicals Index*, the *Handbook of Chemistry and Physics*, and the *Civil Engineering Handbook*. Find out what indexes the library has in your field. There is a list of them in the reference room.

Indexes use a lot of abbreviations, which you should learn to recognize. You probably already know many of these common abbreviations:

bibliog.	bibliography
cond.	condensed
cont.	continued
ed.	editor, edited, edition
il.	illustrated
introd.	introduction
v.	volume
sup.	supplement

The names of the magazines and journals are also abbreviated:

Nat Geog	*National Geographic*
Sci Digest	*Science Digest*
Time	*Time*
NY Times Mag	*New York Times Magazine*
Bsns W	*Business Week*
Harvard Bus R	*Harvard Business Review*

Library Assignment 2: Periodical Indexes

This practice is in reading entries in periodical indexes. Study the entries below and then answer the questions that follow.

ELEPHANTS

Training
Wild elephant roundup in India.
H. Miller. il Nat Geog 135:372–85 Mr'69

GUIDED missile bases
ABM comes to town; deploying Sentinel as an area defense system. P. Moldauer. il Bul Atom Sci 25: 4–6+ Ja'69
Anti the anti-missile; communities fighting to block construction of sites. il Time 93:19 F7'69
Nixon-tailored ABM looks like a fit. il Bsns W p57–8 Mr22'69

INHERITANCE TAX
Estate tax changes coming. il U S News 68:72–4 Ap7'69

INJECTIONS, Hypodermic
Automated injections. Sci Digest 65: 71 F'69

JACKSON, Louis
Westchester trustees warn against unions; summary of address, December 3, 1968. Library J 94:134–5 Ja15'69

JACKSON, Rupert A.
Computer tells what street to pave. Am City 84:9+ Ja'69

NORMAN, Barbara and Tatsumura, Kazuko
Soaring popularity of Japanese restaurants. Holiday 45:58–9+ Mr'69

TWAIN, MARK, pseud. See Clemens, S.L.

X RAYS
Measurement
Search for soft X rays from the galaxy. R.J. Grader and others. il Sky & Tel 37:79–81 F'69
Physiological effects
What you should know about X rays and pregnancy. G.C. Lewis, Jr. and P. Feinstein. Redbook 132:30+ F'69

XENAKIS, Vannis
Toward infinity in sound. il por Time 93:77–8 Mr21'69

YALE DRAMA SCHOOL—see Yale University-Drama School

ZORSA; musical comedy. See Musical comedies, revues, etc.—Criticisms, plots, etc.

1. In what magazine does the article on elephant training appear? Does the article contain any pictures or photographs?

2. How many articles on guided missile bases are indexed?

3. How many articles on X rays are indexed? Are they on the same subtopic or different subtopics? What are the subtopics?

4. What are the names of the authors of the article on X rays and pregnancy?

5. Is there an article about American author Mark Twain? Where should you look to find an article about him?

6. What is the volume number of the article by Vannis Xenakis? What are the page numbers? What is the date of publication? In what magazine did the article appear?

7. What is the title of the article by Rupert A. Jackson?

Library Assignment 3: Using the Library

Plan to spend about one hour in the library completing this assignment. Answer all questions carefully and completely.

CARD CATALOG

1. How many books written by Joyce Carol Oates does the library have? List the call number and title of one of her books. Also give the date and place of publication, and the number of pages in the book.

CALL NUMBER	TITLE	DATE AND PLACE OF PUBLICATION	NUMBER OF PAGES

   Exactly where in the library can you find this book? _____

2. Who wrote the book entitled *The Magic Mountain*? _____

   Is this an English book or a translation? _____

   Where in the library can you find this book? _____

3. Find the cards for two books on nonverbal communication. List their call numbers, titles, authors, and date of publication.

CALL NUMBER	AUTHOR	TITLE	DATE OF PUBLICATION
a.			
b.			

4. Look up a book written *about* John F. Kennedy by a man named O'Donnell.

   What is the title of the book? _____

   Who are the co-authors? _____

5. Under what subject can you find books on the following subjects? (These subjects are too narrow to be listed by themselves; you will have to look under a broader subject.) Consult your dictionary if necessary.

   schizophrenia _____

   malaria _____

   moon exploration _____

   San Andreas fault _____

   totem poles _____

   soil conservation _____

PERIODICAL INDEXES

6. Locate and write the names of three periodical indexes in your major field. Where are these indexes located in the library? Which room? Which shelf? Which table?

Name of Index   *Location*

a. _____

b. _____

c. _____

7. In the *Readers Guide to Periodical Literature*, look up an article written about Alcatraz Island in *Newsweek* magazine in July 1970. Copy the complete reference and explain all of the abbreviations and numbers. _____

_____

_____

_____

_____

_____

8. In one of the three indexes you listed in question 6, look up an article on a subject of your choice. Copy the complete reference, and explain all of the abbreviations and numbers. _____

_____

_____

_____

_____

_____

REFERENCE LIBRARIAN

9. Ask the librarian to look up the most recent statistics on the birth rate in your country. (Your answer should be a percent of births per thousand.)

Country: _____ Year: _____ Birthrate: _____

MICROFILM LIBRARY

10. Look up your birthdate in the *New York Times*. Write the headline of the newspaper on that date: _____

_____

APPENDIX C:

CHART OF TRANSITION SIGNALS

Meaning/ Function	Sentence Connectors	Clause Connectors		Others
		Coordinators	Subordinators	
To introduce an **additional** idea	furthermore moreover in addition	and		another (+ noun) an additional (+ noun)
To introduce an **opposite** idea	on the other hand however in contrast	but yet	although though even though whereas while	in spite of (+ noun) despite (+ noun)
To introduce an **example**	for example for instance e.g.			an example of (+ noun) such as (+ noun)
To introduce a **restatement** or **explanation**	i.e.			
To introduce a **conclusion** or **summary**	in conclusion in summary to conclude to summarize			
To clarify chronological order and order of importance	first (second, third, fourth, etc.) next, last, finally first of all, above all after that since then more important, most important		before after while until as soon as	the first (+ noun) the second (+ noun) before the (+ noun) in the year since the (+ noun) the most important (+ noun)

To introduce a cause or reason		for	because since as	because of due to to result from the result of the effect of X on Y the consequence of
To introduce an effect or result	as a result as a consequence therefore thus consequently hence	so		the cause of the reason for to result in to cause <hr>to have an effect on to affect
To introduce a comparison	similarly likewise also too	and	as just as	like just like alike similar (to) the same as both . . . and not only . . . but also compare to

To introduce a contrast	on the other
	  hand
	in contrast
	however
	by (in)
	  comparison
		but
		yet
			although
			though
			even though
			whereas
			while
				different from
				dissimilar
				unlike
				to differ from
				<hr>to compare to
				to compare with

INDEX

SIMON & SCHUSTER BOOKS FOR YOUNG READERS
An imprint of Simon & Schuster Children's Publishing Division
1230 Avenue of the Americas, New York, New York 10020
Text copyright © 2000 by Douglas Wood
Illustrations copyright © 2000 by Doug Cushman
SIMON & SCHUSTER BOOKS FOR YOUNG READERS is a trademark of Simon & Schuster.
Book design by Anahid Hamparian

The text of this book is set in 20-pt. Garamond Book.
The illustrations are rendered in pen and ink and watercolor.
Printed in Hong Kong
10 9 8 7 6 5 4 3 2
Library of Congress Cataloging-in-Publication Data
Wood, Douglas, 1951-
    What dads can't do / by Douglas Wood ; illustrated by Doug Cushman.
    — 1st ed.
    p.   cm.
    Summary: Describes how dads show love by explaining all the things
      that they cannot do, such as sleeping late, keeping their ties clean,
      and reading books by themselves.
    ISBN 0-689-82620-6
    [1. Fathers—Fiction.] I. Cushman, Doug, ill. II. Title.
    PZ7.W84738Wh 2000
    [E]—dc21
                    98-41773
                    CIP
                    AC

*To dads everywhere,
and the kids who watch
over them
—D.W.*

*For Kelsey and papa Don
—D. C.*

What Dads Can't Do

by
Douglas Wood

pictures by
Doug Cushman

Kreature Kids
DAY CARE

Simon & Schuster Books for Young Readers

There are lots of things
that regular people can do
but dads can't.

Dads can't cross the street
without holding hands.

Dads can push,
  but they can't swing.

Dads can't pitch a baseball very hard

or hit one very far.

When dads play hide-and-seek
  they always get found,

but they have a hard time finding you.

They aren't very good wrestlers.

Dads lose at checkers
    and cards
    and almost every other game.

Dads aren't good at sleeping late.

They can't comb their hair

or shave by themselves.

Dads like to go camping,
  but they need lots of help
    setting up the tent.

And cooking.

Dads like to go fishing,
but they don't like to go alone.

And they need extra practice baiting the hook.

Sometimes dads have a hard time
getting organized.

They can't drive very fast.

Dads seem to have trouble holding on to their money.

Dads can't see you hiding your lima beans
at dinnertime.
Or feeding them to the cat.

They can't eat just one piece
of chocolate cake
or one scoop of ice cream.

Dads like to give baths,
but they can't help
getting all wet.

Dads can't read a book by themselves.

Dads really need to be
kissed good night at bedtime.

Sometimes they leave a night-light on
    because they're a little bit scared of the dark.
They also like to check under the bed for monsters.

And in the closet.

There are so many things that dads can't do
it's a wonder they make it through life
at all.
But dads can't give up.
No matter how tired a dad gets,
or how hard life gets,
a dad never quits.

And most of all,
whatever happens,
a dad never ever stops
loving you.